The Failure of Our Fathers

The Failure of Our Fathers

Family, Gender, and Power in Confederate Alabama

VICTORIA E. OTT

The University of Alabama Press | *Tuscaloosa*

The University of Alabama Press
Tuscaloosa, Alabama 35487-0380
uapress.ua.edu

Copyright © 2023 by the University of Alabama Press
All rights reserved.

Inquiries about reproducing material from this work should
be addressed to the University of Alabama Press.

Typeface: Baskerville

Cover image: Family group before the house in which Gen. Charles S.
Winder (C.S.A.) died; photograph by Timothy H. O'Sullivan, Library
of Congress Prints and Photographs Division
Cover design: David Nees

Cataloging-in-Publication data is available from the Library of Congress.
ISBN: 978-0-8173-2147-5
E-ISBN: 978-0-8173-9435-6

To William "Bill" Nicholas

Contents

List of Illustrations ix

Acknowledgments xi

Introduction 1

1 "Faithfully and Affectionately"
  CLAIMING EQUALITY IN THE ANTEBELLUM ERA, 1820–60 19

2 "Remember Me, with Soft Emotion"
  FAMILY AND HONOR IN WARTIME, 1860–62 57

3 "This Unholy War"
  FAMILIES IN CRISIS, 1863–65 91

4 "There Is a Great Wrong Somewhere"
  THE STATE AND FAMILY IN CONFLICT 119

5 "Oh! How Changed Everything Has Become"
  FAMILIES IN THE POSTWAR STATE 151

Conclusion 175

Notes 179

Bibliography 195

Index 203

Illustrations

1. Montgomery County courthouse in Montgomery, Alabama   37
2. "Industry of Ladies in Clothing the Soldiers, and Zeal in Urging Their Beaux to Go to the War"   67
3. Henry Stokes Figures with an unidentified young man   93
4. "Alabamians Receiving Rations"   124
5. "Scenes in Cotton Land—the Home of the Poor White"   154

Acknowledgments

This book is the product of the kindness and support of many friends, family, and colleagues. When I began this project several years ago, I was fortunate to have the financial and academic support of those at Birmingham-Southern College. Provost Brad Caskey along with my colleagues in the History Department made it possible for me to take advantage of our sabbatical program. The time away from the classroom to devote to research and writing made this book a reality. I also received several summer research stipends from the college, which offered the financial assistance necessary to spend countless hours buried in the archives. I am likewise grateful for the encouragement from the members of my department, Will Hustwit, Randy Law, Mark Lester, and Mark Schantz, whom I consider more as friends than coworkers.

I am deeply indebted to those who took time away from their busy lives to aid in the research and writing of this book. Foremost, Keith Goodwin, my spouse and best friend, was there from the beginning when this study was a mere idea. He went with me on a number of trips to archives and took hundreds of pictures of documents, most of which formed the basis of this work. I am also thankful to Lynn Sherrill for serving as my "assistant" in the archives during one particular summer when I was overwhelmed with sources to review. She quickly learned how to navigate the microfilm machine and became a pro at documenting sources. I am appreciative of my father, Thomas Oliver Ott III, who read drafts of my chapters. He spent hours going over the manuscript, providing important edits and suggestions on how to strengthen my prose. He is not only my father but a mentor whose own talent for historical writing is truly inspiring. Mark Schantz also read a draft of my introduction. His suggestions on how to hone my argument made this book a much stronger work. I would also like to thank Claire Lewis Evans from the University of Alabama Press for encouraging me to finish the book and for all her help in shepherding it through the process of publishing. I am likewise grateful for all the hard work the editorial and production staff at the press put in to bring the book to publication. Finally, I am beholden to the staff at the Alabama Department of Archives and History for putting up with many visits and countless requests to pull collections. They offered assistance at every turn and always with gentle patience.

The work that goes into producing a book is encouraged by our family and friends. I received immeasurable moral support from those known collectively as The Pod: Orlando Carrucini, Jared Heaton, Ruth Hughes, Corey Hults, Natalia Narz, and Jamie Whitehurst. Their love, laughter, and countless hugs kept me motivated even when the weight of the world seemed overwhelming. I am also thankful for the continued support from Valerie Emanoil, Véronique Vanblaere, Mary Donna Luckey, and my brother, John Ott, who all offered their own form of motivation, whether it was a friendly voice or a much-needed pep talk. I would also like to acknowledge the significant role Stephen V. Ash has played in my life. His career as a prolific scholar of the Civil War has inspired generations of historians, myself among them, to follow their passion for history and all the stories still to uncover. Finally, William Nicholas, professor emeritus at Birmingham-Southern College, remains an important fixture in my life. He became my informal mentor during the outset of my career, teaching me about the importance of a liberal arts education in fostering our intellectual curiosity. His own forty-year career in the academy is testimony to his excellence as a professor and historian. It is to him that I dedicate this book.

The Failure of Our Fathers

Introduction

By 1862 a beleaguered and homesick James Garrison dreamed of the day when he would leave the battleground behind him and return to the loving embrace of his family. When not fighting for survival on the battlefield, the soldier of the Twenty-Sixth Alabama Regiment spent most of his days searching for food and his nights struggling against the elements. As he lay on the unforgiving ground with merely a canopy of trees above him, his mind wandered to loving scenes of home and family. What would bring this man, with a young family and bright future, to push his body and mind to the point of exhaustion as he endured the daily trauma of surviving a war? For Garrison, the meaning of his service to the Confederacy, at least in the beginning, was clear. His devotion to the masculine ideals of duty and honor, both to his family and to his country, drove him to risk life and limb to fight enemy invaders from a distant land. Surprisingly, his letters to family mentioned little of his loyalty to the cause of Confederate independence or of his fear of outsiders bent on destruction. Garrison likewise avoided any mention of slavery or the racial hierarchy that the Confederate mission intended to protect.

Rather, family served as his clarion call to enlist, as he reflected on his role as a devoted husband, father, and son. Just two years earlier, he lived comfortably in Fayette, Alabama, with his wife, Harriet, and their three-year-old daughter, Rebecca. Garrison's parents lived close by on a modest farm that anchored the family to the land. Yet he left his family and parents to serve the Confederacy. And though miles from home, James continued to lean on the people whom he left behind, especially during the darkest times. Like his contemporaries in the camps, he spent countless hours writing home to request a catalog of material items to supplement the meager provisions the military provided. Hesitant to ask family to sacrifice for his well-being, he wrote to Harriet, "I have lost my blanket but I have another," yet admitted that he needed more items from home, as "I have only one suit of clothes with me." More revealing, however, were the letters from Garrison seeking emotional support from those whom he had left behind. As his circumstances worsened over time, James questioned whether he could endure the war much longer, revealing, "I went through with it so far but I don't know how long I will." In spite of the suffering he endured, returning to home and family gave him hope to continue. "You must kiss my children for me," he wrote, "for I think of you and them all the time."[1]

Time, however, brought this soldier to question the very cause that he had sworn to defend. By 1863 Confederate conditions on the home and military fronts took a sharp turn, thrusting thousands into a downward spiral of material scarcity and declining morale. These dual calamities drove his desperation to return home to defend and provide for his family. In May of that year, Garrison wrote Harriet, "I ought to be at home plowing this morning. . . . I think that it would benefit me much more than being here lying about doing nothing." It had become clear that the value of family outweighed any allegiance to a cause that undermined his abilities to fulfill his masculine role as provider and protector. Such challenges to Garrison's manhood justified his turning against the war. Even as he remained in the camps, he lamented the loss of the reciprocal relationships within the family that validated his role as the family patriarch. "I am not very well," he lamented. "I would like to be at home so you could wait on me." Garrison and the many like him who stood outside the ranks of Alabama's elites at one time supported the Confederacy as their duty to their family and, as a consequence, the preservation of their standing as honorable, reputable members of society. But the cause that promised security from outside invaders now intruded into the private world of home and family, threatening to destroy the very core of its existence.[2]

This study is about common white families in Alabama during one of the most pivotal epochs in the state's history. It chronicles families that at one point identified with and even supported the Confederate mission to leave the Union and create an independent, slaveholding nation. Using the lens of gender through which to examine their experiences, we gain a more nuanced understanding of the ways in which common whites responded to the war and, in the process, found new avenues to power as a distinct socioeconomic class as Confederate society began to collapse. Common whites drew their value in the Confederate cause from antebellum constructs of manhood and womanhood centered squarely in the context of family and the roles and relationships within it. The idealization of family brought common whites into the conflict to preserve the social and racial hierarchy stemming from the institution of slavery. Family likewise provided a source of continuity and support necessary to sustain their involvement in the conflict.

Yet as the war ravaged Alabama communities and heaped untold hardships on those serving in the army, it ultimately prompted common whites to focus more on mere survival than devotion to the Confederate leadership. In their estimation devotion to fighting the conflict seemed less a priority as their families increasingly stood in peril of ruin. Their ever more dire circumstances outweighed their willingness to remain in the fight and, in the process, brought them into conflict with the elite power structure of the state. These common white civilians and soldiers came to understand their clash with elites as due to the failure of the state to protect its people from the exigencies of war. Out of these growing class tensions, couched in the context of gender identities, rose new relationships between common whites and Alabama's political and social structure during and after the conflict.

Who were the people who constituted Alabama's common white families? To answer that question, we must first understand my use of the phrase "common whites." In this study, I employ it as an umbrella term to include two distinct classes of the South's white population. The first are those from independent landowning families who were either small or non-slaveholders. For those who laid claim to the status of slave owner, their holdings were limited and rarely fixed depending on their economic circumstances. Regardless of their slave-owning status, they never reached the level of wealth and political power to claim membership in Alabama's elite. The second group consisted of poor, landless whites. Poor whites found themselves marginalized in a slavery-driven economy, forced to either seek work for wages or rely on tenant farming. No matter their occupation, all lived in what many travelers to the region described as abject poverty. To verify that those in this study fell within either two of the categories, I examined their personal real-estate property values documented in the Manuscript Schedules of the Census of the US Bureau of the Census from the antebellum and postbellum periods. I confirmed when applicable their slaveholding status by using the Slave Schedules of the US Bureau of the Census.

Certainly, historians have provided a clear understanding of the distinctions between these two groups of the South's non-elites. Beginning with Frank Owsley's early study of those he termed the "plain folk," readers first learn of a middling group of white southerners, often referred to as "yeomanry." He offers a romanticized view of them as "salt-of-the-earth" people who led independent and noncompetitive lives. Independence, whether envisioned or realized, formed the nucleus of their world. And work provided the path to freedom from toiling for mere subsistence and dependence on others for financial support. These core values deeply separated the plain folk from elite planters within the social order. Historian Carl E. Osthaus reaches a similar conclusion, citing that for those tied to the land through farming, "respect for hard work, independence, and the ability to provide for one's own were core values." William Harris and Bruce Collins, in contrast, recognize the divisions between the classes of elites and non-elites but concentrate more on what united them. Harris, for example, makes the case that all southern whites united along racial lines, sharing a sense of white supremacy born out of an agrarian republicanism. Collins likewise offers similar conclusions in seeking to understand why whites, regardless of class interests, united in favor of the Confederacy. He found in particular that investment in agriculture diminished class differences. This emphasis on the lives of independent, landowning farmers as representative of the "plain folk" therefore downplayed the experiences of other non-elite southerners.[3]

More recent historians, however, look deeper into the class of poor whites as separate and unique from the yeomanry. Charles Bolton, for instance, led a movement to understand those living in poverty on their own terms. This effort helped debunk popular stereotypes of poor whites as backward, ill-mannered, and violent "white trash." Exceptions existed, of course, as one looks into the life of notorious criminals such as Edward Isham, whose life seemed more atypical of the poor-white experience but fed into the popular perceptions of this class group. Although the majority shared common cultural values with independent small farmers, the South's poor struggled to maintain a livelihood in the face of slave labor. Historian Jeff Forret identifies their experience through his study of the underground economy shared between poor whites and enslaved men and women. In their economic exchanges, these two groups helped each other supplement their material and dietary needs that circumstances made difficult to procure. This clandestine interaction confounded the South's elites who sought to drive a wedge between whites and Blacks who otherwise shared similar living conditions. Additionally, Keri Leigh Merritt found that slavery devalued poor whites' labor and limited their access to jobs, as employers preferred unfree workers who could be easily controlled and lacked the power to protest their conditions. As a result, poor whites became itinerate laborers and engaged in the underground economy with slaves for subsistence.⁴

For the purposes of this study, the term "common whites" brings together the two classes of non-elites and recognizes their shared cultural position. In particular, both were forced to compete within a slave society that privileged the planter elites above all others. Such use of the terms stems from the work of Bill Cecil-Fronsman and his analysis of common white culture in North Carolina. He identifies that "poor white trash and prosperous yeoman" certainly differed in their nature and lifestyle. Yet what drew them together was that both "were obliged to support a system that worked against their interests." In the case of Alabama's non-elites, a similar sense of duty to protect slavery also existed to the extent that it served to motivate common whites to support the Confederacy. A shared belief that outsiders threatened to undermine their liberties, invade their communities, and, in the process, harm their families brought poor whites and yeomen to join the cause. Others shared a strong view that secession worked against their interests and pledged their loyalty to the Unionists' cause. Yet the concern in this study is with those who bought into the narrative of Confederate nationalism and supported going to war, even at great risk to the security of their family. Non-elites constituted a majority of Confederate civilians and soldiers, endured similar wartime devastations, and, as a result, underwent a transition in their relation to the state. Because of these collective experiences, the term "common whites" seems fitting to identify them.⁵

This study moves away from the historiographical discussion of whether soldiers remained loyal to the war effort or if internal dissent from civilians provided cause for Confederate defeat. Rather, my primary concern is about the conditions that brought common whites, including soldiers, into conflict with the survival of their families and how that conflict redefined their relationship to Alabama's elite power structure. Plenty of scholars have proved that soldiers, elite and common whites alike, remained loyal to the Confederate war effort up to the very end—and that their devotion to fighting remained, despite the gender, class, and racial divisions. Even so, Alabama's common whites found that the growing challenges in sustaining their support for war served as the catalytic agent in an emerging class consciousness that challenged the hegemony of the state's elites.⁶

Family offered common whites a source of power by providing social connections, economic support, and emotional solace. Shared notions of masculinity and race also offered common white men legal rights to control dependents and property similarly to their elite counterparts. And they made those demands in public arenas, specifically the hallowed halls of Alabama's courts. As they moved into the regional conflict between North and South, common white men and women continued to rely on the family to understand the reasons why they should fight to protect the right to secede and form a separate Confederate nation. They conceptualized the Confederacy as a larger family and the state as paternal figures devoted to protect its loyal dependents. Through the rhetorical notions of honor and duty, they came to believe the reciprocal relationship between the fatherly protector and loyal dependents would remain throughout the course of the war. Yet, as total war increased, heaping great economic and emotional burdens on Alabama's common whites, their vision of a familial structure once a source of loyalty to the Confederacy now provided them with cause to question its leaders.[7]

Severe food shortages left in the wake of diminished farm labor and government impressment policies threatened to destroy families. And common whites made demands for relief through high rates of desertion, petitioning state leaders, and, in the case of the Mobile bread riot, public protests. As a result, those from the ranks of common whites in Alabama launched formal and informal resistance aimed at the leaders who continued to demand their sacrifices. The war-torn conditions of the state emboldened common whites to demand action from government officials to stave off the desecration of their families. In doing so they played a central role in shaping state policies concerning civilian aid. Returning to a sense of normalcy after the war proved even harder for common whites, who faced greater struggles in rebuilding their lives as compared to the elites. Challenged by a state left in physical ruins in the wake of war, and on the brink of starvation, these families turned once more to the support of their state. Placing pressure once again on their state leaders, they found a source of power to shape, at least for a time, the postwar political agenda regarding recovery.

Historians have often missed the opportunities to consider the power of gendered studies to enrich Alabama's historical narrative. Many early state histories concentrated on a larger survey of the state's formative period and the emergence of the planter aristocracy in a growing cotton economy. Even studies interested in the wartime experiences of Alabamians generally concentrate more on elite-driven political and economic developments. Malcolm McMillan, in his earlier examination of the gubernatorial years of three wartime leaders, includes the relationship of political policy and the people whom it affected. The more recent work of Christopher McIlwain in *Civil War Alabama* offers a comprehensive study of the state while again emphasizing the political interests of leaders. Other historians have given consideration to the lives of common whites from their perspective and, in the process, revealed their part in Alabama's economic, political, and social culture. Wayne Flynt's *Poor but Proud* provides the groundwork for shifting the focus from the planter class to the poor whites of the state, raising important questions about their daily lives and personal relations. While Flynt covers the years spanning the Civil War and after, his survey of poor whites offers limited conclusions about their agency in wartime Alabama. Bessie Martin's comprehensive study of desertion in Alabama during the war sheds light on the connection between the economic interests of common whites and their reactions to state and Confederate policies. Originally published in 1932, Martin's book introduces readers to everyday individuals in the Civil War, offering a socioeconomic analysis of why men deserted the army. The limitations of her work leave readers questioning what other ways common whites challenged wartime policies out of their best interests. In a more recent study about the southeastern region of the state, Tommy Craig Brown contributes a more complex view of the state's common whites before and during the Civil War. His research adds to the historiography by illuminating the experiences of everyday individuals from this often-overlooked class in Alabama. Perhaps Margaret Storey's research into Alabama Unionists gives us better insight into the state's common whites. Her statewide focus uses multiple sources to bring the lives of common whites into high relief. Although these relatively recent works offer significant insights into the lives of common whites, they remain limited in scope. My work aims to fill a gap in the historiography of common whites in Alabama by placing gender along with race and class at the center of their story. My choice has been to focus solely on those who identified themselves as Confederates, adding to the discourse of the political power of common whites during the war.[8]

Alabama presents a unique backdrop to study common white families in the Civil War South. States emerging from the former British colonies had a long history of development that produced conditions that varied from states formed out of the nineteenth-century push into the trans-Mississippi West. Alabama's early beginnings as a frontier of Georgia and its eventual statehood in 1819 meant that it played catch-up to the long-established states such as Virginia, South Carolina, and Georgia. As historian Thomas Perkins Abernathy asserts, the formative years of Alabama came not during the colonial period but long after, between 1815 and 1828. The resulting effects meant that the state experienced frontierlike conditions well into the nineteenth century. With limited development in the state, families, regardless of socioeconomic conditions, focused more on meeting the day-to-day concerns of life in a new place. They shared the same anxieties over high mortality rates, food sources, and moral education so common in developing areas. Planting roots through the building of homes, churches, government seats, and other institutions thus occupied energies and resources of residents of a nascent state. As a result, frontier conditions slowed the development of a true aristocracy, at least for a time, like that found in older southern states.[9]

Class difference and conflict existed, even as the developing nature of the state tended to keep them beneath the surface. Planter elites along with the yeomanry set themselves apart from their poor white contemporaries by viewing themselves as refined and well-mannered groups. They also tended to view their elevated status as occupying a position of aristocracy. The eventual growth of plantation districts magnified the contrasts in living conditions between elites and common whites. Yet slavery proved the most pronounced display of wealth, making it clear who would come to control the political and economic interests of the state. As historian Paul D. Escott describes, the elites "believed that they were better than the yeomen and were entitled to special influence and privilege." They likewise viewed those whom they considered beneath their aristocratic station as crude, unrefined, and worthy more of paternal care than equal access to political and economic power. Common whites, however, pushed back against such depictions by displaying fierce loyalty to family, work, and religion—attributes that afforded them a sense of group honor. They held fast to the values of "independence, self-reliance, and individualism" that emerged from a democratic culture inherited from the frontier experience of early settlers. As a result, common whites "demanded social respect" and treated the elites as "equals," even requiring shows of reverence from those currying their favor, such as "wealthy office seekers."[10]

Alabama's political culture resembled the democratic spirit visible on the national level by the late 1820s. Common whites, although aware of the growing dominance of the planter elite, still demanded the same political rights of any white man. Even if common whites found office holding an unattainable goal, they recognized the power that their vote carried, especially in state and local elections. The Democratic Party claimed a majority of support in Alabama by the antebellum period. Even as some planter elites aligned with the Whig Party by the 1840s, most remained loyal to the Democratic Party because of its defense of states' rights and because agrarian interests proved the best route to defending slavery amid a growing abolitionist movement.[11]

Common white men likewise perceived the Democratic Party as the best line of defense against challenges to their independence. The debate over the fate of slavery in the newly acquired territories following the Mexican War created a new set of concerns that transformed the political culture of the South, including Alabama. By the 1850s, with the growing tensions between North and South, Alabama's politics increasingly resembled one-party dominance as it became poised to defend its interests against outside attacks. Much of the state's voting population threw their support behind the Democratic Party, seeking to defend slavery and seeking a leader from a new generation of "fire eaters." The emergence of William Lowndes Yancey as the voice of regional independence gave way to a nascent faction of political leaders clamoring for either protection of slavery by the national government or secession from the country.[12]

By 1861 the question of secession produced deep social divisions in Alabama over its fate in the Union. The Hill Country of North Alabama along with the Wiregrass region of Alabama became a bastion of Unionism, while those areas where elite power was firmly entrenched held fast to secession as the South's solution to the slavery question. John Inscoe and Robert Kenzer in *Enemies of the Country* bring together a collection of scholars introducing how family loyalty and regional differences within the South produced a strong cadre of Unionist supporters. Building upon their scholarship, Margaret Storey's study of Unionism in Alabama brings into high relief the contentious nature of the secession debate, which gave the lie to notions of unanimity for southern independence. Storey illustrates that a strong loyalist faction existed within Alabama's population. Rather than rely on a regional model to explain the Unionist position, she argues that family honor and sense of duty brought a minority of Alabamians to lead the charge to remain in the Union. Central to their position was the shared view that "the Union embodied democratic processes that continued to provide fair and just government." Those most vocal Unionists, however, found themselves at odds with the rising tide of Confederates upon passage of the ordinance of secession on January 11, 1861. The loudest proponents of secession were those whose economic investment in slave labor meant they had the greatest to lose by staying in the Union. Common whites, however, invested little in the slave institution and thus lacked the same reasoning as elites to support secession.[13]

But among those who eventually came to identify as Confederate, there was a common connection to secession and eventual war. The rhetorical argument of invading forces imposing their will on an independent people resonated with common whites. The loss of independence at the hands of invaders posed, in their estimation, a real threat to the survival of the family. In situating their personal lives within this public context, the connection between nationalism and family became clear. Confederate supporters envisioned the family as a microcosm of the infant nation, tying protection of the home to defense of the southern home front.

The story of common whites in Civil War Alabama must be told from their perspective, yet uncovering firsthand sources from a socioeconomic group with marginal education and resources can prove a Herculean task. This study draws from a wide spectrum of primary sources involving personal and public records. Searching the archival resources, I uncovered a number of private letters between soldiers and their families, giving voice to Alabama's common whites, as they conveyed their own sentiments about the war and its consequences to the family. These sources reflect the limited education of many in this group, as they often used phonetic spelling in their compositions. Diaries and other personal papers likewise allowed me to see the Civil War from their perspective. I fleshed out their stories using public records, specifically census information and court records, which provided nuanced details of their status and their personal relationships. Those writing about common whites also provided significant insight into their relationship to elites. For instance, travelers' accounts bring insights into the biases popular culture held toward common whites and the ways those biases shaped how others related to them. The many newspapers throughout the state likewise offer a balance between reporting the facts of common white conditions and inherent prejudices regarding their circumstances, especially as they related to the state government and its policies. The totality of these records provides a deeper, more complex narrative of how the common white majority negotiated and understood their place in Alabama before, during, and immediately after the Civil War.

The subjects of this study come from a wide sampling of the state's diverse regions. Alabama's vast resources and access to major waterways offered varied economic opportunities for common whites. Early migrants to the state came from older states, such as North and South Carolina, Georgia, and Virginia, escaping conditions such as soil exhaustion and searching for new farming opportunities. Most tended to reside in areas of the state that offered the most affordable access to farming, while others worked as artisans, mechanics, and even laborers in the scant number of textile mills in the state. The area typically referred to as North Alabama laid claim to the Tennessee Valley and Hill Country regions, where one could find extremes of wealth and poverty intermingling in the countryside. The areas gave way to the growth of grand estates with a large force of enslaved laborers. This wealth, however, meant that common whites fought against the current of the planter minority, as they too searched for economic independence and upward mobility. Although most of the state's common whites hailed from its northern portion, some, isolated by its mountainous geography, sought residency in the prosperous Black Belt region with its many plantation estates peppering the countryside. The southern portion of the state likewise produced vast contrasts in wealth and power from those in the Wiregrass and Coastal regions. A good number of the state's poorer citizens came from the neighboring Piney Woods in the southeastern portion of the state, where farming proved more arduous than in the rich, fertile lands just north of them. Still, those who make up the narrative of this study represent the varying circumstances and access to upward mobility shaped by the diverse geography of the state.

To fully understand why a study of Alabama's common white families is warranted, we must consider what set them apart from the state's elites, the enslaved, and free people of color. Their place within the racial ordering, membership in a distinct socioeconomic class, and adherence to conventional gender prescriptions governing men and women converged to create a unique family experience unlike any other social and racial groups in the state. How did these three categories of race, class, and gender play such a significant role? First, life within a slaveholding economy meant that race defined one's place in the social order. Members of the planter minority carefully crafted a narrative of white supremacy to justify race-based slavery for life. Common whites, regardless of their socioeconomic conditions, shared with elites a higher place in the racial order, providing them with a sense of equality with their elite counterparts. Political leaders reinforced this racial ordering by creating an environment that created divisions between African Americans and common whites, muting any sort of shared sense of class consciousness. Poor whites and the yeomanry understood that their elevated position in the social hierarchy provided them with a sense of power. Although they lacked the material comforts and political clout of elites, their independence and freedom stood in stark contrast to the dependency and restrictions of enslaved men and women. Leadership within the southern region constructed policies that not only worked in their political and economic interests but also secured the devotion of common whites to the racial order. The lack of property requirements granted all white men the right to vote, but few common white males held political office. This absence of representation from their socioeconomic class left most susceptible to the influence of slave owners. A vote for the slaveholding interests, whether it benefited their own livelihood or not, meant more than securing the institution itself. It meant support for a racial order that provided them with a higher status within the larger social hierarchy. In the context of defending white supremacy, one sees the intersection of race and class in defining the identity of common whites as a socioeconomic group.[14]

Second, while their "whiteness" elevated them in the racial ordering of southern society, common whites clearly occupied a lower socioeconomic class position than the elites. Scholars such as Anna Gayle Fry and W. G. Robertson writing on early Alabama emphasize that an elite class of planters or "aristocrats" moved to Alabama right after statehood and brought with them a distinctive culture that set them apart from other, less prosperous whites. Alabamians, regardless of race, became acutely aware that the elites' wealth allowed them to invest in and expand the plantation economy, including ownership of enslaved people, in the state. The prosperity of the planter minority also led to differences in material conditions, political leadership, credit opportunities, and land ownership that made it clear that they occupied the highest level of the state's social ordering. As discussed above, class divisions also emerged in the geographical landscape of the state. For example, the elites investing in the cotton kingdom settled on the rich soil of the Black Belt region. Those of the yeomenry and poor whites moved into the mountainous regions of northern Alabama as well as the Piney Woods region of the southeastern portion. The port city of Mobile also offered a unique culture of urban distinction that included a mixture of socioeconomic interests. A growing sense of inequality and limited opportunities for upward social mobility emerged from this diverse landscape. In response, elites made a concerted political and economic effort to diminish a class consciousness among white and Black southerners. Throughout the 1830s and 1840s, poor whites shared with enslaved people a class consciousness shaped by oppression and marginalization. Such an underclass threatened the very existence of the slave institution and planter dominance. Seeking the means of sustaining their place in the hierarchy of southern political and economic culture, slaveholders resorted to various legal and extralegal means to gain non-slaveholders' loyalty to the institution and to drive a wedge between poor whites and slaves. The Civil War challenged the relationships between the common white majority and their planter counterparts, for whom they bore much of the wartime hardships. Although similar studies of other southern states exist, their focus has been mostly on how these growing class conflicts manifested themselves in the economic and political discourse during and after the war.[15]

Finally, gender provided the key to overcoming the limitations resulting from membership in the common white class. Members of the poor white and yeomen classes called on popular concepts of manhood and womanhood in their private and public lives to claim power in a world dominated by the planter minority. Gender, whether in the roles they played or in the relationships they forged, figured prominently in how common whites conceptualized the world around them. Situating this analysis within the family allows us to move beyond the binary understanding of gender—the male versus female paradigm—to dive deeper into the reciprocal relationships and mutual interests of men and women in and outside the home. In their roles within the household and their connections to the state and its leaders, common whites stood on equal footing with those elevated in the social order, at least through the rhetorical constructions of gender. In essence they laid claim to the same gender ideals to which elites identified in their own lives. Although conflict between the elite and common whites existed due to the overwhelming advantages the former held over the latter, for the most part class lines seemed blurred when making similar claims to feminine and masculine identities.

They carried this link between the personal world of family and the public world of duty and reputation into the secession and war period.

The Confederate cause allowed common whites to center themselves in the mainstream of the sociopolitical culture by once again calling on the power of gendered rhetoric. Men leaned on notions of masculine honor and duty to the family as cause for fighting a war that did little to protect their interests. Antebellum cultural norms defined men's masculinity in the context of their roles within the family and their reciprocal relationships with its dependents. Historian Stephen Berry's study of southern masculinity reveals that the identity of men depended on their relationships with and validation from the women, especially their spouses, in their lives. As the South moved toward war, these same masculine expectations guided the construction of Confederate nationalism. In her work on the political agency of white women and enslaved people of the South, Stephanie McCurry contends that Confederate support involved a masculine conception of what the war was about and that "the voters and the soldiers" shared a fraternal connection to the cause. White women, within this political culture, assumed images of "objects of protection symbolic and real." The gendered rhetoric of male protector and female bodies in danger provided a language that drew elites and common whites together in a shared goal. Women likewise envisioned their support for the war in terms of their maternal and domestic roles. Continuing their prewar responsibilities of nurturing family members and producing household supplies allowed common white women to create their own political identity within the context of the Confederate effort. In particular, they found a source of civic power within the private world of the home and family. Their emotional and material support they once assumed in the antebellum era now took on significance in the public world of military supply and soldier morale.[16]

Yet the war's toll on common whites eroded their willingness to sacrifice family and the comforts of domesticity for the long term. Notions of duty and honor rooted in gender identities provided their voice to express their frustration with the war's economic and emotional hardships. Risking the label of "Tory" or "traitor" for deserting the army or rioting to demand food for the starving threatened to impugn one's public reputation. Yet to do so in the name of family provided men and women the rationale to protest conditions and to question the war effort. Even more so, the elites, many of whom influenced public policies that countered the interests of common whites, bore fewer sacrifices at home, causing class relations of the antebellum era to change. A good example of this transformation is found among common white women. McCurry demonstrates how common white women, especially the poorer wives of soldiers, discovered a new position of power in their relationship to the state. In trying to defend their families against imminent starvation, "they forged a politics of subsistence" that allowed them to lay claim to political power. The emergence of a new feminine identity that McCurry defines as the "soldier's wife" gave way to a campaign, whether through formal or informal means, to seek justice from the state. In doing so they placed enough pressure on state leaders that they had little choice but to heed the demands of white women when determining many of their policies regarding civilian aid. Men too experienced a transition in sentiment as the war wore down the will of soldiers to remain in the fight. Just as men called on the ideology of masculine protection of vulnerable women to enter the war, they likewise used the same reasoning for questioning the continuation of war. Hearing news of civilian suffering with little support from the military or state threatened their masculine identities as providers and protectors of the family. War no longer meant the protecting their loved ones, but rather a clear and imminent threat to their survival. Common white men and women came to see a war waged not in the interest of the family, but rather in the economic and political interests of the state's elites. Rooted in the convergence of race, class, and gender identities, the narrative of common white families in Alabama reveals the power from within this social group to claim public agency throughout the course of the war and beyond.[17]

The chapters of this book move chronologically to illuminate the war's transformative effect in the lives of common whites. Chapter 1 situates their story in the antebellum period from statehood to the eve of the war. I explore the centrality of family in the personal identities of men and women but also their connections to public power. Relegated to the margins of Alabama's economic and political mainstream due to the control of planter elites, common whites sought alternative sources of power in order to claim the same rights and responsibilities of an honorable man or woman. One important source of this power came from the court system, in particular the divorce records and criminal cases involving nonelites forced to defend their public reputations. Valuing the gendered ideals of respectable behavior allowed common whites to stand on equal footing with elites and thus quieted class conflicts lying beneath the surface.

Chapters 2 and 3 explore the wartime experiences of men and women from their own perspective and, for the most part, in their own words. I first demonstrate why and how those who supported the Confederacy portrayed their loyalty, whether by joining the army or through their service on the home front. The family factored significantly as a rationale to join the Confederate cause, even if reluctantly. Those left on the home front likewise provided a source of material support and emotional comfort in the first two years of the war. Thus, family became the primary motivational factor sustaining common whites regardless of the sacrifices they endured. Next my research turns to the sources and expressions of discontent among common whites, whose situation worsened as conditions soured in the army and at home. The ideal of family that had at one time buttressed their support now became the source of their discontent. This chapter offers, from the voices of common whites, the reasoning for their growing frustration with the war as the family they sought to protect now stood in peril.

The final two chapters illustrate the agency of common whites in shaping the public policies during and after the war. Men and women demanded from their paternal leaders a response to wartime privations and the threat to family security. Their response in wartime proved less than adequate in responding to the needs of non-elites. And they felt the full weight of their discontent as they turned against the war in personal and public demonstrations. The last chapter brings common whites into the immediate years after the Civil War. From the end of the war to the 1870s, the situation for common whites reached a crisis level as the state faced a war-torn landscape that needed to be rebuilt, while facing a new set of circumstances that threatened to destroy many families. Once again, declining conditions forced state leaders to take action to keep a majority of their population from starving. As a result, common whites again drove public policy, at least for a short time. By the 1870s state leaders turned their interests to reestablishing Democratic Party power, developing industry, restructuring agricultural labor, and restoring white supremacy in a postemancipation world as the future of Alabama in a new South.

The gendered world of family provided the rationale and motivation for common whites to assert agency in Confederate Alabama. Calling on a prewar culture of familial duty and honor to which they long held fast, they used it to negotiate the consequences of military service and home-front sacrifice. Conditions at home and in the military called on all southerners to sacrifice, while for middling and poor households, their preexisting socioeconomic status exacerbated their difficult situation. Living in a world that privileged the wealth and civic power of the planter elites, this group turned to the ideals and responsibility of family to help endure material privation, emotional turmoil, and physical danger. Family also provided the justification to turn against the war by rebelling against the paternal power of the Confederacy and the state. When James Garrison wrote about his desire to return to the comforts of home, he revealed the extent to which family informed the power of common whites in the Confederate experience. Sadly, though, Union troops captured Garrison during the Battle of Gettysburg, and he spent the remaining months of his life imprisoned at Fort Delaware, until his death in November of 1863. Although Garrison made the ultimate sacrifice, his story demonstrates the many common white Confederates who refused to bend to the slaveholders' pressures to preserve the status quo. Rather, they emerged as agents of change for Alabama in their quest to determine the fate of their own lives.

1

"Faithfully and Affectionately"

Claiming Equality in the Antebellum Era, 1820–60

Traveling through Alabama, Thomas Hamilton, an English author, bleakly described an environment peppered with underdeveloped lands, inhabited by a crude population possessing little moral conviction. "There are no smart houses or equipages, nor indeed any demonstration of opulence, of amusements of any kind I heard nothing," he wrote as he started his tour northward from the Gulf Coast city of Mobile. At one point an immigrant to the state confirmed Hamilton's conclusions, informing him that "the man that comes here, sir, only exchanges one set of evils for another; he is obliged to mingle with a most profane and godless set." As Hamilton continued his move onward to the capital city of Montgomery, his assessment of conditions in the state remained the same. He expected the trappings of a refined town familiar to a worldly traveler but to his disappointment found little by way of adequate accommodations, noting that "there is not one tolerable house." Even the place where he boarded for the night resembled a dormitory with "beds full of vermin." Although he emphasized a lack of refinement and structure in the state, Hamilton continually commented on a notable air of opportunity among the white population. He wholeheartedly believed that, as one resident aptly summarized to him, "They may not get rich here, but they will be sure, if they are sober, industrious, and do not suffer from the climate, to escape from poverty."[1]

Hamilton's observations came in 1831, just twelve years after Alabama achieved statehood. The physical landscape was still in the process of developing into the prosperous cotton kingdom already booming in neighboring states. Large portions of the land remained undeveloped, and social institutions such as churches and schools continued to grow. These frontierlike conditions in Alabama bred a sense of egalitarianism among the diverse population of white immigrants. While differences and, at times, antagonisms existed between the powerful wealthy minority and those of lesser means, the slow development of the state muted those contrasts. In the decades from statehood to the onset of the Civil War, Alabama remained a land in which the possibility of upward mobility and prosperity continued to exist, whether realized or not. In most cases the chances of moving from the status of common white to elite planter were relatively slim. As their access to the economic prosperity shared by elites began to narrow, common whites found other areas in which to create a level playing field. The family, and the roles and relationships within it, provided that sense of a common experience shared among all whites in the state. The desire to create a better life for their loved ones, the reliance on kinship ties, and the fierce protection of family reputation created a space in which the common whites, although marginalized economically, could stand equally with their aristocratic "betters." Neither wealth nor the lack thereof defined one's claim to protect and provide for their family; rather, their status as free, white members of the state granted those rights. As a result, men and women alike linked their valued honor as individuals to the reputation of the family and fought fiercely to protect it.[2]

Alabama's long history began with the settling of Native American peoples, namely, the Mississippians. As the first inhabitants of the state, they reached the peak of their culture around 1300 ACE and were known for their many diverse communities. By the 1600s the Mississippian culture morphed into several distinct tribes, identified by their language, known as the Cherokees, Creek, Chickasaw, and Choctaw. These groups maintained their presence in Alabama and began a trade with whites moving into the territory. Such early trade relations created a middle ground between primarily Scottish immigrants and local Native American groups that became the foundation for the early fur trade in the area. With the defeat of the Creeks after 1815, the Federal Road became the main passage of migrants, and they began to pour into the territory.[3]

The white settlers who moved into the territory did so out of a desire to seek new land and, with it, a chance to improve their standard of living. The cotton boom in the South incentivized this movement westward. One could perhaps find their fortune through investment in cotton. Yet the required land and slave labor to create a place in the plantation economy precluded the majority of whites from joining the ranks of the wealthiest planters. Competition for new lands driven by soil exhaustion and economic competition meant the majority of those who came to the Alabama Territory claimed membership among the yeomen and poor whites who constituted the population of common whites. They came from areas of Georgia, Virginia, and North and South Carolina and saw acquisition of land in the territory as a direct route to financial independence. Land, as the most important commodity, was difficult to obtain in especially fertile and productive areas such as Virginia and the Carolinas. Those who came with wealth invested in the prime areas of the state along the Black Belt region, known for its fertile soil, and laid the foundation for Alabama's elite planter class. The clear majority, however, owned little property, including slaves, and came with fewer resources to begin a farming venture. Historians of early Alabama have described these conditions as "primitive" and stated that the lack of developed farms created food shortages and other hardships when first settling the state. As historian Leah Rawls Atkins describes, "life on the frontier was hard, drab, and confining." Regardless, migrants continued to filter into the territory in numbers that began to alarm the neighboring, older states about the potential for depopulation. Due to their lack of wealth, most of these new arrivals intended to squat on public domain lands until they could obtain a full title to them once they had been surveyed and placed on the market. Common whites recognized signs that not all would share in the prosperity of the state's early years. They could merely look down the road for evidence of the narrowing opportunities for upward mobility, as their wealthier neighbors began to replace their modest cabins with grand mansions. Other signs of the elites' growing influence took on subtler tones, especially in the world of politics.[4]

The political environment created a space in which white men regardless of their class group could, at least by all appearances, find a seat at the table. The Alabama constitution, adopted in 1819, embodied the spirit of Jacksonian democracy. Rhetorical constructions of the common man as the source of "true" American democracy resonated in the state, especially given its rugged, frontierlike conditions in its early years. As with many states created in the post-Revolution, the need to open the vote to as many white male residents as possible proved necessary to meet the requirements for statehood. When delegates constructed Alabama's constitution, they ensured that universal white male suffrage prevailed. Gone were the property, tax, or militia service requirements; now the white male population, regardless of socioeconomic status, would decide their officeholders. These liberalized voting rights meant that common whites could find a path to citizenship often denied to them in the older southern states. As a result, an alliance between yeomen and poor whites emerged that gave them a substantial presence in the political process as the majority of the state's population. Wealthy planters who held or aspired to hold political office understood the value of the common white man's vote and courted his favor through public events, barbeques, and campaign rallies. Within this democratic atmosphere, common whites were welcome participants but solely as voters; the elites firmly controlled the state's political culture as the primary officeholders.[5]

State leaders did, however, recognize the importance of addressing the interests of their common white constituents. Certainly some of those politicians did so purely out of a desire to garner their votes. Others, however, demonstrated a true advocacy of their interests, as seen in the debate over land distribution. Nearly a decade before the Civil War, only 4.4 million acres of the state's 32 million acres were what was considered improved, or developed, land. In the 1820s the state legislature requested that Congress keep land prices to their "true value" and reduce the minimum acreage and price to forty acres at twenty-five cents per acre. In addition, they asked that those squatters who had already established themselves in the state be allowed first right to purchase the property. Thus, for many of the state's farmers, the hope of obtaining land appeared a reality even as late as the 1850s. Common whites turned to their state and national legislators to advocate for their interest in obtaining land and to pass policies that were not just favorable to the elite classes. Due to such power as a voting bloc, common whites understood that they could hold some sway over issues such as land distribution.[6]

As advocates of the issues concerning common whites, elites needed to appear relatable to their voters. Such men ran for office on the idea that they shared the same identity as a "common man," often downplaying any semblance of privilege or elitism. One such example was that of Williamson Robert Winfield Cobb, from small farming communities of the northeastern portion of the state. Although a member of the state's elite class, he emphasized his limited education and familiarity with the common white population. His primary cause was the accessibility of land and protection of property from confiscation due to debts. As a representative of a district of small farmers, he easily defeated his planter opponent in his bid for Congress. Felix Grundy McConnell likewise served a district of small farmers and emerged as an advocate of homestead legislation that offered greater access to land ownership. Like Cobb, McConnell presented himself as one who denounced privilege and advocated for legislation for the common man. He found support among the hill regions of the state, winning election to state office in 1838, and later served in Congress, beginning in 1843. Another champion of small farming interests was William Russell Smith, who, like Cobb and McConnell, gained most of his supporters from the mountainous areas of the state occupied primarily by common whites. Smith also believed that land ownership was the clearest means of protecting those constituents and creating equal opportunity amid a growing powerful planter class in the state.[7]

By all measures, the availability of land fueled perceptions that economic opportunities awaited common whites, as they migrated to Alabama. And they could turn to tangible examples of upward mobility through stories of those who achieved a level of success. Joel Spigener, for example, moved from South Carolina when the price and availability of land there prohibited him from expanding his farm. In 1833 Joel chose to relocate to Alabama with his family and would later call for his stepbrother William Oliver, also from South Carolina, to come as soon as he thought the conditions were safe. Spigener settled in central Alabama along the lower portion of the Coosa River. His wife, children, sister, and seven enslaved people accompanied him on the journey. Once settled, he wrote to William describing favorably the land but that he would have to squat until the government had determined how land would be sold. In another letter Joel explains that while the water and fishing were good, "there will be no society for a few years, as the Country is so newly Settled." Still, the potential for the Spigener family to move up the socioeconomic ladder, perhaps into the realm of planter, proved worth the uncertainty of settling a new land. Smith Lipscomb also found Alabama ripe with opportunities for upward mobility, as he chose to relocate his family from South Carolina in 1845. Obviously lacking the financial security and investment in enslaved labor that the Spigener family possessed, Lipscomb still risked his family's comfort and security as he attempted to make a life for them in Alabama. At first the family had little choice but to squat on a plot of land. Those early years indeed became so difficult that his wife worked as a seamstress while Lipscomb concentrated on growing the farm. Fifteen years later his efforts had clearly paid off, as he had grown into a rather prosperous planter with investment in cotton and livestock. It was these rags-to-riches stories of men like Spigener and Lipscomb that gave hope to Alabama's common whites of one day achieving that status of elite.[8]

Along with their sense of political worth and perceived opportunities for economic success, common whites also shared with elites the values of independence and self-reliance. As one historian notes, the planter class "was neither closed nor homogeneous." Those smaller planters tended to live more like their yeoman brothers "in comfortable circumstances" whose sense of self depended upon "the sense of independence and authority which their position in society gave them." The early conditions of settlers living on small plantations demonstrates how those who moved began with very little and developed better conditions over time. One traveler to the state observed such a spirit of self-reliance while staying in the home of Duncan Macmillan. He learned that Macmillan had "settled in the country about ten years ago, and ha[d] seventy acres cleared by his own industry." Harriet Martineau, an English writer who visited near Montgomery, recognized that even among the planters, the pioneer conditions bred a sense of common culture among all whites that placed less emphasis on refinement and more on the attributes of a self-made man. "The result is a society which it is a punishment to its best members to live in," she wrote in 1837, adding that "there is pedantry in those who read; prejudice in those who do not." She concluded that the conditions created a society in which men and women displayed crude mannerisms "and an absence of all reference to the higher, the real objects of life."[9]

The blurring of class distinctions likewise appeared in the social behaviors of whites, due mainly to the slow pace of development in the state. It seemed at least in the first two decades after statehood that common whites and elites living in Alabama behaved more alike than differently. The elite culture of the antebellum South characteristic of older states to their east had yet to take shape. As travelers to the state noted, even in the Black Belt region occupied by the growing planter class, a lack of sophistication existed regarding manners and morals. Outside observers tended to fixate on instances of violence and debauchery, most notably the result of alcohol consumption. Frederick Olmsted, while traveling through Alabama, believed that few distinctions existed between planters and the poorer socioeconomic groups, namely, when observing their behavior. He wrote that in one instance the planters aboard a boat carrying cotton "were usually well dressed, but were a rough, coarse style of people, drinking a great deal, and most of the time under a little alcoholic excitement." Olmsted praised what he considered an independent spirit of the planter but denounced their appearance as "unrateable by dress, taste, forms, and expenditures." Another traveler as late as 1835 also recorded the behaviors of planters from the state and described them in ways often associated with the stereotypes of common whites rather than elites. While taking a boat to various locales, he noted that "some of the passengers were kind and communicative, but others were too fond of gambling and spitting, and smoking to permit the enjoyment of much comfort." He saved his harshest criticisms of Alabamians for those who had "an inordinate love of tobacco," seeing the habit as a common yet abhorrent behavior of men from all backgrounds.[10]

The architecture of homes in Alabama provided further evidence of the state's frontier conditions that prolonged the blurring of class distinctions. For example, the Black Belt region settled rather quickly in the 1820s with the development of newspapers, stores, boarding houses, and schools, all made possible by the growing plantation wealth in the area. Yet planters' homes still appeared rather modest in that decade. Even Perry County, an area included in the Black Belt region, resembled more of a backcountry settlement with primitive log cabins as the primary residences for more than two decades after its founding in 1819. In fact, the first generation of families to settle in Perry were squatters who migrated to the area in search of new farm lands. With such frontier conditions, especially in an area that would eventually house the state's wealthiest residents, the distinctions in living conditions that came to separate common and elite whites took time to develop. But, with the entrance of consumerism and material culture by the 1840s, the separation of socioeconomic classes grew more pronounced when it came to homes. Coosa County, for example, in east-central Alabama, became a formal part of the state as late as 1832 after the Creeks ceded the remainder of their lands. Although Coosa would become a vital part of the state's cotton economy, it would take nearly two decades to develop its infrastructure. The primary unit of housing for residents thus remained the basic log cabin. Even as late as 1850, homes with framed structures were limited and modest, and ranged in size from the single-room cabin to the more extravagant two-story homes. The majority of residents, however, lived in a "two room or double log house, with a hall of ten or twelve feet between."[11]

Alabama also trailed older states in developing basic institutions such as schools and churches. As early as 1818, missionaries, such as those sent by the Presbyterian Church, attempted to establish religion in what many perceived as "ignorance, superstition, and wickedness" among the early population. One missionary, Hiland Hubbard, spent time in the Alabama Territory and delivered a report on the state of religion. He remarked that "in these several places, the people were almost, or entirely destitute of the preaching of the Gospel." Hubbard attributed the limited religious institutions to the lack of ministers willing to relocate. He believed that while there was a noticeable population who were "grossly immoral and ignorant," there were many who sought religious instruction and needed a minister. This binary view of the morality of settlers seemed popular among missionaries: the people were either desirous of an established church or prone to vice. Nonetheless, as Alabama developed as a state, the establishment of permanent churches became more evident. Schools in the state followed a similar trend, having established a statewide school system as late as 1856. Frederick Olmsted, while visiting Alabama in 1852 and 1853, noted that what was hailed as the premier "Young Ladies' College" in Selma consisted merely of a "brick barrack" with no grounds and was "forlorn in expression." During James Stuart's visit to Alabama, the Scottish writer and journalist remarked that his hostess on one occasion admitted that she liked the state "were it not for the want of schools for her children." Perhaps one reason for the protracted time to establish formal churches and schools resulted from the access to supplies. As in the case of Coosa County, the simple construction and meager furnishings of churches and schools were due, in part, to a lack of sawmills. Even with the state's abundance of natural resources, without access to the means to process them, communities like Coosa experienced lengthy periods of development. Residents brought cut lumber into the county through long hauls that proved rather cumbersome in the early period of settlement. Still, by the time Alabama's structural growth seemed to catch up with older southern states, the growing sectional tensions between North and South had already begun to take shape.[12]

Race likewise played a crucial role in downplaying the growing imbalance of economic and political power in favor of the state's elites. From the beginning of statehood, Alabama clearly situated itself among the South's prominent slave states. Hopeful planters who migrated to the state either brought with them or purchased enslaved men and women to provide the necessary labor to generate their wealth. Yet, noticeably, most common whites possessed little of the state's enslaved population, owning fewer than ten unfree laborers, if any at all. So why then support an institution that tended to marginalize those with little investment in it? Scholars take varying approaches to the issue of slavery as it related to class relations. As one historian contends, common whites challenged very little about slavery and, instead, supported it. They served on slave patrols, voted for proslavery leaders, and eventually risked their lives to preserve the institution. Frank Owsley argued that they never possessed a Marxian sense of class consciousness, but rather revered elites and saw hope in that they would one day rise to their status as slave owners themselves. On the other hand, Eugene Genovese contends that planter hegemony kept class conflict at bay as elites garnered a paternalistic loyalty from common whites due to their wealth and political power. Other evidence indicates that common whites did challenge the elites by fighting for expansion of political rights and pushed back against the cultural superiority of elites. But the issue of race created by the presence of slavery perhaps drew the two classes together more than kept them apart, whether intentionally or not.[13]

By the antebellum period, growing threats to slavery created a sense of urgency among elites to protect the ties that bound members of the white population together. The abolitionist movement, gaining momentum by the 1830s, placed pressures on elites and state leaders to defend the institution. Expansion of antislavery societies coupled with emerging political discourse against slavery's movement westward sounded alarms among Alabama's leaders. It became clear that a defense of slavery needed to involve the support of the common white majority. To that end, the planter minority constructed a narrative of white supremacy that created an elevated space for common whites in the social ordering. One historian asserts that "racism provided the glue to hold white society together" and that slavery "made all white men equal." Leaders even pointed to what they saw as evidence of "wage slavery" among northern white factory workers that fueled class conflict. They argued that such a conflict just never materialized in a culture that placed all whites above the class of unfree African Americans. As John C. Calhoun announced, the division within southern society was between "white and black" rather than "rich and poor." Calhoun's words resonated among many common whites, even non-slaveholders, who sought validation in the social order despite their economic and political marginalization. Many other ties reinforced this sense of a higher class based on race. Kinship, for example, sometimes bound elites and common whites together. In addition, common whites could turn to their elite neighbors for help in farming, in forms such as renting labor, use of a cotton gin, or purchasing supplies. Tommy Craig Brown found such evidence of these business transactions in the Piney Woods region of the state. He concludes that despite the varying investment in the actual system itself, ranging from non-slaveholder to small slaveholder, all common whites "embraced both the expansion of the cotton economy and the institution of slavery that made it possible."[14]

Yet we must be careful to avoid painting all common whites with a broad brush. The poorest members of the common white population perhaps had greater cause to challenge such racial unity. Hardened attitudes toward the elites along with their impoverished living conditions and limited access to political power seemed more aligned with the situation of enslaved individuals. As historian Keri Leigh Merritt contends, poor whites tended to blame their circumstances on slavery and the elites bent on protecting and expanding it. Their resentment, however, threatened the racial order. Thus, when necessary, state leaders relied on the law to drive a wedge between poor whites and enslaved people and free people of color. For instance, they outlawed interracial sexual relationships and banned the underground exchange of goods across racial lines. Authorities even used extralegal means in the form of vigilante violence against those who dared challenge "both slavery and the southern social hierarchy." The efforts to create a common culture of "whiteness" fed into their eventual defense against growing incursions on the slave institution. As the debates over the fate of southern states grew increasingly loud, so did the discussions of what was at stake for common whites if slavery were abolished.[15]

Although conditions in antebellum Alabama helped to downplay class differences, striking contrasts developed between common white and elite residents. A visible indicator of these differences emerged in the settlement patterns of whites in the state. By the antebellum era, Alabama's communities clearly displayed a division between socioeconomic groups. For instance, planters with more wealth to purchase fertile land in the Black Belt region settled what would become a notable plantation district in the state. Common whites with fewer savings or less access to credit constituted the majority in northern Alabama and in the mountainous regions of the state where land tended to be cheaper. This geographic separation of common whites from elites in the state contributed to a sense of class difference that could, at times, fuel resentment. For example, Madison County, located in the northern portion of the state, was home to a large planter community where elites gained "commercial and political advantages" that, on occasion, "aroused the antagonism of men who were not financially independent."[16]

Alabama's legal system likewise reflected the divisions between common whites and elites concerning their financial and community resources. Many of those convicted of crimes came from among the poorest common whites, because they lacked the financial support or kinship ties to avoid prosecution. As a result, they petitioned the courts for help in avoiding stiff penalties that, unlike their elite counterparts, they had no means to pay for. Their petitions for leniency often cited their dire circumstances as reason for avoiding prison, fines, or both. By the late 1830s, Alabama created a state prison to handle men incarcerated for crimes ranging from horse thievery to murder. Yet the state also set in place a process for inmates to petition for their release that began with demonstrating good behavior within the prison and support from the community outside it. Many of those requesting pardons, parole, or clemency cited their dire financial circumstances, a contributing factor for their incarceration, as cause for their release. In 1823 Joseph Turnbull of Jackson County was tried and convicted of horse stealing and fined $30, which he was unable to pay. The court placed him in custody and sentenced him to branding and thirty-nine lashes "on his bare back." A petition to the governor from "the citizens of Jackson County" claimed that Turnbull was "a very poor man in aid with a family of small children to support" and therefore should be set free. The petitioners argued that a group of men persuaded him to take the horse, that he did not commit the crime of his own volition. Another case occurring in the early 1820s involved two men who each received thirty-nine lashes, jail time, and a $100 fine for running "a common whore house and disorderly house" in the city of Mobile. The court followed through with the lashes and the jail time but realized that the men had little means to pay the fine. The judge in the case, J. C. Mitchell, submitted a petition to the governor to waive the fine and force the men to leave the city. He intended to shut down the brothel that, according to the judge, "was a disgrace to the city . . . and the scene of riots and quarreling to the great injury and disturbance of the public peace."[17]

Other areas of Alabama's social landscape revealed evidence of class divisions between elites and common whites. In particular, common whites performed differently in the culture of violence and honor so deeply embedded in the antebellum South. In a masculine world protective of public reputation, southern white men called on the familiar act of dueling to restore one's good standing or to seek retribution for other wrongs done to them. With dueling came a tradition of protocol reserved for the ranks of the elites. Selecting weapons and place as well as choosing a second to stand in for the participant all played out as public theater for the sake of restoring honor. Yet, for common whites, dueling in the high culture of elites stood outside what seemed familiar to them. Rather, a man restored his reputation through the physical violence, primarily fist-fighting, more familiar to their culture. As Keri Leigh Merritt asserts, fighting "helped create a way of measuring a man's worth without relying on occupation or wealth." Additionally, notions of preserving honor allowed common whites to claim ideas of masculine behavior and identity similar to those of wealthy men. Settling disputes that often led to fistfights, as opposed to a formal duel, played a critical role in a common white man's culture.[18]

Court records provide evidence of the sacred role of violence in protecting a man's reputation. In Clarke County the court convicted a man of the last name Hammonds for assault and battery. He received a $65 fine plus a jail sentence. Hammonds had very little income and therefore could not pay. A petition went before the court asking that the judge waive the fine, as it would "increase his public debt without any public benefit." The petitioners rooted their defense of Hammonds's release in the notion that he was acting out of honor rather than malice in instigating the fight. Thomas Adams and his son, both of Lauderdale County, also landed in jail after a physical fight. The record is unclear whether the father and son were fighting each other or others. Regardless, Thomas could not pay the court costs of $50. The petition to have the costs waived stated that while Thomas was guilty, there was "no damage done or blood drawn." Being a man of modest financial means, Thomas, the petitioners argued, could not afford to be away from his family of thirteen, all of whom were "dependent entirely on his exertions for their support and maintenance." The petitioners emphasized that since Thomas acted out of his duty to protect his standing in the community, the court should show leniency. Daniel West likewise landed himself in court after using violence to deal with a challenge to his reputation. In 1820 a Tuscaloosa County court convicted him of assault and battery and fined him $100. Supporters of West claimed that he was "a peaceable and orderly citizen" and that therefore the court should waive the fine. Regardless of the outcome in their cases, the common denominator is that these men connected violence with protection of honor, even when asking for leniency from the courts.[19]

In some cases men resorted to violence when they believed their livelihood was at stake. A man's good standing in his community directly affected his ability to do business. Any slight against his integrity, for example, could mean the loss of potential customers or other financial relationships, placing his role as breadwinner in jeopardy. In the case of James of Lawrence County, he had little choice but to resort to violence to protect his standing as an honest citizen. In 1825 a man in the county accused James of starting a rumor that he had stolen corn. James, now put in the position of slanderer, vehemently denied the accusation. Yet his accuser, along with two other companions, confronted James at a corn mill and demanded that he fight them in order to settle the dispute. James tried to avoid the fight but eventually felt he had no alternative but to battle the man. In the course of the fight, James got the best of the man and "several times called on the deceased to cry enough." Unfortunately, James ended the fight by killing the man, and authorities took him into custody. He eventually received a conviction of manslaughter and was sentenced to prison. Yet, in accordance with the culture of honor, James had merely exercised his duty to defend his reputation, especially as it involved his work at the corn mill. Even the community stepped in to defend James's actions. After his conviction over two hundred citizens signed a petition on behalf of James asking that the governor release him, citing that he was a good man and a son of "a soldier of the Revolution." They argued that James had little financial means and a large family to support, and given the circumstances of the fight, the courts would be justified in waiving the fine. James had followed the code of conduct in a physical conflict intended to restore honor, and unfortunately his opponent lost his life in the process. The community rallied around James and insisted that he be freed from all penalties so as to continue supporting his family.[20]

Amid the growing divide between common whites and their elite counterparts, the former found in family an arena in which to demand equal rights and opportunity. The economic reality of prewar Alabama was that by 1860 a visible planter class controlled the center of economic and political life, and occupied a position as the state's aristocracy. The majority of the white population, however, consisted of numbers of common whites who, despite their economic and political limitations, claimed the same rights as elites to protect their families. They railed against anything that seemed to challenge those rights and fiercely defended their reputations as men and women devoted to their roles in the family. Men claimed their power as the head of the home by protecting and providing for their dependents. Women too asserted their authority in the home as mothers and wives who sought great value in their domestic and maternal roles within the family. Any question of their ability to sustain a viable family life had to be eliminated, through either private or public means. It is from their perceptions of family as the center of their existence that they created a path from the margins to the mainstream of life in antebellum Alabama.

Family formed the heart and soul of common white culture in antebellum Alabama. Foremost, men and women leaned on family for comfort during emotional trials. For instance, as a new migrant to the state, Christianah Spigener wrote to her sister-in-law in 1833 noting her deep sense of homesickness. "When I first came out here," she wrote, "I would of given all I was worth to of been back there." She noted, however, that the isolation from extended kin eventually passed as she settled into the routines of domesticity. Still, the trials of moving to a new state with few family ties meant depending on immediate family for support. For example, Joel Spigener described how his wife had little choice but to endure poor health conditions while trying to nurse their daughter, who had also fallen ill. Having just lost the child of one of his cousins to the dreaded scarlet fever, the family felt an even greater sense of anxiety when anyone became sick. To mitigate their fears, they came to rely solely on the comfort from the immediate family, rather than on their extended kinship network from their previous home. Dependence on family therefore became a key to survival for many common whites. This dependency was made even more significant when families experienced death. Margaret Miles Gillis, for example, underwent a significant transformation when her mother passed away. With the father and remaining siblings left to fend for themselves, Margaret, a young woman herself, assumed many of the domestic duties. Despite such hard times, family became the source of comfort and solace for common whites. Turning inward toward the relationships within the domestic circle created a sense of identity and belonging that created a valued sense of self.[21]

Such was the case in the life of Sarah Rodgers Rousseau Espy. Born December 7, 1815, Sarah started life in Madison, Georgia. Her father, Hiram Rousseau, moved his family to Alabama around 1834, to Cherokee County. Eventually, Sarah married Thomas Espy from Cassville, Georgia, becoming his second wife. The couple lived in Georgia until 1849, when they moved to Cherokee County, Alabama, so that Thomas could seek better-paying work. She resided in Alabama throughout her marriage and the birth of her seven children. Sarah's husband, however, died in 1860, leaving the family to maintain their farm as a source of financial support. Like many women, Sarah entrusted the settlement of her husband's affairs to a male friend, described as Mr. E in her diary. By July of 1860, the financial state of the family grew alarming for Sarah, as she expressed fear that they would not survive the hardships. "We are feeling badly and lonely and destitute tonight," she wrote, "for we are weak and look forward to hard struggle with an unfeeling world." Yet, with many of her children old enough to work, Sarah found solace in the support of her family to sustain the farm.[22]

The labor of family members took on significant meaning for common whites, serving as a significant tie that bound them together. For many southerners, the core values within the family consisted of "respect for hard work, independence, and the ability to provide for one's own." Work, in essence, served as the means to escape dependence and was more than often a family endeavor. All members of the family, regardless of age or gender, performed some labor vital to the survival of the home. Most common whites regarded idleness as a flaw and a path to dependence. A good example of the centrality of work is found in common white women. They maintained the essential domestic tasks of cooking, cleaning, and child care, but oftentimes stepped outside the home to perform other forms of labor. They joined their husbands in cultivating crops or assisted in a family business outside of farming. They likewise helped supplement the family income by using their domestic skills to make clothing to sell and to take on boarders. Women also found employment in the scant textile mills in antebellum Alabama. The majority of female employees tended to be young and unmarried, providing wages for the family income. But mill owners also allowed married women to work, earning between $6 and $12 a month. Other occupations for women included "spinning, weaving, sewing, cooking, and washing." Work therefore defined a woman's daily life as well as contributed to the independence of the family by providing crucial economic support.[23]

Social activities also reflected a similar connection between work and family so deeply embedded in common white culture. One of the most common events was the assembly of a new home when families turned to their neighbors for help. Community members willingly lent their labor in the construction process especially for reputable families deemed worthy of their time. Home construction also brought people together, fostering closer bonds and providing entertainment. During such events in Coosa County, for example, tales of "hunting feats, stirring incidents, interesting exploits, or political matters" regaled participants, making the arduous work seem "more like a good-natured social gathering than the hard work it was." The women's roles during the house raising also focused on production of either food or domestic items. "Some of the neighbor women," as noted, "would come in and help get up the dinner and supper, for usually both meals were eaten on such occasions." Women also engaged in quilting circles while men built the home. They would serve the men their meals, then ate separately while their male counterparts "rested, smoked chewed their tobacco and cracked their jokes." Although work defined these activities, they became vital sources for social interaction familiar to them as a socioeconomic class.[24]

Other social events proved rowdier and less productive in nature. In the era of Jacksonian politics, democratic participation made the common man's vote more valuable. Community barbeques, for instance, served as one way to court the voters, helping candidates during election season. A local group would organize the event, providing food and alcohol, and then invite candidates to offer campaign speeches and mingle with the crowds. Not everyone approved of the meetings, but it was a typical way to reach out to the common white male. Other typically male-centered activities could also become quite raucous at times. Gambling likewise became a fixture in the male popular culture. Such activities did receive negative attention, as "complaints were made that gamesters . . . often assumed an air of importance because they were noticed by prominent men." Yet the draw of gambling reached across class lines, as sons of elite families mingled with the common whites when engaged in such activities. The masculine nature of certain social activities drew men of all stations to "the crossroads store, the militia muster, and the barbeque," where for many "horseplay was the rule . . . and assemblies usually ended in drunkenness and fighting." Such physical altercations, however, appeared less about violence and more about sport, with the victor proving his brawn. While a growing movement for temperance emerged within the religious culture of Alabama, alcohol consumption remained a common presence in most social activities involving males only.[25]

Religious faith figured prominently in Alabama's common white culture. The church provided a central location for community interaction and a sense of purpose through faith. In a culture that often viewed common whites as uncouth or uncultured, perhaps even vulgar, their expression of religious conviction countered the negative stereotypes and helped protect the family's public reputation. Hiland Hubbard, who reported to the Presbytery of South Carolina about his missionary work in Alabama in 1818, cited rampant sin "with eagerness in many of the fashionable amusements of the present day." Yet Hubbard recognized the benefits of establishing a church in the territory of Alabama. He noted that "there are a few, who appear to be feelingly affected with a sense of their situation, and are anxious to obtain a preacher . . . to build them up in holy things." With an eager community of devotees, he saw that the Presbyterian Church could establish a foothold in the soon-to-be state. He appeared especially interested in areas around the Black Warrior River where "commercial advantages" could draw a great deal of financial support for a church. He warned, however, that they needed to act quickly to keep "dangerous men" from settling in the area. Most common whites identified themselves as either Methodist or Baptist. And as the state's population increased, their involvement in the church served a vital purpose in their lives. Christianah Spigener, for example, wrote in 1833 that while she felt a sense of homesickness for her family, she found the people in her new community in central Alabama a "religious kind of people mostly." She joined the Methodist Church in part to connect with her neighbors but also as a means to express her faith, a cultural identification key to common whites. But her involvement in the church took on even more meaning, as she wrote, "I still feel Determined to Serve my God while I live. It is my only comfort here in the world of troubles."[26]

Cultural identity in the prewar South emerged from the relationships and responsibilities situated in the family and the larger community. Intricate kinship ties helped inform the hierarchical power structure that privileged the elite, slaveholding classes. The legitimacy of their community leadership, whether in the world of politics or business, depended on a paternalistic image rooted in their ability to provide for the material and physical protection of their families and their enslaved "family." Kinship relations also provided the power of family name to buttress their community reputation. In this culture that identified the "best men" to lead through paternalistic obligations, a great emphasis was placed on traditional family ideals that defined male and female roles. Society viewed men as heads of families who provided for their dependents, and women as supportive wives and mothers who maintained the domestic responsibilities of the home. Parents expected their children to mirror these conventional gender behaviors as training to one day assume their places in the adult world. This narrative of traditional family values found in an ideal nuclear structure became the social script that elite white southerners aspired to perform.[27]

Obviously, family duty and relations as a source of power and identity extended beyond the elite classes of the Old South. Common whites also drew from notions of masculine and feminine responsibilities within the context of family life to assert the power to protect reputation, property, and even their lives. By claiming a right to perform the same gender roles as did members of the planter class, these men and women exhibited a sense of equality in an unequal world. Men demanded the right to perform their masculine duty to provide for the protection and security of their families and made this clear in their daily community transactions. Their concern with their dependents demonstrating proper gendered behavior also illustrated their concern for securing a respectable reputation, something valued in a world deeply immersed in notions of honor and duty. Protecting the family's public image, then, involved an assertion of power in the community's eyes. Women too found that holding men responsible for fulfilling their paternalistic duties enhanced their domestic power in their relationships to their husbands, fathers, and brothers. And a man's failure to act as the "good man" altogether allowed women to expand the barriers of the female world into civic life by demanding that the community step in as the surrogate provider and protector.

The value of gender roles within the family is most evident in the divorce petitions of the chancery courts and criminal court records in Alabama. Once one moves beyond the contentious and many times hyperbolic descriptions vilifying spouses, we can see the purpose gender had in protecting one's position in the community. In particular, the rhetorical constructions of male and female propriety provided a narrative for couples seeking a dissolution of their marriage. Men and women each stressed that they had performed their masculine or feminine duty to the family without failing. The common narrative of these cases became one of the dutiful wife unable to perform her marital roles due to the obstacles set forth by a morally corrupt spouse. The same emerged as husbands sought separation and eventually divorce. They played the honorable husband whose wife had impugned his masculine reputation, in most cases by committing adultery.

Historians recognize the valuable insights divorce cases offer in understanding how southerners used the legal system as a source of power. Laura Edwards's study of North and South Carolina asserts that "ordinary people"—those she identifies as women, enslaved and free people of color, and poor whites—found in localized law a system that allowed them to "challenge the actions of individual patriarchs" but not patriarchal domination. Edwards distinguishes that state law recognized only "free men," mainly white, wealthier men, and left the local courts to deal with all others as long as it kept the social order in check. In other words, those deemed powerless according to the rules of subordination in slaveholding states could wield some authority in local laws in the name of keeping the peace. The elite, male power structure defined patriarchy in relation to those considered subordinate to the law. But they understood that to maintain social order they would have to allow ordinary people a place to take their grievances, especially in instances of divorce. White women, for example, could

Figure 1. Montgomery County Courthouse in Montgomery, Alabama, 1854. One of the many public spaces where couples pursued divorce petitions in the antebellum period. Alabama Department of Archives and History.

claim power to assert control over the means and relationships in their lives without defying the social order. Loren Schweninger offers similar conclusions about how the legal system served as a venue to assert social power in a strictly ordered slaveholding culture. His study, although focusing more on the experiences of elite white women, delves deeper into the ways that divorce offered women a place to challenge patriarchal authority and at the same time reinforce the racial and social ordering. Because his subjects are slaveholding elites, Schweninger deals more with causation of divorce than with the development of the legal system to handle such cases.[28]

Allison Dorothy Fredette's study of relationships in the upper South reveals a much different perspective on the reasons for marriage and the causes of divorce. Focusing on West Virginia and Kentucky, Fredette contends that those geographically separated from the more established marital traditions of the slaveholding South created a different meaning of marriage and divorce. She explains how couples sought divorce not as a means of protecting or challenging patriarchal order, but rather as a way to preserve a "blend of mutuality, individualism, and contracturalism." In the older southern states to the east, "divorce represented a threat to power, control, and the slave system itself," whereas in the more frontier-like areas of the upper South, failure to live up to roles in marriage presented a threat to the family's survival.[29]

Alabama's handling of divorce cases developed to meet the needs of common whites while serving the cause of protecting social hierarchy. Socioeconomic conditions of common whites made it necessary to forge relationships primarily out of mutuality and a marital contract necessary for survival in the antebellum era. Romantic love and companionate marriage played a role, but the idea of a marital union as a relationship of reciprocity remained paramount. On the other hand, Alabama's place in the Deep South's firm commitment to cotton and slavery meant that divorce posed some challenges to the social order of the state. Alabama's divorce cases thus demonstrate a form of localized law reflecting the situation of a still-developing state while embracing the patriarchal culture important to protecting a slaveholding economy. All of these conditions shaped the cause and defense of divorce for common white couples. Those seeking an end to their marriage went before the chancery court with a petition to file for divorce. If the petition was granted, the bill of divorce went before the Alabama legislature for a final decision. This practice, which lasted until 1855, exemplifies the distinction between local and state laws. Chancery courts heard the cases for divorce and determined the validity of the petition, thus keeping these cases on the local level. If the courts granted the petition, it then became a matter of public law, which fell under the purview of the state. Because cases started within the realm of localized law, courts often rejected petitions due to reconciliation or based on a lack of evidence supporting the claims of wrongdoing. Regardless of their results, these divorce petitions bring into sharp relief the efforts of common whites to assert power within the court system. And the arguments used in divorce cases reveal just how important ideas of proper gender behavior—demonstrations of manhood and womanhood—played in asserting that power. As with divorce petitions found in other southern states, men and women "struggled to strike just the right tone of virtuous victimization" in their defense. They attempted to shape a narrative that "portrayed themselves as dutiful wives and husbands who had endured long years of suffering" at the hands of their depraved spouses.[30]

Courts typically started review of petitions with the intention of reuniting families and repairing marriages. After all, divorce appeared to challenge the validity of the southern social order. It implied, in essence, a failure of a gender system so intricately woven into a slaveholding society. Such efforts to heal discord in the family fell, first and foremost, under the responsibility of the husband. The case of Egbert Crossman of Wilcox County shows the courts' willingness to dismiss cases of abandonment based on the failure of the husband to manage his dependents or control their behavior. It was up to the husband to bring his family members in line with his patriarchal authority. Egbert and his wife, Nancy, married in 1827 in Massachusetts and had two children over the course of their union. In 1834 Egbert made the decision to relocate the family to Alabama. Egbert mosved ahead of the family to establish a home, during which time he maintained a relationship with Nancy through correspondence. However, letters from her eventually ceased to come, and after several attempts to contact Nancy's brother and sister, he learned that she had no desire to move south. Egbert therefore testified to the court that she had "voluntarily left her bed and board for the space of three years with the intention of abandonment."[31]

The court, however, viewed the case very differently. The authorities argued that Egbert could have gone to Massachusetts to convince his family to relocate to Alabama, yet he had failed to make any effort. When he claimed that such a trip "was impracticable or even inconvenient for him to do so," the court disagreed and refused to grant his petition for a divorce. In the court's estimation, Egbert neglected his masculine obligations, and they exposed a perceived weakness in him, namely, that he had not exerted the necessary authority to control his dependents. In the end, the court ordered Egbert to pay the court costs and dismissed the petition. Aside from their efforts to reunite families, courts heard varied reasons as to why they should move forward with a man's petition to leave the marriage.[32]

One significant reason stemmed from a man's ability to even produce a family. Being able to father children reinforced a man's masculine image by validating his fertility and sexual virility. Yet, when a woman found that she could not bear children, she placed her spouse's masculine identity at risk and therefore created grounds for a divorce. Malcome A. McKinnon, of Talladega County, for example, sought a divorce from his wife, Sarah, whom he had married in 1845. In 1849 he alleged that "he has never been able to have sexual intercourse" and blamed it on Sarah's "apathy and physical inaptitude for the marriage state." As the central paternal figure in the home, the role of father held special meaning for men. It meant the continuation of family lineage and validated their role as the head of the household. For those of modest economic means, like Malcome, children also helped to expand the labor force on the farm or in a family business. Malcome did not intend to impugn the reputation of his wife, merely to show her inability to perform her marital duties. He expressed a deep respect for his wife and remorsefulness over her "defect" that created a relationship "of gloom . . . without a single hope to light up a dim and cheerless future." Sarah's inability or unwillingness to be intimate with her husband placed social pressure on Malcome to end rather than to remain in the marriage. The court, however, disagreed with him and dismissed the bill.[33]

Husbands seeking divorce most commonly alleged adultery on the part of their wives. And in many cases the claims proved true. As historian Victoria E. Bynum found, "a familiar pattern of escaping one man by taking up with another" existed among poor white women. Denied the same legal rights and access to financial self-sufficiency, poorer women lacked the resources to leave a marriage on their own. Their only recourse came through the power to seek a new mate, even if they never legally divorced their first one. Moving on to another relationship, for example, was a means of escaping possible physical abuse at the hands of their husbands. A man's inability to support his family also motivated a woman to pursue another man to protect them. Yet the public typically focused more on the act of adultery as a violation of proper female behavior than on women's lack of access to other means of support.[34]

In the patriarchal culture of the Old South, society viewed a woman's behavior as a direct reflection on the character and reputation of the male head of the home. If a woman strayed from the marriage, it was imperative that the husband seek some means of clearing his name and demonstrate that he exercised all resources to fulfill his duties as a husband. Such was the case of Campbell Jefferson of Talladega County, Alabama, who testified in 1848 that during his marriage to Lydia Margaret Jefferson he had fulfilled his responsibilities as a dutiful and supportive husband. In 1846 Lydia abandoned the Jefferson household, leaving Campbell vulnerable to public speculation about his ability to offer a secure, stable family life. Placed on the defensive, he noted that when the couple married in 1844, he entered a "matrimonial alliance" in which he fulfilled his role "with cheerfulness and affections" and "provided for her comfort and sustenance." However, when rumors began that she had moved in with another man in St. Clair County, he faced further scrutiny from his community. James Franklin likewise confronted a similar challenge to his reputation when his wife took up with another man. Nancy Franklin allegedly had "voluntarily" left his "bed and board" to reside with Bennett Gibson. In fact, Nancy and Bennett, after also moving to St. Clair County, began to refer to themselves as husband and wife. In his defense James testified that he had been forced to "live by himself at home destitute of all that domestic place and connubial bliss which in the married state can only result from a union with an honorable and virtuous woman," which, as James attempted to prove to the court, Nancy was not. The chancery court approved his petition, and the Alabama legislature believed James's assertions, granting his divorce.[35]

Assertions of abandonment figured prominently in cases of husbands filing a petition for divorce. The emasculating effects of a wife leaving her husband for another man, and thus rejecting him as a spouse, created a need to reclaim his masculine identity in the public courts. James W. Johnson of Russell County, for example, sought a divorce from Mary Johnson just two years after they married in 1855. James stated that Mary had "disregarded the solemnities of the marriage vow" since they married, by allegedly having an affair with "one John Hadley." He continued to paint her in a negative light by arguing that she had actually had affairs with several men over the course of two years' marriage. Thomas Williams, also of Russell County, sought a divorce on similar grounds a year after his marriage to Eliza Williams. He testified that he had "provided her with all the necessaries and comforts of life suitable" to his financial means. He further claimed that "without any good cause," she had "voluntarily abandoned the bed and board . . . and still remains separate and apart from him." Eliza had moved to Georgia at the point of the trial, and she refused to return, implying that she had taken up residency with another man. Given her absence from the trial, the judge had reason to believe Thomas's testimony and thus approved his petition for a divorce.[36]

Efforts to impugn the reputation of their wayward wives also included claims of prostitution. For women, maintaining the image of a proper woman, devoid of sexual scandal, was important in protecting not only her reputation but also that of her male head of household. Accusations of sexual impropriety could potentially harm a woman's reputation, rendering her unable to find a spouse. And if her personal conduct violated the terms of respectable behavior, it implied that her husband lacked the masculine authority to control his dependents. Yet the allegation of prostitution typically came from a husband attempting to explain his wife's infidelity or her desire to leave the marriage. In the case of James Clark of Perry County, the court heard testimony that his wife, Nancy, admitted that she engaged in "illicit intercourse," and, James contended, she refused to cease her behavior. The original petition for divorce in 1850 included allegations of "abandonment, adultery, and infidelity." The couple married in 1838 in North Carolina and then moved to Alabama. According to James's testimony, they "got along reasonably well together" despite his long absences from the home due to work. He contended that on one occasion after returning home, friends "intimated to him hints and allusions . . . that the conduct of his wife was constantly not prudent." James, in contrast, portrayed himself as a hardworking, industrious husband who strove "to labor with a cheerful good heart and to accumulate a competency for future comfort and support." However, as the marriage continued, it became clear that Nancy cared little that her husband knew of her extramarital affairs and, as James claimed, "was insolent, insulting, and abusive" toward him. What seemed egregious to the court was that Nancy blatantly admitted to having affairs and supposedly felt no remorse for them. James named two particular men with whom Nancy had engaged in a relationship and referred to her behavior as "base prostitution." He furthered his claims of her illicit, and illegal, behavior by questioning the paternity of their two children, citing that his wife had been involved in "indiscriminate intercourse with other men." The final straw was that Nancy failed to appear in court to refute the accusations, leaving authorities to believe James's side of events. They granted his petition for divorce, and the Alabama legislature approved the act in the 1851–52 session.[37]

Husbands trod carefully when using accusations of prostitution. Claiming his wife engaged in illegal sexual conduct placed his own reputation in jeopardy. In essence, the patriarchal society of the Old South viewed a wife's turn to prostitution as a husband's inability to keep his dependents in line and ensure their well-being. To avoid such accusations, men, such as Byrd Forsyth, carefully constructed a perception of themselves as the upstanding, proper husband who did all that they could to provide for their families. Married in 1854, Byrd and his wife, Mary, moved from Georgia to Alabama. He contended that when they married, he believed her to be "a virtuous woman." He charged that after their wedding she proved herself to be "faithless to her marriage vows" and that his wife engaged in "criminal sexual intercourse . . . with diverse persons." He further told the court that his wife since filing a petition for divorce was "living the life of a common prostitute." Putting forth such a narrative allowed him to preserve his image as the proper husband, while placing blame for their doomed marriage on Mary's moral failing.[38]

An unfaithful wife found herself in the position of having to defend her own reputation. Sexual impropriety violated the gendered agreement that wives served their husbands dutifully in exchange for protection and financial support. And a woman accused of prostitution or sexual misconduct ran the risk of never finding a future spouse. In many court cases where husbands accused their wives of adultery, there were others that showed women's willingness to defend their reputation. Robert Gibson, a small farmer in Russell County, claimed that his wife Elizabeth had engaged in an adulterous relationship with Henry Hunt in 1857. A year later Elizabeth received a summons to appear in court to answer to the accusation. Robert had been married before to another woman, Lucinda, during which time they had six children. He later left Lucinda to assume a marital relationship with Elizabeth, even though they were not legally married. Regardless, Robert argued that he learned of Elizabeth's affair on August 3, 1858, after which he left her and began the process of petitioning for a divorce. Elizabeth, however, gave a conflicting, albeit disturbing, response to his accusations. She contended that on the day that Robert learned of the supposed affair, he remained in the home and shared their bed. In a strange twist, Elizabeth testified that during that day she was deprived of sleep due to caring for a sick enslaved boy her husband owned. Over the course of caring for the child, she felt "much exhausted from the loss of sleep and rest" and to finally get some sleep "drank a small quantity of brandy or whiskey." After that she fell asleep for several hours and then awoke groggy and confused. She went into the kitchen to oversee preparation of dinner, when the female slave of Henry Hunt, the man with whom Elizabeth allegedly had the affair, "urged and entreated her to drink . . . about a spoon full" of liquor. Elizabeth claims that after drinking the liquor "her head began to dod," becoming "utterly insensible," and had no recollection of walking from the kitchen to her bedroom. Elizabeth leveled a surprising accusation that she woke up the next morning with her husband in their bed and with an ominous feeling that she had been drugged.[39]

Elizabeth's testimony served, in part, to counter the claims that she was an adulterous wife. Rather, she asserted that she had remained faithful and implied that perhaps Robert was attempting to harm her. She argued that Robert "did not treat her with affection and kindness" even though she had been "an obedient, constant, and faithful wife." In fact, she testified that he had threatened to "get rid of her" and that if he could not do so, "he would kill her." His reasoning, she stated, was that "he intended to have a third wife," and she stood in the way. Elizabeth claimed she had proof that on one occasion her husband actually attempted to kill her by cutting her throat and "inflicted a severe wound upon her neck the scar from which wound she still bears." The implication was that either Robert, Henry, or both had conspired with the female slave to drug Elizabeth as a means to either kill her or, at the very least, stage the scene to appear as if she had engaged in intercourse with another man. Either scenario, Elizabeth asked the court to grant her alimony to avoid destitution. She reasoned that she deserved financial support as the good wife who was not the adulterer Robert had maintained but rather the victim of his violence and cruelty. In the end, however, Elizabeth admitted that even though she had taken up residency with her father, she continued a romantic relationship with Robert. In the court's eyes, such actions invalidated her claims and they dismissed the petition for the divorce.[40]

Sometimes shaping the narrative of divorce petitions came down to proving who had wronged the other the most. To restore one's reputation and, in the case of most wives, seek material support, common whites found it important to convince the courts that a most grievous wrong had taken place. In 1833 David White of Wilcox County filed a petition for a divorce from his wife, Jemimah White. The couple had been married for thirty years and produced eight children. Yet, as David claimed, Jemimah "has never been a dutiful and obedient wife . . . has left his bed and bord for the space of four years with intention of abandonment." He further charged that she continued to cause him "injury" by incurring debt in his name. Jemimah returned the accusations with her own charge that David's failure to live up to his masculine duty caused the family great public embarrassment. She claimed that over the course of their marriage, David engaged in upward of twenty extramarital affairs and fathered a child. Jemimah cited that he had boasted "in the presence . . . of their mutual children and grandchildren that he had had improper intercourse with twenty women some of whom were married women." When she attempted to confront her husband about his actions, Jemimah testified that "he left her and left her 'entirely destitute.'" She told the court she had no intention of divorcing David and that, if given the opportunity, she would still fulfill her domestic duties even though he wanted nothing more to do with her. Her counter bill, known as a "crop bill," was intended to have the courts ensure that David would provide for her material support rather than offer a counterpetition for a divorce. Both David and Jemimah attempted to use the court to establish that each had played their role as the proper spouse while the other had failed to do so. Before Jemimah could petition for spousal support, thus placing David in the position of having to defend his masculine honor, he presented a bill for divorce claiming that his wife had abandoned him. Regardless of the claims, the court dismissed the petition.[41]

While men sought divorces as a means to guard their public reputation, women used the courts as a shield from physical abuse and economic destitution. In a slaveholding society that demanded the subordination of women, the courts offered the best route to challenging "individual patriarchs" without threatening the patriarchal order in a larger social context. For common white women, this meant seeking protection from a man who had failed in his duties as head of the family. To assert such a defense for ending a marriage required women to prove they had lived up to their end of the marital bargain. Successful cases for divorce usually involved presenting oneself as the devoted wife and mother who had lived up to the southern dictates of proper womanhood. Women did not intend to undermine or challenge the patriarchal system by leaving the marriage but rather demanded help from the legal system. When women fell victim to wayward or violent husbands, as were many of the cases, it was the responsibility of the courts to step into the place of protector, thus reinforcing the larger world of male privilege. In this context women, as subordinates, "shaped the legal terms of patriarchy, even though they did not alter the legal principles of subordination." Power in that sense could exist as "a means to an end," and that end was to preserve the social order.[42]

Women seeking divorce crafted narratives intended to gain sympathy from the courts. Ann M. Brown of Wilcox County, for example, filed a bill for divorce on the grounds of enduring physical and emotional abuse at the hands of her husband, Morgan G. Brown. Ann took great care to express in her testimony that the treatment was unprovoked and undeserved. This approach was particularly necessary given the nature of the nineteenth-century legal system. Legal authorities typically viewed domestic violence as a private issue, leaving it to members of the household to resolve the matter. A social structure that elevated men as the head of the household also acknowledged that a husband, at times, would need to punish his dependents, including his wife, as long as he refrained from excessive force. When Ann took her case to the court, she assumed the burden of proving that she "had always acted towards him as a kind affectionate and obedient wife" and that Morgan exceeded the limits of his paternal authority in his physical abuse. Her dependency on Morgan as a financial provider had left her unable to fulfill her duties as a mother to their two children once she left the marriage. She added that, in addition to abuse, Morgan's failure to manage the household finances sent the family into a state of financial destitution that "compelled her to rely for subsistence."[43]

Ann Brown, however, made the case for her divorce by emphasizing her husband Morgan's failures as the patriarch of their family. She portrayed him as a cruel head of the home who, in succumbing to alcoholism, hurt rather than cared for his dependents. The original bill of divorce stated that Morgan "had wasted the means of support for his family," leaving Ann to an economic state "approaching want." She further asserted that he failed to act as a sensitive marital companion, citing that "at a time when she most needed his kindness and protection" that he "beat bruise[d] and cruelly and inhumanly treat her." Ann emphasized Morgan's dishonorable behavior by claiming that he had "expelled her from his house." With Ann gone, he continued to live in ill repute, "lingering out a wretched existence, the miserable mark of his folly and intemperance." Morgan, however, attempted to redeem his reputation as a responsible husband. He rebuked her claims that he had forced her to leave the home by testifying she willingly left. Morgan accentuated his wife's failure, arguing that she had not performed her role "as a dutiful and loving wife" and that her state of economic dependency was the result of her decision to leave the home. The court, however, believed that sufficient evidence existed for his "cruel and barbarous behavior" and ruled in favor of the divorce.[44]

Women most commonly sought divorce based on accusations of domestic violence. Judges often viewed spousal abuse as a private issue among family and found that "lesser forms" of domestic violence were necessary for a patriarch to assert control over his subordinates. Serious cases that resulted in injury or threatened loss of life, however, garnered attention from the courts. Excessive abuse signaled a flaw in the patriarchal system and thus required the courts to step in to restore social harmony. Thus, seeking a divorce on the grounds of abuse allowed women to shape the legal confines of just how much power patriarchs wielded over their subordinates. In a South where "domestic violence remained a constant," women demanded authority to control those terms of marriage. Mary Ann Collier, for instance, sought a divorce from her husband, Augustus Collier, in 1854, after the couple was married for nearly five years. She testified to the court that during the course of the marriage, she "was bestowing on him all manner of kindness" but that he was prone to extreme anger that bordered on mental torture. Although no allegation of physical abuse existed, there appears substantial evidence of emotional abuse by using threats of violence. Mary accused Augustus of threatening to "whip and kick" her, and on a few occasions he told her that "he would knock her brains out together with many other barbarous and inhuman threats." Mary employed a common practice of women in the courts by asking members of the community to speak on her behalf. Her petition included corroborating witnesses such as Elizabeth Johnson, who witnessed several outbursts by Augustus. She noted that he treated her in a "rough and cruel" manner and, indeed, that he had threatened to kill her by "knocking her brains out." She noted that the tumultuous relationship between Mary and her husband lasted the entire length of the marriage. Johnson further noted that Augustus would leave the home for months at a time with no provisions of "food nor clothing" for Mary, which meant she had to turn to friends in her community for support.[45]

The extremes of domestic violence demonstrate the vulnerability of subordinates in a culture in which men held ultimate authority in the home. In the case of Mahala Mansell, she filed for a petition for divorce after nearly ten years of marriage. Her husband, John Mansell, was an independent farmer in Bibb County with a small amount of property and a few slaves. Mahala testified that for some time after their marriage, the couple lived together "harmoniously," with a few setbacks due to John's bouts of "occasional intemperance" after having consumed liquor. She contended, however, that the intermittent drinking had grown into a "confirmed habit" that led to his cruel behavior toward her and a "total disregard to all the duties of a husband and a father." He often threatened to kill Mahala and "degrade her in the person of her servants." John's behavior reached a horrific climax when one day he "violently assaulted and beat and bruised" Mahala, leaving her with "marks" that lasted several weeks after the assault. Over the course of their marriage, the couple had four children, the youngest being nine months at the beginning of their court case. As a result of John's alcoholism, he left his family destitute and in need of financial relief. Mahala specifically requested that the court prohibit her husband from selling off property the family desperately needed for support. She claimed that he had already sold off one of their slaves who "was a gift from her father." Mahala argued that due to her children's dependency on her for support and the failure of John to meet his responsibilities, the court needed to exercise authority on her behalf.[46]

John attempted a defense against the label of an alcoholic and abusive husband, as it threatened to tarnish his reputation. He admitted to being intoxicated on occasion but denied the allegations of "cruel and intemperate treatment." More importantly, the charge that he neglected his obligations as provider seemed far worse, and he claimed that he was never drunk to the point to "make him neglect his business or be unable to attend to it or to forget his duty to his family." Rather, John blamed Mahala's mother and her meddling in the marriage as the source of their problems. He testified that on one occasion he left for a week to earn money painting a house in Perry County. During that time Mahala's mother, he contended, "said to her [Mahala] that she would not live with a man who would leave her a week at a time." In an attempt to further deflect blame, he argued that the incident during which he struck Mahala was his attempt to restrain her after she attacked him. He said that "one morning she refused to have breakfast prepared" for him and that she claimed she would "never prepare another meal for him." At that point, he claimed, "she immediately made at him for a fight, he caught her and held her without attempting to injure her in any way untill she called the negro woman to assist her he then struck her twice but not violently her neck was somewhat scratched in his attempt to hold her." According to John's account, he was an innocent victim of Mahala's disregard for her obedience to him and failure to trust him, and he "has always loved" her "most devotedly." Yet Mahala's accusations of abuse proved stronger than John's efforts to redirect blame, and the court granted the petition for a divorce.[47]

While the courts viewed domestic violence as a private matter, they were willing to step in to protect women facing extreme cases of abuse. Zelpha Reach of Bibb County endured frequent verbal and physical abuse from her husband, Jeremiah. She stated in her petition for divorce that he "failed in the performance of almost all his duties as a husband and has frequently treated her with great violence in a cruel and barbarous and inhuman manner." The abuse became so severe that he often left "marks and bruises" on Zelpha. She pleaded with the court that she did nothing to warrant the violence, but rather had performed her domestic and marital duties. But still Jeremiah "threatened to destroy her life" and forced her to leave the home, after which she escaped to her father's household. She returned to Jeremiah, after which he abused her again; she alleged that he "beat her with his fists, rods and pulled her hair." After that final incident, Zelpha returned to her father's home and filed a petition for divorce.[48]

Jeremiah, seeing his reputation at stake, responded to her claims of abuse by blaming Zelpha. He cited that from the beginning they actually had a happy marriage, but that it was Zelpha who caused the turmoil by engaging in a sexual affair with an enslaved man owned by her father. Jeremiah claimed that from the start of their marriage, he intended to "cherish and sustained his wife" but that she taunted him with the affair. Zelpha, according to Jeremiah, lacked the virtue of a good wife, and it was she who abused him, thus leaving him no choice but to resort to corporal punishment. He alleged, for example, that Zelpha disregarded his feelings and "added insult to injury already inflicted by intentionally defiling her finger and rubbing it" on his nose. It was at that point, Jeremiah testified, he struck Zelpha, "though in great moderation," believing that such abuse was his "imperative duty" as a good husband. To underscore his accusations of Zelpha being an improper and immoral wife, he went on to assert that she had contracted a "loathsome disease." Yet after an examination of Zelpha's body, the court found no proof of any disease and argued that while a husband had a duty to punish his dependents, including his wife, he must refrain from any "conduct as shall endanger life or health." The court found Jeremiah "unfit for the station of a husband and unworthy of the affections of a wife" and granted the petition for divorce.[49]

Women often navigated the court process much more easily with the material support and public testimonies of their kin. The corroborating evidence from friends, relatives, and other community members strengthened their cases by substantiating a woman's credibility before the courts. Huldah Johnson of Bibb County turned to her family when her husband, Spencer Johnson, became physically and emotionally abusive toward her. The couple married in 1840 and had two daughters over the course of their marriage. In 1852 Huldah testified in the chancery court that soon after they wed, her husband "treated her with great indignity and cruelty" that lasted through the course of their marriage. She testified that during fits of jealousy, Spencer would "charge her with having illicit intercourse," resulting in his inflicting "corporal punishment . . . with a switch and by choking her." After the first incident, Huldah escaped to her father's home, where he eventually convinced her to return to Spencer. Two weeks into their reunion, Spencer grew violent once more and even began to deny paternity of their first daughter. Huldah left again to stay with her father, but given the family's poor financial state, she felt it necessary to return to her husband. The situation grew worse when she became pregnant with her second child. It seemed Spencer accepted the second child and that all was fine until "in a fit of rage" in the confinement stage of her pregnancy, he "pushed her out of the bed and threatened to kill her." It was at this point that Huldah went again to live with her family. Eventually she returned to Spencer out of desperation, having very little financial support from her family. Although Huldah sought protection from Spencer by relying on her family, she remained with her husband, and the bill for divorce was dismissed for "want of prosecution."[50]

Amanda Dortch also turned to her family for support when her husband left the home. The couple married in 1839 and moved to Bibb County just a few years later. Shortly after the move, her husband, James Dortch, abandoned the home and moved to North Carolina. Amanda went before the court to seek a divorce from her husband. Like many women in the courts, she had a male family member address the court on her behalf. Her father testified that she had "faithfully and affectionately discharged all the duties of a wife" but that James had "failed in the performance of almost all the duties of a husband." Given that the Amanda found herself destitute and without support from James, she sought aid from her family. In fact, James had taken all the money his wife had earned "by her industry" and fled. Seeking help from her father, Amanda asked him to testify to the courts that her conditions had become so dire that she had gone back to live with her family. By the time that the court granted the divorce, she remained in the home of her father, calling it her "proper home." Zelpha Reach, also of Bibb County, found herself in a similar situation after her husband forced her to leave the home with just a few of her possessions. During their tumultuous marriage that began in 1845, Jeremiah Reach became abusive toward Zelpha. After each confrontation, Jeremiah forced her to leave the home and "flee to her father's" given that she had no means of support or protection.[51]

Husbands accused of abuse attempted to salvage their reputations by deflecting the allegations. Use of excessive physical abuse threatened his public image as a protector of his dependents. Husbands therefore sought ways to minimize claims of abuse, oftentimes blaming members of their community for fabricating stories out of malice. Such was the case of Margaret Jane Dye of Talladega County, who petitioned for a divorce from her husband, Weldon Dye. Margaret turned to the court for protection in 1849 after nearly six years of marriage that produced one son, James. She claimed that just one year after they married, Weldon began to treat her "in a cruel barbarous and inhuman manner." She left Weldon shortly after the abuse began, at which time she gave birth to their son. Since their separation Weldon, according to Margaret, threatened to take their son from her, despite his very young age. She argued that she feared Weldon would take the child "by force . . . unless prevented by the order or decree" from the court. Her main concern was that Weldon, if he took custody of the child, would be unable to provide "proper care and attention" to him. According to the depositions in the case, Margaret had the means to support her child by relying on community members and her family. The implication was that Weldon had failed in his dual role as protector and provider, thus leaving Margaret dependent on others. Having his reputation questioned in the courts, Weldon then provided his statement of defense in which he blamed outside influences on the demise of their marriage.[52]

As a man of little property, Weldon's reputation as a faithful husband and father was his only conduit to the public world of respectability. When he provided his statement, Weldon offered great detail about how people in the community meddled in their private lives and convinced Margaret to make the allegations of abuse. It was true that Henry Click, also of Talladega County, served as Margaret's petitioner to the court, providing guidance throughout the process of filing, and speaking at times on her behalf. Yet Weldon portrayed Click's and others' help in Margaret's case as less than altruistic. He asserted that Click along with John Bass and "others by hints and insinuations and persuasions . . . poisoned her mind" against him. Weldon likewise denied "that he treated said Margaret in a cruel barbarous and inhuman manner." Perhaps the interference of community members stemmed from Weldon's severe criticisms of them, which he admitted in his statement.[53]

The case became questionable as conflicting testimonies from community members painted Weldon as either a violent, threatening husband or a "quiet and peaceable" man. One witness testified that Weldon consistently threatened his wife and that, in a sort of murder-suicide plot, "he went to bed with an open knife under his head and threatened to kill himself before morning and proposed to kill her also if she was willing." The deposition of Thomas Elliott corroborated the proposition of a murder-suicide scenario. He further stated that Weldon had indeed threatened to take their young child away from Margaret, by force if necessary. Yet, when John Bass provided his testimony, it became clear that he and Weldon had a rather strained relationship. It appears that Weldon had a problem with Bass because he was wealthier, owned slaves, and had provided the home in which he and Margaret lived. An incident between the two men exacerbated their animosities. On one occasion, Bass passed by Weldon without speaking to him, leaving him to feel as if he had been snubbed.[54]

The sentiment of the court slowly turned in Weldon's favor as the testimonies continued. Margaret Weldon had on her side the statements of John Bass, who also provided her with some financial assistance. Further, Margaret stood to inherit property and three slaves on the condition that she leave Weldon. To restore his good standing and honor in the community, Weldon had several witnesses speak on his behalf. Many of them testified that "his deportment as correct as any citizen" and that "his temper is not worse than that of ordinary men." The court ultimately sided with Weldon and dismissed the bill of divorce. The final record stated that, in its determination, he "was the victim of the most melancholy feelings and deeply despondent at one time during his matrimonial conviction," which caused the threats of ending his and Margaret's lives. Yet the court saw any threats as unfounded and that intentions of putting "her life, health, or persons in danger" had little substance. The court then took aim at Margaret, citing that during Weldon's "dark hour of his unmanly despondency," she had little sympathy for him and rather than offer support for Weldon succumbed to the influences of outsiders. As to the claims that Weldon failed to provide for his child, the court favored him once again, stating that he provided for the children of his first marriage and therefore could do the same for young James. The outcome of this case was quite significant, as it demonstrated a kind of reversal of power through the use of the court. Weldon, who according to the 1850 census had no property of his own, could stand in court to defend his honor that had been threatened by Bass, a member of the wealthier class. This rare case of gender relations trumping the power of class hierarchy left Weldon a vindicated man in the public eye.[55]

Women also used the courts to protect them from economic vulnerability resulting from their dependency on a failed patriarch. Property claims appeared in most of the divorce petitions. As Laura Edwards contends, property "symbolized the balance of authority between husbands and wives," and when that balance appeared disrupted, the courts stepped in to act as protector. In particular, women turned to the courts to seek financial protection from husbands who abandoned the home, leaving them without the traditional income of the male head of household. Even if she worked for some sort of wages, the inequality in pay between men and women meant that she could find herself destitute and unable to provide for her children if her husband left the home. Many women emphasized this economic vulnerability when they went before the court. Antonello Green of Wilcox County filed a petition for divorce from James Green. As the petition stated, Antonello claimed that James had "disentered the bed and board" for a span of three years. Without a formal divorce, Antonello was not free to remarry, thus reducing her ability to seek support from another man. Elizabeth Holloway, of Perry County, sought a divorce from her husband, Washington, in 1842, claiming that she had "discharged the duties of a wife with affection and fidelity." To demonstrate Washington's moral failure as a man and a husband, she accused him of living with another woman, during which time he "conduct[ed] himself . . . disgraceful." She further argued that because she acted the part of the dutiful wife, her husband had no just cause to leave her. The court agreed with Elizabeth and granted her petition for a divorce. The same allegations of abandonment also led Eliza Osborne to seek help from the chancery court of Russell County. Eliza and Francis Osborne married in the early 1850s in Georgia, then moved to Alabama shortly after. The couple had a son together. Yet after their move to the state, Eliza claimed that Francis abandoned her and the child and "refused to return home." She cited that throughout their marriage, she was "a faithful and affectionate wife . . . and [had] done and performed all the duties of a faithful wife." After publication of the divorce decree appeared in the local newspaper, and the lack of response from Francis, the court granted the divorce.[56]

Women likewise sought avenues to economic power through the courts. Namely, they sought protection from the gendered culture of the Old South that recognized a husband's control over his wife's property. When Guilford Olive of Russell County filed a petition to divorce his wife, he possessed rights over the estate that she had brought into the marriage. He stated that she abandoned the home even though he "endeavored to the best of his ability to discharge all the duties and obligations" of a proper husband. However, by the time Guilford filed the petition in 1853, the couple lived separately. Just four years later, his wife Isabella Oliver went before the court again, this time seeking protection of her property from Guilford. She cited that she had some land and a few slaves and that his claims to her possessions stemmed from the fact that he had little property of his own. Rather than rule in favor of the male, the court recognized that Isabella had a right to maintain her own property separate from her former husband and cited in her favor. In other cases, the courts recognized the financial dependency of women and required husbands to provide some payment to their former wives. Whether living separately or formally divorced, common white women understood that their socioeconomic status could put them in a state of destitution without some assistance. In the case of Elva Jenkins, of Wilcox County, the couple lived apart but never divorced. Yet the court ordered her husband, Edwin, to pay her $250. Although the case made for this payment is absent from the court record, the money certainly provided Elva with some economic support.[57]

The Alabama that Thomas Hamilton and other visitors experienced was one that reflected the characteristics of a developing state in the cotton kingdom. Backcountry culture mingled with the sophistication of a refined planter class staking claims in the state. Yet the sense that Alabama still held promises of upward mobility and a chance of a better life pervaded the lives of common whites who came to the state seeking a fresh start. Although both common whites and the planter elites sought out a better life in antebellum Alabama, clear differences in the social lifestyle, economic opportunities, and political power existed between the two groups. The contrasts were striking but at times muted by a shared value system of independence, self-reliance, and honor. Through those common values, whites, at times, wanted the same things. They valued family as the channel through which one could express a sense of honor and protect public reputation. It was through the family that common whites, too, asserted power in a culture that often marginalized them economically and politically. The defense of one's masculine or feminine identity within the space of family served as a tool with which common whites constructed a public identity and laid claim to the same values as their elite counterparts. Moving into the era of the Civil War, the muted class differences created an atmosphere in which common whites accepted the notions of protecting their culture from intruders. And such a need to secure their families would lead them into the battlefield and onto the stage of home-front sacrifice. Both men and women continued to see their gendered identities as connected to the defense of their homes and communities, and to the preservation of family honor.

2

"Remember Me, with Soft Emotion"

Family and Honor in Wartime, 1860–62

When William Moxley departed his modest farm in Coffee County to help organize Bullock's Guards, he left behind a heartbroken and pregnant Emily, who refused to concede any justification for his leaving. To her, the war and its cause were unwanted intrusions on their personal lives. Emily and William married in 1853 and eventually had six children. William served as a community physician but also maintained a farm, since his practice provided little income in a county composed primarily of common whites. Throughout William's absence, the couple exchanged letters that tell the intimacies of a husband and wife trying to come to terms with their separation. Emily's correspondences lacked the typical patriotic rhetoric that lauded the masculine duty of those who enlisted. Rather, she wrote her husband despondent letters detailing the hardships of life without him, even going so far as to claim "we are all nearly heart broken" over his absence.[1]

William, on the other hand, expressed patriotic sentiment in defending his choice to serve. His motivation sprang from his patriarchal responsibility to protect his home from invaders and to secure the good name of his family. "But my dear," he wrote to her in September 1861, "if I should be killed, never regret, for it would be the best legacy I could leave you and my children." As an officer in the guards, William too understood the necessity of heeding the call to serve the nascent Confederacy if it succeeded in creating an independent nation. Yet his reasoning for fighting for what pro-Confederate leaders lauded as a "just cause" did little to counterbalance the hardships Emily endured without her sole provider. Left with an unscrupulous guardian of the family finances while battling constant sadness and the physical strains of a difficult pregnancy, Emily struggled to maintain a happy, stable domestic circle. Still, the couple endured declining conditions on the home front and in the military by attempting to maintain a semblance of a normal family life during their separation. For the first two years of the war, common whites like the Moxleys conceptualized their place within the Confederacy through the lens of family. Victory, they believed, necessitated some sacrifices that family members would have to make, even at the expense of their own comfort and security.[2]

Common whites in support of the Confederacy understood the meaning of secession and war in terms of family in two distinct ways. First, they believed in the rationale to secede and form a separate Confederate nation to preserve slavery as a fight for family. Clearly, the planter minority held greater economic and political stock in protecting the institution. Therefore, those framing the rhetoric of Confederate nationalism needed to provide a narrative that garnered support from the wider common white population if they were to wage a total war. Family offered that reasoning as to why common white men and women should sacrifice for the Confederate cause. Defending the Confederacy meant defense of their individual families from invaders and preservation of their public honor. Even more so, they absorbed the message of the Confederacy as a larger family, and the state as the patriarch dedicated to protecting its loyal dependents from the exigencies of war. They understood of course that with war came a level of sacrifice for civilians and soldiers alike; yet common whites maintained that whatever trials their loved ones faced in war, they could lean on the state as the metaphorical head of family. And as long as the state continued to protect the family, they could, at least for a time, remain loyal.

Second, family offered a more tangible means of sustaining support for the Confederacy. The roles men and women played in the family became a vital source of material and emotional assistance, as they faced separation, sadness, and potential death. Necessary connections to the masculine and feminine roles of fathers and mothers/husbands and wives therefore provided a sense of normalcy that allowed common whites to reconcile risking their lives and their livelihood to fight for the Confederacy. Men continued to assert an influence as father figures by providing advice and even financial support in their absence. Women too found solace in an expanded vision of domesticity that involved their traditional roles as well as taking on greater responsibilities on the farms. Even when conditions seemed difficult to bear for those at home and on the front, they turned to sentimental imagery and religious convictions situated within the family to overcome the emotional strains. Their devotion to family honor that helped define their identity in the antebellum period thus became the call for their loyalty and service to the Confederacy. And as long as Alabama's leaders as representatives of the Confederacy upheld their promises to ensure the safety of their families, they would continue to seek ways to sustain their support.

Family, work, and religious faith figured prominently among common white families even as the threat of war loomed on the horizon. Economic and other responsibilities of domestic life left little time to contemplate the sectional conflict or engage in public secession debates. The diary of Sarah Espy of Cherokee County reveals the constant struggles of common whites in the day-to-day survival of their families. Espy's husband, like many of her class, engaged in subsistence farming and raised a modest number of livestock to sell in the community market. From the early entries of her diary, beginning in 1858, most of her concerns focused on the weather, daily domestic duties, and child care. With her husband's death in 1860, however, her entries took a different tone as she struggled to settle his business affairs. After giving power of attorney to a male community member whom she trusted, Espy expressed a deep concern over her limited means of financial support. Although her household included two enslaved individuals, Espy lived a modest lifestyle characteristic of the common white demographic. Economic concerns coupled with the death of her husband brought Espy great anxiety about the family's future in the summer of 1860: "We are feeling badly and lonely and destitute . . . for we are weak and look forward to [a] hard struggle with an unfeeling world."[3]

Zillah Haynie Brandon likewise focused more on the financial and spiritual well-being of her family than on the political conflict taking shape. Zillah was born in 1801 and lost her parents early in her life. Sent to live with foster parents, she completed one year of formal education before turning her energies toward work. Zillah married Francis Lawson Brandon in 1822, and the couple eventually had nine children. By 1851 they relocated to Cherokee County, Alabama, where Francis attempted to establish a farm. The couple enjoyed modest financial success within a decade, having a total property value of $6,300 and five enslaved people. Zillah kept a diary beginning in 1855, filling the pages with recollections of her life up to that point. Yet she also documented her daily activities in her contemporary life, remarking mainly on the business ventures of her elder sons and reporting on the sickness and death of kin. As among most common whites, religion played a major role in her daily life, as both a source of faith and social interaction. Zillah also divulged the many physical ailments she endured as a woman reaching her sixties. Her other concerns dealt with the weather, in particular a flood that threatened the state of the farm. For the most part, she, like Espy, fixated more on the daily routines of family life than the brewing regional conflict.[4]

The concerns of family in the antebellum period likewise remained a greater priority for the Jackson family of Covington County. Situated in the Piney Woods region of the state, the family relied primarily on their small farm for an income. Just months before the war commenced, Mary Jackson, the matriarch of the family, wrote to family members mainly about their faith than the potential for war. She emphasized often the necessity of religious life and the hope that her children would "come to the general meetings" held in her community. Invitations to visit home figured equally in her letters. Like any mother whose sons had married and lived away from home, she implored them to visit her and bring their new brides. Writing frequently to her children, she kept them up to date on the farm and family news. Only in passing does Jackson mention the "great deal of talk about war." Her primary concern was to maintain the familial relations that defined her world. Only after her son's enlistment in the army did the letters among the Jackson family turn to matters of war.[5]

Although immersed in their daily routines, common whites had little choice but to turn their attention to the regional conflict already taking shape. Sarah Espy recognized the heated struggles between the North and South and what they could mean for white southerners. The impending presidential election grabbed her attention, and she expressed her support for the southern candidate John C. Breckinridge. Secessionist supporters were the most outspoken advocates for his candidacy, but Espy believed him to be the best candidate to maintain the Union, reasoning that "the country is getting in a deplorable state owing to the depredations committed by the Abolition . . . the safety of the country depend on who is elected to the presidency. May that man be union loving Breckinridge." Espy eventually joined the chorus of common whites in favor of secession. She conceived of "abolitionists and negroes" as posing the greatest threat to social order and heralded a split from the Union if they continued. When news of Abraham Lincoln's election reached Cherokee County, Espy concluded that the process of secession meant the potential of war.

Although she supported the Confederate cause, she expressed some hesitation about what it meant for her family, fearing that it was "the beginning of woe." Zillah Brandon echoed Espy's support of the cause. "We must submit to a cruel and wicked oppressor," she wrote, "or we must be independent by an appeal to arms." She laid blame for the war at the feet of the federal government, stating, "It is a well authenticated fact . . . that the seceding states sent delegates to adjust an amicable settlement ere this war commenced, but they were spurned."[6]

Most of the population, North and South, believed that the conflict would be short-lived. Soldiers and civilians often expressed an optimistic hope of merely a brief disruption or inconvenience to their daily lives. Such was the case among Alabama's common whites. James Jackson wrote to his brothers in May of 1861 describing the enthusiasm throughout his camps and encouraged them to consider enlisting. He was convinced that the war would be but a temporary condition when he asked his brothers, "Come down here and let's go together. I have a notion of trying a while." Many refused to concede that they would remain separated from loved ones for longer than a month or two. Benjamin Jackson, stationed in Tupelo, Mississippi, reassured his wife, Martha, "I don't think this war will last much longer." John Cotton, father of seven from Coosa County, also comforted his wife by writing that he thought the war would end shortly and that he would return to the family soon after. As with many others, William McCullough took to heart the rumors the "rite smart taulk of pece" and that the prospect of reuniting with his family would come swiftly.[7]

Some assumed that even if the war lingered on, the soldier would have some flexibility regarding length of service. Mike Holmes of Henry County, for example, expressed a similar perception of volunteering after he left home to serve in the Sixth Alabama Volunteer Infantry. Holmes felt so assured that he would have some control over determining when and for how long he served that he instructed his brother how they should divide up military duty among them. He wrote in September of 1861 that only one family member should serve at a time, out of concern for their aging parents. "There is one thing I wanted," he urged, "and that is under no sercumstancis to joining the army till I come home." Conceiving service as driven by the demands of the soldiers, he instructed his brother to stay home as "one of us is enough at a time if you was to leave I don't know what would become of our folks." Not until the first Confederate conscription laws of 1862 did most realize that they would serve much longer.[8]

For most common whites, the public campaigns to support the war in the name of family honor compelled them to support the Confederate mission. Men and women connected the sacrifices necessary for the cause with securing the home and its members from "invaders" outside the South. Confederate and state leaders, as the greater patriarchs of the people, encouraged such connectivity to rally citizens and sustain their patriotism. "Any of us have is at stake on this great issue of the day," one observer noted, "not only our property but ourselves our wives, children, kindred and characters." In a proclamation Gov. John Gill Shorter encouraged male citizens to join a home guard for the defense of communities. He noted that "such organization is necessary, not only to quiet any domestic troubles which may arise, but to defend our hearthstones against desecration by an invading foe." Even the press used the patriarchal imagery of the state to encourage female patriotism and material contributions. In a July 1862 article, one author scolded women for what he saw as a decline in enthusiasm for supplying the troops. "We hope the patriotic zeal of industrious ladies is not flagging," he declared; "the ladies have acted well their part, so far. We cannot doubt that they will remain true to the cause and look to their own future." Such public declarations to the general population utilized the rhetorical device of home and family as a means of providing service, in whatever form, to the Confederate cause, and any less would mean the demise of their family's future.[9]

Men turned to the familial ideal to justify enlisting in a war that took them away from their loved ones. More specifically, men maintained that their service fulfilled an honorable duty to defend their homes as a microcosm of a larger Confederate community. Historian James McPherson contends that duty served as a "binding moral obligation involving reciprocity" in which one had a responsibility to serve the country "under whose protection one had lived." Avoiding such service threatened to tarnish a man's public reputation and, by extension, that of his family. Common white men absorbed the messages of Confederate nationalism, moving them to serve in the military. For example, James Zachariah Branscomb of Union Springs kept regular correspondence with his sister Lucinda Branscomb Hunter. His early letters reveal a deep support for Alabama's right to secede from the Union in the wake of Lincoln's election. He, along with several of his male neighbors, joined the Southern Rifles after the state seceded in January 1861 in anticipation of going to battle. While he acknowledged the sadness of leaving Union Springs and his family behind,

James remained in "high glee" as he and his friends departed for the new Confederate capital in Montgomery.[10]

But, more so, protection of their manhood stirred common white men to enlist. Men discussed their service with loved ones in terms of their duty to protect public reputation. A man's display of bravery by enlisting enhanced his masculine image so tightly connected to the family's standing in the community. James Branscomb, although inspired by political events, also saw enlistment as a way to preserve his family's honor. With all five of her brothers serving in the Fifth Alabama Infantry, his sister sought to understand their military service that threatened to tear their family apart. James responded by assuring her that "if neither of your brothers should never return there should be one consoling thought, that we gave our lives in an honorable cause." James made the same connections to the masculine duty to fight when writing to one of his brothers. He proclaimed in one letter that "the son of the south must rally. . . . A man that won't fight now has not got a soul." Even as the prospect of death weighed heavy on the members of the Branscomb family, James offered these words of comfort: "I felt that I was doing my duty. I may never return to you all again it is true, but feel assured I will. But if the worst comes to the worst I shall feel contented with my lot. Though I may be reaped at the harvest of death, it will be only to water the tree of liberty."[11]

Common white men also relied on notions of duty when facing the dangers associated with service. As a young, single soldier in the army, D. D. Bonner wrote to Mary Loftis, a potential love interest, that his service in the army was born out of his faith in God, writing, "I think if I get kild or if I die I only have but one time to die." For Bonner, death was an ultimate sacrifice necessary for a "just cause," and his survival would thus be "the will of God." John Davenport, of Montgomery County, wrote frequently to his wife, Mary Jane, after he enlisted with the First Battalion, Company G. Despite the sadness associated with their separation, he reminded Mary Jane in an August 1862 letter that "if I should fall remember I am fighting for Liberty for you and our Little ones and for the rites and Liberty of others." Just a few months later, he reiterated the same sentiment but with greater detail about the perils soldiers confronted for the sake of their families. "I hope you and them may yet live to enjoy the rights and liberitys for which I now am fressing all nit on the forsen ground or snow or waiding the cold and freesing rivers," he wrote. Going on to depict the more tortuous hardships of a soldier, he described being on guard post "in the cold and darkesom nit and the nite damp freesing my beard and hear in tags of ice sheckles around my face" all on the behalf of the family's security. "I take my post as cheerful as I would a good worm bed or breckfirst when cold weet hungry and sleepy," John declared, "and I hope wa all my live to spend yet meney bright and happy days together."[12]

Women too embraced the idealization of male kin enlisting as beneficial to the family's reputation. Zillah Brandon turned to gendered identity to come to terms with the potential dangers her two soldier sons faced. In one entry Zillah wrote that although she feared for the life of her son James, she hoped that he would represent the family properly by offering a solid moral influence in the camps. "I have become better reconciled," she wrote, "knowing that James is a man of God, will speak when moved upon by the Holy Ghost and teach his fellow soldiers to look for the promise of Christ's coming." Elizabeth Danielly likewise expressed the notion that her husband's service reflected well on the family. Although she longed for the day when "you may return home to your fireside to little ones," she concluded that only victory held the noble cause for returning home. "I don't think they can ever whip us," she wrote, "and if they do we had better be dead some time."[13]

Letters including sentimental reflections on familial scenes demonstrated the connection between home and the call to service. John Cotton wrote to his wife in 1862, "I never new what pleasure home afforded to a man before. If it were not for the love of my country and family and the patriotism that bury in my bosom for them I would bee glad to come home and stay there." Even as he expressed sadness over the time away from his young children, Cotton saw the relation between family and his service in the army, noting that "if it had not have been the love I have for them and my country I would have been ther now." Frances Danielly, of Randolph County, wrote to his wife, Elizabeth, about similar family sentiments when explaining the cause of his service. While receiving medical care in a civilian home, Frances described women providing aid "like mothers to sick soldiers." He drew parallels between his home and the domestic-like situation of the other patients who were "like brothers to me."[14]

Oftentimes men rationalized enlisting by comparing themselves to those who either avoided service or fought for the Union. Writing on Christmas Day of 1862, Frances Danielly cited his masculine duty to remain loyal, as he expressed resentment toward suspected deserters in his home community. He noted rumors that "tories" had "risen" in Randolph County and that he "can't help being uneasy about the poor women and children that will have to suffer by such as that for there is not men enough there to support them now." He connected his fears of vulnerable women and children to his notion of a just cause, arguing, "I hope the day is not far distant when our cause will be recognised as just and this war have an end though I am not tired of fighting for our Rights and Liberties which I am determined to contend for." He reserved his greatest contempt for those whom he saw as shirking their duty to serve. "When I hear of citizens of my county turning deserters from the army out of the jail," he wrote, "it made my blood boil." Northern soldiers also fell into that category of dishonorable men. Grant Taylor, who served in the Fortieth Alabama Infantry Regiment, leaned on images of exacting revenge on a disreputable enemy as motivation for fighting. He wrote to Malinda, his wife residing in Tuscaloosa County, "I sometimes think who it is that has brought this distress on us and I get almost desperate and feel that I should not fear to meet them in the deadly conflict." He concluded that he felt "almost a[n]xious to be led against this vandal horde, this destroyer of our peace." As the war dragged on, Robert Williams likewise wrote to his wife, Mittie, expressing his desire to seek revenge on shameful Union troops. He noted that with each military engagement, he felt closer to eliminating those whom he saw as the cause of war and the primary threat to their family.[15]

The use of bravado in letters home denotes a masculine posturing that reinforced their sense of purpose to serve. Detailed descriptions of fighting the enemy or enduring rough conditions underscored the link between duty to the Confederacy and protecting the family. Henry Bray, a gas fitter from Montgomery who joined the Seventeenth Alabama Infantry, often extolled the valor and bravery of the soldiers in his company. In one letter home, he mentioned that if men from the community wanted to join the war, "join owr company for it is the best Co. they can get in to," and reminded his family that "it is better to be a brave volinter than a drafted man." His hyperbolic depictions of his bravery continued as he discussed confronting the enemy. "I am very sorry to hear that the einvaders are in owr state," he wrote to his mother, "it make my blood boil to hear of the depredations they have done since they landed in owr soil and I hope soon to measure arms with the hireling despradodoes." His desire to see the enemy merely ramped up his masculine rhetoric when he proclaimed, "I wish very much that we were going there to defend my mother state wich is now in peril." In a following letter to his mother, Bray repeated his assurance that his fellow soldiers could secure a victory, boasting that their instructor deemed their company "the most intelligent" and could "learn the quickest of any set me he ever had to learn."[16]

Bray tended to save his most overblown descriptions of his abilities for his brother. In an 1862 letter, he declared, "The Yankees can't fight in the bushes like the Rebels," and, "I am one of the greatest bush fighters now of the age. I can charge bayonets over a brush heap in double quick time after a Yankee and make him show me the bottom of his foot mighty quick." Bray's depictions provided that necessary motivation to first enlist in the military and then sustain his service. He insisted, "Never will I lay down my musket until the inhuman scoundrels are driven from our sweet isle or I am laid low with the rest of our brave Shiloh boys." These typical assertions of masculine bravery and bravado, however, would begin to subside as the war continued into its third year, as I explore in the following chapter.[17]

Those common whites who supported the Confederacy did express trepidation over the uncertain changes war would bring to their lives. Sarah Espy, despite reasoning that the Confederate cause was just, feared that the departure of male kin for the military, along with the potential chaos of war, would cause her great distress. "I feel badly," she wrote in March of 1861, "for when the war commence when is it to end and what dire consequences will not fall on us! I fear our happy days are all gone." Zillah Brandon also understood the possible effect war would have as she faced the possibility of her five sons enlisting in the Confederate army. When two of her sons, James and Hines, left for the front, she intimated that their absence "amounted to an agony." Writing to her sisters, Martha Jackson expressed a sadness over their brothers' service in the army, noting that "there is nothing in this world but trouble for us to see." Her husband, Benjamin, likewise appeared to question his decision to enlist, as he expressed fears over his fate. "If I were to write all my troubles in this cruel war," he confided, "it would not interest you at all. . . . My desire is to live to get home and see them calculated to take care of themselves and you, if you should live to get old."[18]

The comfort of family along with its material support sustained the will of common whites to make difficult sacrifices in the first two years of the war. Family offered solace to those at home enduring great emotional pain in the face of prolonged separation and homesickness. And they called on idyllic family scenes to offer hope of one day being reunited. Early into the conflict, common whites realized the importance of family in meeting also the material needs of those serving in the army. In essence, the household, as the central location of the family, and the masculine and feminine roles within it filled critical voids created by the Confederate government's call to arms. Men and women leaned on each other to aid with provisions that the Confederate and state leaders lacked the means to provide.

Historians identify the connections between labor in the home and aid to those in the camps as crucial to maintaining a long-term commitment to war. LeeAnn Whites, for example, identifies this connection as a household supply line vital to surviving the war. Soldiers received meager dietary provisions and thus turned to civilian family members, especially women, to provide sustenance. Soldiers' aid societies and local suppliers did what they could, but their efforts did not include the emotional attachment that family offered, as Edwards contends. Family also stepped in as the primary suppliers of clothing and other material goods, typically produced in the home, when the military failed to do so. These examples of the household supply line reveal "the way household relations persisted, even as those relationships warred against distance, distress, and sadly, the death" of loved

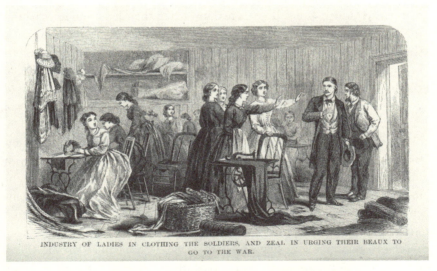

Figure 2. "Industry of Ladies in Clothing the Soldiers, and Zeal in Urging Their Beaux to Go to the War." Originally published in *The South* by John Townsend Trowbridge (1866), this illustration depicts the crucial role women played in supporting the Confederacy and maintaining the domestic supply line during the war. Alabama Department of Archives and History.

ones brought on by war. Similar evidence among Alabama's common white families substantiates Edwards's argument. As long as families continued fulfilling emotional and material needs, despite the state's limited help, then common whites found reason to sustain their support for the Confederacy.[19]

Confederate patriotism sweeping across the state by early 1861 reached into the personal lives of common white women of Alabama. Historians illuminate that war often heightened women's civic activism and created new spaces in which they could express their political beliefs. The politically charged atmosphere that war produced allowed public affairs to invade the domestic arena, while the civic domain became a place of informal political exchanges. The most notable evidence of women's political activism comes from those whose membership in the elite class afforded them leisure time to be civically involved. Women's political participation took place in the domestic setting, where they engaged in war work, hosted patriotic gatherings, and discussed their support for the Confederacy. Soldiers' aid societies and hospitals also became socially acceptable locations for women to express their politicization in their work.[20]

Women from common white families also found political agency in the call to serve the cause. Rarely with free time to volunteer in the activities of their wealthier sisters, they turned inward to their feminine roles within the home and family to express their support for the war. The women transformed their normal tasks of household production into expressions of support and self-sacrifice both as forms of patriotism and as emotional comfort. While they had always been the manufacturers of household goods, their relationship to those duties changed in wartime. Patriotism, in part, drove their desire to supply family members on the front. But they likewise saw those roles as essential to keeping their male kin safe and comfortable while away from home. They filled their letters and diaries with discussions of domestic production that they saw as necessary to sustaining the war effort. Such contributions fit neatly into the confines of women's duty to help supply a family that traditionally relied on the labor of women for material support.

Foremost among the items soldiers solicited from female kin was clothing. Men from the state's elite mustered in to the army with a variety of clothing, while those from lesser means came into service with merely a change of clothes that they carried "in a sack over their shoulders." Thus, common white soldiers depended on female kin to resupply them with clothing. In her diary Sarah Espy illuminated the invaluable role she played in supplementing the clothing of her sons serving in the Confederate army. Rather than resent the added burden to her workday, she saw it as a way to ensure the comfort of her sons despite their separation from the home. For instance, when Columbus Espy, one of Sarah's sons, wrote in September of 1861 that he needed clothes, she acquiesced. Lucinda Branscomb Hunter also wrote frequently to her brothers on the front asking if they needed homemade supplies, in particular clothing. Even young, single women joined their older sisters in providing clothing to soldiers. Margaret Miles Gillis, a young woman from Lowndes County, recorded in her diary that as a company of Alabama guards camped out in her small town, an officer "brought out some shirts for us to make for them, and Sis C sis Mollie, sis Sallie and I made one apiece." Young Mary Loftis also sent clothing to her future husband, who responded with gratitude over the much-needed supplies. For female youths like Gillis and Loftis, providing supplies with soldiers fulfilled their need to interact with members of their peer group while displaying a sense of patriotic support in their communities.[21]

This source of clothing proved especially important to soldiers whose socioeconomic situation limited their access to basic necessities, or when the army lacked means to provide them. As LeeAnn Whites found, the inadequacy of military supplies made the household supply line even more significant as the military consistently ran low on "boots, socks, gloves, hats, or overcoats." This situation elevated the importance of women's domestic work, as it helped fill those gaps. For example, James Jackson, a physician from Chambers County, depended on a regular shipment of items from home. He insisted in one letter that he was "waiting impatiently" for a box of provisions and hoped his mother would "send me a box every week or two." Such items from home proved essential for Jackson, who, although a local doctor, possessed very little in personal property. Concerns over dropping temperatures also prompted William Riley Jones to ask his wife to make clothes for him, especially a coat and socks, as well as a blanket, "all for winter." Frances Danielly likewise requested clothing from his wife, noting that he would need pants "near the coller of our uniform as possible." Joseph Wesson of Talladega County also called on his wife to send "a pear of britches" as soon as she could prepare them. Benjamin Jackson, on the other hand, requested a long list of items, including shirts, pants, vest and "drawers," and with some urgency that she "prepare these things as quickly as you can."[22]

As men settled into military service, they attempted to re-create the comforts of home to ease the stress of camp life. These attempts oftentimes meant taking on roles typically reserved for female kin back home. Some even bragged about their newfound abilities to handle domestic chores. One young soldier boasted to his female relatives, "I can cook as good as any woman can." After some time in the camp he said "to tell the girls that they said bee fore I left that I would not wash my close clean but I can was as clene as any of them." Grant Taylor also wrote home detailing his new skills as a cook in the camps. "I had to cook three days this week," he wrote to his wife. "I think if I stay long in camps I will learn something about cooking." He goes on to boast that she "ought to see me making up doe in a big pan for 15 men. I get on my knees and put the pan between my knees and then work it into a perfect oil." Aside from the inconveniences of camp life, William Thomas Jackson, of Coosa County, detailed the variety of food that the soldiers learned to cook for each other. "We draw fresh beef five days in a week verry nice," he wrote to his wife, "and a teacup full of salt every four days for seven men. We draw rice, sugar and flour every four days." All these they turned into meals for several soldiers despite the meager portions. Additionally, he bragged about his success in preparing a comfortable living space, noting that "it is given up that we have the best bunk in camps."[23]

Regardless of their efforts to re-create the comforts of domestic life, common white soldiers expressed their dissatisfaction with daily conditions. The most common concerns were lack of quality food and living arrangements. In November of 1861, Cornelius Wright wrote to his parents, "We have nothing but beef and bread to eat and some coffee but very little of it." John Cotton wrote to his wife in 1862 complaining about food preparation in the camps, noting, "We get a plenty to eat but it is badly Cooked we had nothing fit to Cook with." He described many of the available food items, such as "meal flour pickle pork pickled beef and some times fresh beef rice sugar molasses"—adding that they lacked the kitchen tools to turn them into decent meals. Soldiers likewise raised concerns about their living arrangements. Henry Bray wrote to his mother, Marian, that he stayed in a comfortable home and had a "soft plank to sleep on," but other soldiers had to brave the elements without shelter. Cornelius also included a description of his poor living quarters in his letter home, noting, "I do not know how we will stay here at this place it is one of the worst campground I ever saw in my life." Another source of grousing came from the daily work assignments for the soldiers. W. V. Fleming, for example, mentioned to his wife that "the duty that we have to perform," while camped in Mobile, "is tolerable hard at this time."[24]

Benjamin Jackson refused to temper his discomfort with camp life and often described conditions as worse than mere inconveniences. Writing to his sister in June of 1861, Benjamin complained that the weather added to already difficult living quarters. "I have been at this place for nearly two weeks," he wrote, "and I have not slept in a tent since I have been here." He described that on rainy nights they had only a blanket to shield them. Yet rather than blame the military directly for the scarcity of shelter, he directed his rancor toward the quality of equipment, noting that "we have not got any tents worth anything, so you may guess we have a bad time of it, for it rained all night last night and all today as well." A constant concern for Benjamin was the health of the soldiers, which he saw as declining due to their heavy workload in the camps. "There is a great deal of sickness in our company," he revealed, "and it makes the duty very hard on the rest. What time we are not on guard nor on detail to work we have to drill. . . . I think that when I get home I can know what hard times are." Benjamin held back little when describing camp life to his wife, especially when it came to the disciplining of soldiers. In one letter he reported the punishment of three men for deserting, detailing that they "were tied to a post with their hands stretched as high . . . were given thirty nine lashes on their naked backs with a leather strap tacked on to a stick." He further claimed that the men's heads were shaved, and they were "drummed out of the service to the tune of 'Yankee Doodle.'"[25]

Another recurring issue in the camps was rampant illness and the general health of soldiers. Early in the war, men wrote home describing various afflictions, most commonly measles, moving through the camps. Luckily for Frances Danielly, his company seemed spared from an outbreak of the virus in September of 1861, but the larger regiment experienced many cases of the malaise. He reported that within a month "there [were] over a thousand men in this regiment and about 500 of them able to drill" and blamed the reduction in manpower on "measles and mumps" in the camps. Many others reported being sick themselves. D. G. Holcombe wrote to his relatives that after being exposed to "all the bad weather," he suffered from a "verry bad Coald." Others worried about the prospect of dying from sickness. Thomas Owen admitted his fears to his father when revealing they had "lost 9 of our boys," while H. S. Strom distrusted the hospital because, in his estimation, "we have the sorryist dockters her I ever saw."[26]

Although soldiers groused about the hardships of military life, they found reasons to remain positive about the war and its cause in those first two years. Their masculine sense of duty to the Confederate cause helped them to justify enduring hard conditions in the camps. In 1861 D. G. Holcombe encouraged his loved ones to "not study about mee for I have plenty to eat and plenty to ware and I don't think that you ought to cear." He reminded them to "jest look at the men that has left their wives and children and that all." They countered depictions of rough conditions with their sense or a higher purpose to serve the Confederacy. D. D. Bonner wrote to Mary Loftis, "I have now found out what hardtimes is," yet he countered, "I have come to the conclusion that I will content myself anyway. We have never suffered a great deal for anything to eat although our rations have been cut pretty short at times." Another young man writing to young Mary echoed the sentiment of sacrificing for a greater cause when he proclaimed, "I am not keen to get into a fight but I am ready when I am called on to do my duty." Writing to his wife, Martha, Benjamin Jackson also resolved that "it is not worthwhile to complain since it does no good," but rather he held to the hope that "when I get back home we can all enjoy the freedom of the Confederate States together." And J. M. Stubbs wrote to his wife that regardless of their constant marching, "the boys are as good bunch as ever the glorious sunny South has given birth to" and that "just let them hear of the enemy and they holler for pay and perten the march." In a letter to his wife, Grant Taylor grumbled at the "way of living" but believed "it is for our good." These same sentiments of fighting for a higher cause that drew common white men away from their homes provided, in part, the fuel to continue fighting, even as they confronted the realities of camp life.[27]

Despite such hardships, letters home often downplayed the sometimes unbearable camp conditions. Most of these correspondences stemmed from soldiers' attempts to ease their family's concerns over their well-being. Despite the crude nature of his encampment near Huntsville, Alabama, in October of 1861, Frances Danielly found ways to make life comfortable, writing to his wife that "we have cleaned out our camp and fixed all up." One month later Frances advised Elizabeth that she should hold off on sending clothes, as they "are all good and more of them than I can pack in my knapsack." Thomas Smyrl likewise stated his faith that the Confederate government would take care of the soldiers and that she should keep all supplies for the family. "Dont give your self any uneasiness about my clothing," he informed her. "I can draw clothes from the Government to do me . . . if the Confed cant clothes us I think it a poor chance." John Cotton wrote encouraging words home that "we get a plenty to eat and a plenty to give our horses," while Henry Bray confided to his mother that despite the quality of food, "it all helps to fill up and I suppose that's all the Confederacy cares for so they keep our belly full with something." William Riley Jones described "hard times" to his wife, Fannie, but promised that he had enough to eat to the point of gaining weight. Leonard Land, a young man still living with his parents in Washington County, enlisted in Company G of the Twenty-Third Alabama Infantry. Although homesick, Leonard reassured his parents that "we have fine times here plenty to eat and drink."[28]

Furloughs provided some hope of easing the stress of military life. Most men believed that after a time of service they would receive a reprieve, especially if stationed near their home or after a particularly strenuous battle. Even if the prospects of furloughs seemed unlikely in those cases, they expected that one day their time would come. Henry Bray seemed little bothered when looked over for a furlough, reasoning that at the time, they needed as many troops as possible. He held fast to the idea that as soon as more men came to replenish the ranks, he would be next for a furlough. William Thomas Jackson wrote to his wife that the only leaves granted were for those "that have no clothese." Yet he speculated that perhaps some soldiers "will tell lies from the beginning and by talking hard, begeing, maby he get six or an eight day furlow." Most soldiers kept up their spirits by seeing the prospect of returning home for a visit. Kinnon Lee, a small farmer from Covington County, quipped that the only furloughs allowed were for sick soldiers and that "perhaps I can get a sick furlow" by feigning an illness. Like Lee, most soldiers recognized that as long as they were able-bodied, they would remain in the camps. Though disappointed by their chances of a visit home, few saw this as a military failure, but rather as a necessity given rampant illness in the camps. As evidenced in Frances Danielly's letter to his wife, "there is no chance for me to come as yet they do not give any furloughs now only sick furloughs and I now able for Duty."[29]

Regardless of treacherous camp conditions, relationships with their families emerged as the most significant source for sustaining morale among common white men. Continuing their typical role as head of the household minimized the intrusion of war into their personal lives and fostered a sense of normalcy. Men specifically asserted their role as provider and protector for the family, even if at a distance. Husbands often sent letters instructing wives on how to run the farm, deal with financial issues, and handle other related duties typically overseen by men. Such intricate directions meant that they could maintain power over their household and, in the process, protect it in their absence. Kinnon Lee wrote to his wife about how to use money that he sent home, namely, to "pay all your debts" and "to buy corn and wheat enough to do you next year." John Davenport directed his wife on a number of issues regarding his family's finances and state of their farm. In September of 1862, he informed his wife that she should use their money to purchase corn and install a chimney in their house for the winter. Just a few months later, he instructed her on how to maintain the corn crop and care for their cows. Also unwilling to relinquish his role as the family breadwinner, Thomas Smyrl advised his wife on ways to provide income for the family. In one letter home, he informed her that he was "expressing" a pair of shoes to her that she could sell. He also promised to send her money for home expenses. William McCullough likewise asserted his position as head of the family when he directed his wife to collect on debts owed to him. He reasoned that she should "try to get it an liv on it as you see."[30]

Ensuring the continuation of the farm meant the family could survive during the extended absences of husbands and fathers. And trusting their wives and other loved ones with the upkeep of the farm was all that men could do while away. Husbands especially refused to relinquish total control and, as result, sent detailed instructions on how to run the farm in their absence. William Thomas Jackson was twenty-four and newly married when the war began. He came from a large family and maintained a close relationship with his mother and siblings, especially after the death of his father when he was just a teenager. After he enlisted in the Confederate army, William had to leave the family farm and all the responsibilities to his wife and mother. Yet he refused to give up control and asserted a presence from afar by offering meticulous directions on what to do in all matters related to the farm. Writing in December of 1862, he instructed his wife, Mary Ellen, on how to care for the family's meat supply and other food sources for the family's survival. When selling meat from the farm, he advised her to get "as much for the meet as you could get any whers else. . . . sell it for as much as you can get." Yet he also instructed her to "keep as much as you will have salt to save and be careful to kill it in verry cold wether and dont put on any more salt than just what you think it will take to save it." He contended that she should keep to his instruction in order to "bring you more money next sumer" and that "you dont know how much it will take to do you."[31]

William's directions grew more specific as his army service continued. He often wrote that he hoped to return home to care for the farm. But he soon realized that he had to entrust the farming responsibilities to Mary Ellen. However, he refused to give up complete control of the farm, perhaps out of a desire to preserve his masculine identity or to quell his fears over the family's survival. At one point he expressed concerns over the family's finances, citing that Mary Ellen should collect on his debts and sell one of their cows. He sent her a list of points on how to prepare the farm for "making a crop and something to go upon another year." William requested that his wife clear a place to grow corn, repair part of a fence, plant patches of cotton, and prepare a space to grow potatoes and peas. On the other hand, he instructed his mother, who he feared took on too many responsibilities in his absence, to refrain from such arduous work. He wrote to her, "I want you not to trouble yourself about matters and things there at home and I dont want you to expose yourself in seeing and tending to my things there at home." His largest concern was the extra strain that his absence would have on her health. "You know that the chills is very hard to break anyway and especially at this season of the year," he wrote, "if you dont take the very best care of yourself that you will have them all winter." William advised her that "rather than for you to expose yourself tending to my business, I had A heap rather you would let it go undone. . . . I had A heap rather loose every thing than to cause you to be sick and to suffer." As a means of alleviating the added burdens on the women he left behind, William hoped that his father-in-law would "hire a hand" to help with the farm.[32]

For John Cotton, his management of the farm from afar offered assurance that his large family would be cared for during the conflict. John, at the onset of the war, had seven children, whom he raised on a small farm in Coosa County. When he enlisted in 1862, he left his wife, Mariah, in charge of their modest property holdings. Similar to many who volunteered for the army, John believed that the war would last but a little while—until, he estimated, the "wheat gets ripe." Most of his letters to Mariah expressed a reluctance to give her control of the farm. He often expressed hope that he could "bee there and see how things are going on and look around a little rite to me how my wheat is doing and how things are going on." Yet, as the reality that his time in service might last longer, he began to advise his wife on how to care for the farm. His main concerns focused on the condition of his wheat crop and the prospect of it being "ruined with rust." By June of 1862, his letters became more specific in the tasks he expected her to complete: "If I dont get to come back home you must do the best you can have that wheat and barley thrashed as soon as you can and turn the hogs in and dont let the pares nor ases in and have the ry cut and thrashed." John's concerns about his family's financial state in his absence could be seen in his comments about the rising costs of goods. In particular, he advised her on what items to sell for additional income. By mid-November of that year, his anxieties over the state of the farm increased as it became clear that he would remain in the army longer than he anticipated. "Rite to me how your stock is doing," he inquired, "and if you have sold any pork yet and if you have killed any beef yet or sold any on foot and what you got for it." He emphasized the need for his wife to assume responsibility of the farm, despite his obvious inability to trust her completely. "I want you to cary on your business as if you never expected to see me any more," he wrote, "do the best you can and you will please me if I dont come home you must make your arrangements for another year." A conflict between serving in the army and serving the family emerged for John by early 1863, as he concluded, "I dont no when I will get to come to see you all." Trying to ease his fears, he used the family's limited funds to hire additional labor to handle the heavy physical tasks of preparing and maintaining the farm. Although he recognized he needed to rely on Mariah to run the farm, he was unwilling to completely entrust its care to her.[33]

Women recognized their newfound roles and sought their husbands' advice on matters of the farm. Such solicitations reflected yet again the traditional gendered protocol among couples in which the wife deferred to their husband's input on farm-related matters. Although John Cotton expected his wife to run the farm with competency, he received several letters from her asking what to do about the sale of crops: "You must rite me all the good advice you can for I need advice." Mariah also expressed concern about how to spend money and asked her husband again to send instructions on the matter. Similarly, Malinda Taylor wrote her husband asking for assistance on selling livestock and planting crops, even though she leaned on her neighbors for help. Throughout most of their correspondence, Malinda demonstrated a sense of insecurity in taking over the family farm and a need for her husband's input.[34]

Some reports about farming conditions reinforced men's anxieties about leaving behind their familial duties. Fannie Jones, of Fayette, sent an update to William that the prospect of a bountiful harvest of their corn, wheat, and rye seemed low on their modest farm. The same was true for Benjamin Jackson as he served in the Thirty-Third Alabama Infantry. His wife sent him letters detailing bleak conditions on their farm. "I will say to you that we did not make any [corn] in the swamp at all worth naming," Martha wrote, "we have not made bread, though I hope we will not perish." Jane Brooks Lindsey also had less-than-stellar news to report about the status of their farm in Coosa County. She revealed that their hogs "didn't grow much," and that the tobacco crop was poor, although "the ears of corn are very large."[35]

At times a husband's insistence on asserting his masculine role while away created tensions between him and his wife. Women who demonstrated an aptitude at taking control of the family farm confronted husbands who, in some cases, refused to recognize their ability to assume those duties. Elizabeth Danielly proudly reported to her husband the success of their crops. "The women that has got any spunk about them," she wrote, "is trying to make a living them that never did work is doing nothing still." In a letter to her husband, Malinda Taylor informed her husband that she successfully negotiated for a better price for their livestock. She also offered prideful descriptions of growing the crop on her own and the confidence that came with knowing she could run the farm on her own. Malinda proclaimed to Grant, "I tell you I am getting to be a splendid farmer. All I like [lack] being a man is the pants and something els."[36]

Regardless of women's increased confidence, some husbands refused to relinquish total control and insisted on a trusted male to oversee some, if not all, matters related to the farm. Although Malinda informed Grant of her success as a farmer, she received a letter asking her to rely on extended kin to help her in his absence. John Gwyn wrote to his wife that in preparation for the winter, he intended to ask neighbors to help chop wood. Benjamin Jackson likewise requested that his wife allow her father to take control of any money that he sent home, making decisions on the best way to spend it. Others also relied on extended kin to step in and care for the family. Kinnon Lee encouraged his wife to move in with family to ease her financial struggles. He agreed that "do what you think Best if Peace is not made this year you will have hard road to travel unless some boddy helps you." Henry Bostic, of Coffee County, relied on a man he called Brother Huggins to help his wife. He charged the man with purchasing food supplies for the family as well as everyday items such as paper. Throughout many of his correspondences, Henry referred to Brother Huggins as a trusted assistant and provider for his wife and family. Yet his wife persisted in her choice of a farm hand whom Bostic distrusted. In regard to a man named Jack, he questioned whether he would be able to perform the work. "I dont want you to hiar him unless he will agree to clear about 8 or 10 achers and fence it ove whar the hog pen is," he insisted. Their disagreement over who should assist the family did insert a level of tension in their relationship. Bostic, however, had little choice but to concede to his wife's decisions during his absence.[37]

For William and Emily Moxley, the issue of who should oversee the family's finances strained their relationship to near the breaking point. William relied on his small farm to supplement his modest income as a physician. When William enlisted, the farm took on greater importance, as his absence eliminated his pay as a doctor. He left his family in his wife's care but placed the burden of financial dealings with his brother Daniel "Newton" Moxley. Adding support to the Moxley household was Appleton Justice, a trusted friend, who was a small merchant in the community. Both men played a crucial role in providing Emily with all the assistance she needed. Yet early on in William's absence, the two men left in charge clashed over business affairs, and Emily found herself caught in the middle. At first the two seemed to agree on affairs relating to her purchasing food supplies. But soon after, in October of 1861, the two had a falling-out after Justice refused to sell Newton "spirits" on credit from his business. Later that month Newton informed Emily that she should no longer allow Justice to "have any thing to do with your affairs." She indicated to her husband that despite Newton's warnings, she considered Justice "the last friend" she had as someone from whom she could purchase supplies.[38]

In the end, Newton Moxley showed himself to be more of a source of frustration than of help for Emily. As his care for his brother's family grew less frequent, Emily was forced to depend more on Justice for supplies. The issue stemmed from a matter of the family's corn. Emily wrote to William that his brother was angry over a neighbor, Charles Malloy, who refused to hand over the corn that he had stored for them. Newton went so far as to threaten to "take out an attachment" as a means of legal action against

Malloy. Yet as time passed, Newton grew increasing negligent of the Moxley household, and William turned to Justice to retrieve his corn. He wrote to Emily that he proved more reliable than his brother. When Newton did resurface, he demanded that she cease all business with Justice, which Emily refused. The negligence on Newton's part continued as he failed to settle debts owed to William and delayed selling land that could help supplement the family income. Emily wrote to her husband that "it looks like he is very tired of me and the children. . . . he is not willing to do any thing for me and them." By December of 1861, Emily realized that she had become a burden to Newton and confided to her husband, "I will be glad when [he is] with you, for I can do as well with out him as I can with him, for he does me no good at all." In subsequent letters Emily revealed to her husband that she was growing dependent on Justice to provide supplies on credit. Rather than admonish his brother for doing little to protect his family, William deemed Emily's reliance on the merchant the most egregious affront to his reputation. "You know I have always been willing to furnish you with any thing needed I could furnish," he wrote. "If you need any thing let me know it, for [I] expect to furnish it for you."[39]

Even with diminished control over the livelihood of their families, common white men could at least offer some military pay to send home. Male kin relied on military pay to offset the financial burdens of family effected by their absence. For one, compensation allowed them to purchase basic household necessities rather than depend on loved ones to provide them. But, even more so, men hoped military pay would allow them the continued role of family provider so closely associated with their masculine identity. Henry Bray wrote to his brother that he needed money to buy clothing and food but that the military was slow to act. "I recon we will geted payed in a day or so," he wrote, "or so at lest I hope so for I done with out money long enuf." Benjamin Stubbs wrote home that he hoped they would "receive our bounty," which he expected would be around $75. W. C. McCullough informed his wife, "I have fifty dollars for you if I cant get a chans to send it to you witch I think I will in a fue days." The Jackson family likewise anticipated that Benjamin would start to receive regular pay for his service. In their case Benjamin asked his father-in-law to determine how best to spend the money he sent home, rather than leave it to his wife's discretion. "We have not got our money yet," he wrote to him, "but I think we will get it before long. I will send you money as soon as I get a chance."[40]

The assertion of patriarchal power from afar included policing the behavior of their dependents. The fierce protection of community reputation among common whites before the war now took on greater importance as couples lived apart. Common white men grew especially anxious over losing some control over their wives' propriety. These concerns stemmed from the value of public reputation within common white culture. For a husband, his role in protecting that reputation offered proof of his manhood and good standing in the community. For example, during his absence from home, William Moxley grew increasingly concerned about his wife's personal habits. In particular, he pleaded with his wife in several letters to "quit the use of snuff." Women of the poorer socioeconomic classes commonly used snuff. Yet William abhorred the thought of his wife using tobacco in his absence and even offered to quit smoking his pipe if she would do the same. As a physician, William's pleas originated, in part, from his fear of the health effects. "My dear, it is for your good that I make the request," he wrote in December 1861. "I would not deny you any thing that would afford you Comfort or Happiness that would not be an injury to you." His insistence that she take his advice, however, illuminated a much deeper concern. In his request for her to end the practice, he attempted to direct his wife in proper conduct, arguing that the practice "was questionable." William Thomas Jackson likewise scolded his wife for her reaction when handling a situation with hiring help for the farm; in particular the way that she described the situation seemed more unsettling to him than the problems with finding a farmhand. "You said that you dident intend to be shit on in no such way," he wrote to her. "Now any other word would have done just as well as that and please let me never see that word in another letter from you."[41]

Grant Taylor also took issue with his wife Malinda's behavior during his absence. He became particularly concerned after hearing that she had hosted a holiday party for young men and women at their home. Feeling uneasy about the gathering, she disclosed the events of the evening in a letter to Grant, who was encamped in Spanish Fort, Alabama. In his return correspondence, he admonished his wife for having such a gathering, arguing, "You know I always had serious objections to having parties at my house and more especially at such a time as this for several reasons." His largest concern was that her opening their home to company without his presence would leave her vulnerable to gossip, fearing that "designing persons both men and women use such times to carry on their sinful communications." He further warned that "young men brag about staying at parties up there till late in the night and then go home with the girls through the old pine fields alone and you know that the morals of people were never so low as now." To Grant, the actions of the youths reflected on his wife and his household and would make them targets of accusations of impropriety. "And then another thing," he warned her, "is people are so ready to talk about women living alone as you are." Without his watchful eye over the family, Grant feared that they would face public rebuke and noted that "you need not think your former good name will screen you if a disgraceful talk should be started about you, for I tell you nay, though you may be ever so innocent which I doubt not you would be." In the end, Grant agreed to drop the issue if she promised to excercise better judgment for the remainder of his absence.[42]

Additionally, men expressed concerns over the treatment of family members at the hands of their community. Understanding that their absence kept them from being the protector of the family name, they wrote frequently instructing loved ones on how to handle any slights against their reputation. In one letter home, Frances Danielly defended his father-in-law, who endured criticisms for staying home from the war. He wrote to his wife concerned about people "that put out that tale on your Pa about not being a loyal man but that is a lye for he is as loyal as any man." He insisted that her father demonstrated his loyalism through small acts, such as helping Confederate soldiers passing through their community. "I dont care when he is," he argued, "he stop his horses and cary the soldiers home when he . . . to be ploughing and that is the thanks he git?" John Davenport inquired frequently about gossip around their community, especially if anyone "impose or slite you or my sweet Little Children and who seams to be truly our friends." He seemed particularly worried over how people treated her in his absence and asked if anyone "misuse you in eney way." William Hobson likewise worried about his family's reputation after learning of a physical altercation involving a loved one. "I was very sary to her that dan mack cut windom," he declared. "I wish I had bin at home when he was there I would lete hom know ede what a knife was maid fur."[43]

Rumors of disloyalty threatened not only the reputation of the individual man but also that of all family members. Such was the case of Henry Bray when he heard of community members creating rumors that he had delayed enlisting in the army. He responded to the accusations that it was "a false report and I don't care who told it, they told a lie certain." Henry continued his defense, claiming, "I never kept nothing from

[you] and had it not been for you, Ma, I would have been in the Army six months before I did so don't take any of the blame on yourself." In response to what he considered malicious gossip meant to tarnish his family's reputation, he asked his mother to send him the name of "who told the tale on me" and threatened that "if it was a man, tell him I am good for his meat when I get back and if it is a woman, tell Sis Mary to give her a mauling and oblige her brother."[44]

Women also took particular interest in the behavior of their male kin during their service in the military. Their concerns stemmed primarily from their role as moral guardian of the family. Stories of drinking, gambling, and prostitution within the camps reached the home front and caused much distress among female kin left to wonder if their male counterparts could resist temptation. When the Confederate draft threatened to take her youngest son away, Sarah Espy confided in her diary that she feared "he may be inticed by wicked men into bad habits." Elizabeth Taylor Teer wrote to her brother and husband imploring them to ask respectfully, noting that she would "pray that you may forebeare the temptation of camp life." Oftentimes, women encouraged men to participate in religious meetings in the camps or, at the least, to remember their faith. In a letter to her son, Marian Davis reminded him that "if you are absent in person, you are not absent in our hearts for we send our prayers up to our Maker for your happy conversion daily." Hoping to steer him in the right direction, she wrote, "Son, you must pray for yourself if you wish to be a Christian. You must make an effort. Mind not that which the world sayest unto you for they cannot save you in the hour of death. Pray to the Lord to forgive your sins."[45]

Male kin responded by sending reassurances that they behaved honorably by reflecting on their religious convictions. James Zachariah Branscomb, for example, reassured Eliza, his mother, that he remained devoted to his religious faith and that such devotion helped him through the hardships of military life. "Dear Mother," he wrote, "you can't imagin how I feel when I think of you on your knees at the family altar, supplicating the throne of Grace for me at the hour of retiring . . . but I am glad that I can tell you that I never as yet been out of my place as a soldier." James also reminded his sister of his religious devotion, emphasizing that he attended Sunday services regularly in the camps. And, in an 1863 letter, he boasted to her that there was "good work going on in the regt. Now, we have prayer meeting four times a week. . . . May this good work continue."

Grant Taylor wrote to his wife promising her that his religious faith would help him to combat the temptations in the camps. The same held true for William Riley Jones when he wrote to his wife, Fannie, noting, "I see moore sin an weakness her in camps than I evr saw in life before." He further confided that "it some times makes mee trimel to her and see what I do tho I am wicked my self I neede an want the prairs of all Christen people." William, however, recognized the difficulties in keeping his faith, admitting to Fannie, "I hant hurd nary surmons in five or six months nor hant hurd nary prair in two months religion is all most gone down her."[46]

Amid separation, distress, and death, common white families turned inward to the family for emotional strength through forms of sentimentalism and religious faith. Sentimental reflections of family life helped combat homesickness among soldiers and eased the constant worry of those they left behind. Letters including emotional descriptions of domestic scenes provided the catharsis soldiers needed to mitigate the loneliness of separation. Common themes included fantasizing about favorite foods, envisioning oneself surrounded by loved ones, and offering flowery expressions of romantic love. Moreover, men and women turned to their religious faith as a form of emotional venting, helping them face the potential of death. Turning to idyllic images of home life provided the psychological security for common white families. And, it offered reassurances of continued relationships within the family. In essence, the home provided the mental therapy to endure long-term anguish that helped sustain men and women's support for the war.

Notions of one day returning to the domestic circle figured prominently in sentimental expressions. James Zachariah Branscomb explained to his sister in 1863 that having been in the army since the onset of the war, he looked forward to the day when he could "shake hands with you and your children." The prospect of a furlough likewise intensified Branscomb's goal of making it through military engagements to see his family again. "Sister," he wrote Lucinda, "these years absent from those that are so dear him causes a heart to beat as it never did before when he soon expects to meet those dear ones, to meet Father, Mother, Brothers, Sisters after all I have born will be the happiest day of my life." John Wesley Branscomb, the brother of James and Lucinda, echoed the sentiment of reunion in a letter to his sister: "I almost despair when I think childhoods home but the thought of meeting again gives me pleasure. I am not dissatisfied with my home only when I am lonesome." William Riley Jones took a humorous approach to his desire to be home. In addressing his sisters, he asked, "Tell thim that i wood bee as proud to see thim as i wood a bar fight in the winter time." Conversely, in a later letter to his wife, Jones adopted a more somber tone when divulging his homesickness. "I want to see you the worst that i ever did in my life," he wrote in September of 1862. "The longer i stay away the worse i want to see you my love is like un to a founten of water that naver gose dry it till flows for ever to wards you if i wast to go to the end of the Earth i naver wood for get you." Henry Bray likewise saw the prospect of reunion as a time of celebration. When contemplating the upcoming Fourth of July holiday, he declared to his youngest sister, "How I wish I could be with you all tomorrow. I am afraid my holiday is far distant yet but when it does come you ought to see me making tracks for that sweet little spot they call home in double quick time."[47]

Children played prominently in the sentimental expression of fathers who sought comfort in their paternal connections to home. Feeling the pains of being away from his young child, William Riley Jones asked his wife to "take the best cear of our babe." His separation from home brought even greater sadness when he learned that his youngest child became ill. "I could a have bin thar to a hopoe wate on hime when he was sick," he wrote. "I dremp about him the other night i saw hime as plane as i ever did in my life i felt like he was sick when i wake." Oftentimes fathers focused on their children's daily lives, especially in the areas of education and behavior, as a way to express their affections. Frances Danielly, for example, directed his young daughter to learn to read, and Jimmy, his son, to "be a good boy." W. V. Fleming likewise implored his daughter to make sure that she watched her behavior and to "tell the rest of the children to be good children." Joseph Wesson asked his sons to "bee smart boys" and his daughter to "bee a smart girl," while John Cotton advised his child to "lern a heap and bee kind to her teacher and lern to rite." More frequently fathers became sentimental toward their children, as Grant Taylor demonstrated when he wrote his family, "I would long to embrace them and you if there were any chance. . . . Oh how my heart swelled in my throat as I thought of sweet Mary." Malinda, his wife, encouraged the emotional connection to his children in her response: "They say they want to see you so bad they dont know what to do. Jimmy wants me to wright to you that he prays to God to leet you come home. Matthew says you have got a heap of Yankes to cill before you can come home. Little Mary is the sweetist little thing I ever saw. . . . Buddy says he tries to bee good and works hard."

Fathers found such emotional connections a way to channel their sadness over separation from family.[48]

For the Moxley family, the imagery of a loved one at home added to, rather than eased, the emotional strain of separation. Emily Moxley revealed the overwhelming sadness she felt with her husband William off at war. She, like many wives, looked for ways to feel close to their loved ones. "You told me to comb my hair ever time I thought of you," she revealed. "That is out of my power, for I would do nothing but comb it, for there is not one minute in the day but what I think of you." Emily, however, described to William how she thought about their time together, noting, "Ever where I go, there is where we have been together seting, walking, talking, standing, or lieing. There is always something to bring you in my mind. There is your clothes, your old hat. They look so natural." Ultimately, finding ways to remember William during their separation left a grieving Emily with little comfort. She wrote to him, "This paper is wet with your wife's tears. They are shed for you, for one that I love more than heart can tell or words can express."[49]

Romantic exchanges between husbands and wives provided other familiar forms of sentimental expression. These types of love letters also offered them a source of normalcy as they reaffirmed traditional gender behavior among couples. In a letter to his wife, Henry Bostic touched on scenes of affection when he playfully asked, "How wold you like to hang your arms Around my Neck?" Thomas Smyrl likewise reassured his wife of their romantic connection, reminding her of "the weeks the Months the years that has been so pleasantly spent by us as man and wife." Other husbands offered more titillating details about the physical intimacies they missed. "I have strange feelings when I contemplate your likeness," Grant Taylor wrote to Malinda. "How natural you look. How I yearn to press those silent lips to mine and hear those sweet words of love fall from them once more." Husbands often framed their amorous expressions in the form of poetry in their letters. Offering a few poetic lines, even at the end of a letter, permitted men the freedom to reassert their masculine identity while observing nineteenth-century forms of sentimentalism. John Cotton, for example, composed a poem to encourage his wife to write to him: "Now in a fare land I rome, fare from my friend at home, but I hope the time is near, when shall all meet again, I have not herd from home since I left there." An eighteen-year-old, Samuel King Vann, reassured his future wife of his continuing affections when he wrote, "Remember me, with soft emotions, and believe I think on thee." Mary Loftis received a similar letter offering a flirtatious message from a potential suitor who wrote to her, "I think of the tho far away, I think of the both nite and day, I think of the and then I sigh, I think of the and all most cry." John Davenport's letter home included a poem reminding his wife that their separation was for a greater cause:

> But when the dream awakes me, the beet for revelee, I am sadly disappointed, I can butlook for thee, I will take my post on deauty, whear ever it comes to hand, in protection of my mary and my dear native land.[50]

Even single young men and women found romantic letters a source of emotional support. Correspondences replaced face-to-face courtship rituals in the antebellum South and allowed them to continue the social traditions familiar to their youth culture. Young men turned to notions of valor and honor as a soldier to enhance their masculine identity and, in turn, their appeal to eligible women. James Zachariah Branscomb, for example, wrote frequently to his sister asking about the young women in their community and insisted that she speak highly of his military service to enhance his image among them. "I want you to have a sweetheart picked out for me when I get home," he wrote. "Give all the girls my pious regards." In a subsequent letter, James charged his sister with finding a "sweetheart" and to "tell her about me so she may know what to depend on when I come." The notion of returning to a potential romantic relationship seemed to lighten James's spirits in his letter to Lucinda: "I am going immediately to courting and I shall wish your judgment. So get to work now and let me know soon who she is so I will know whether to come home like a soldier or like a gentlemen." Samuel King Vann courted his future wife through their letters and often asked about the prospects of marriage. "I hope you will remain my sweetheart until I once more return," he wrote. "And then I ask a hard and serious question to answer but I hope you will answer it with great satisfaction." In a subsequent letter, he continued to assert his masculine role and asked her again about marriage, adding, "I ask this sincerely and with heartfelt emotion, and I hope you will not make any delay."[51]

Mary Loftis received several letters from young men in her community seeking familiar courtship relations. Their contents demonstrate the desire of young men and women to replicate the prewar gendered behaviors of courting couples. C. H. Bonner wrote to Mary, "Give my love to all the girls," and H. S. Strom asked her, "Tel the girls they must not for get me for I think of them every day." Strom furthered his romantic entreaties, writing, "I wish it was so I cold be with you now but I can't my injoyment is no more with you I am afraid." G. Davis likewise sent flirtatious letters to Mary reasserting his desires for potential courtships. "You must remember me to all of the girls of my acquaintances," he asked. "I often think of the girls that is old friends and what has past be fore this wear come on. . . . I am hopes the girls will not for git the boys. . . . We often talk a bout the girls it is the young Ladies whom we have so much pleasure with althow we are surprised of it all now." These exchanges between youths created a connection to home that helped ease the homesickness of soldiers and provided a connection to the world they left behind.[52]

Soldiers' sentimentalism often reflected on the rituals of family life. Frequently, men wrote letters discussing food and the women who prepared it. Food conjured up nostalgic feelings of home while reinforcing connections to loved ones through the ritual of dining together. James Garrison admitted to his wife that he dreamed of the day when he could return home and enjoy a family meal. In one letter he detailed all the types of food that he wanted his wife to prepare for him upon his return, including "a heap of water melons . . . and cornbeef and a few snaps and rosen and a fride chicken." Newton Davis also discussed how much he missed having dinner with his family. "I often long for the good things at home," he wrote his wife, Bettie, "and I hope that it will not be long before I shall be permitted to enjoy them." Benjamin Jackson, of Convington County, lightheartedly instructed his sister that when the watermelons of the farm were ripe, she should "send me one in a letter if you can seal it up." James Crowder, of Chambers County, reminisced that he longed for his mother's cooking and hoped to survive the war to enjoy another of her meals. He likewise reflected on the types of food he missed the most. "I have not eat no corne bread since I eat that up that I started from home with," he lamented. "I wood give a half a dolar for one litle cake of corn now just to sea how hit would taste."[53]

Scenes of enjoying family rituals around food at times worsened homesickness. While stationed in Camp Lee, William Thomas Jackson often used food to express his sadness about being away from home and his young daughter. He confided to Mary Ellen, his wife, "I almost envy you tho think that you are at home eating buiscuit and butter and taters and good hog head and feet and spare ribs and eating up all my goobers and hear I am in old furginny and get nothing but beef and old ginger bread." But in that same letter he reassured her, "Yet I get tolerable plenty to eat." Letters like these were less about the actual material conditions of camp life than about reconnecting to home. Thus, William revealed to Mary Ellen that he longed to come home "to healp you eat some of them back bones you spoke of" but resolved that "it is all in vain." Regardless of whether it mitigated or exacerbated homesickness, common white soldiers sought solace in scenes of reuniting family around the rituals associated with food. Moreover, the idealization of sharing food with loved ones reminded men of the reason why they served the Confederacy: to protect the sanctity and security of family. Benjamin Jackson also turned to images of home and the food served at the family table as a source of comfort. He wrote home that he would "give anything . . . to see you all and get some bacon, collards, cucumbers, watermelons and roasting ears. There is no chance to get such here." Later he wrote to his wife that he missed the food from his mother, especially "her beans and collards" but that "wishing does no good."[54]

To deal with the anguish of separation, common whites also drew on the religious traditions that brought family together. Women especially found their faith as a way to assert some power over their circumstances. Sarah Espy, for instance, turned to her religious faith as she faced the prospect of federal troops entering her community, writing in her diary that she hoped "the good Lord will not allow them to come, but turn them back to their own country to live in peace." When the enemy finally came that summer, she again relied on her religious faith. "May the good Lord grant we may never have such another trial pass through," she wrote, "but may He fight for us against the mighty." Emily Moxley leaned on her spiritual beliefs to deal with her separation from her husband, believing that she must "trust in providence for the better." By 1862 Emily continued to depend on prayer as a source of hope for family reunion, writing to William, "God grant that we may gain the victory and all can go home to familiys in our country now." Zillah Brandon called on her piety to come to terms with the loss of her two sons, James and Hines. News that James died in a hospital reached Zillah in May of 1862. Two months later Hines, the youngest of her sons, passed away in a hospital in Gainesville, Alabama. Her faith took precedence as she sought to overcome her grief, resolving "like twin brothers, they were linked by a threefold cord that will ever beautify the Christian name. And as Saul and Jonathan, they were pleasant in life, so they were barely separated in death."[55]

Common white soldiers likewise turned to religious faith as they confronted the possibility of death during their service. Whether surrounded by casualties on the battlefield or sickness in the camps, soldiers depended on religious sentiment as one way to vent their fears and find a source of courage. Soldiers, moreover, often called upon religious imagery to help ease the pain of separation from loved ones and to reassure them that they would one day be reunited, even if in death. Benjamin Jackson reflected on home life and the routine of attending "meetings" together as a family. He frequently boasted to his wife about his frequent attendance of religious services in the camps. "I heard very good preaching to day here in our regiment," he wrote in 1862. "We have a preacher that is going to preach for us as long as we stay here." Jackson hoped to return home, yet, as the chances of a furlough seemed slim, he turned to his faith to deal with his homesickness, believing that "if it is the will of God we shall meet again." William Jones also used faith to navigate the separation from his family: "i hav got the faith to beleaves that i will go home once more to live with you again. . . . i hope that God will be with me throo all of undertakens and ceap mee from all harm i think of him bowth night and day . . . i pray for help from god every day in my life for you and the babe."[56]

Grant Taylor likewise turned to his faith to navigate the painful separation from his family and the fear of never returning to them. "Pray for me," he wrote to his wife, Malinda, "and try to be reconciled God can take care of me here as well as there." She returned his religious sentiment as a tool for managing the grief of separation, writing that she prayed for him "night and morning" and would "kneel alone and pray to God." Grant agreed with the notion that God would intervene on their behalf and reunite the family. "I believe we will meet again," he assured Malinda, "for I have prayed with all the faith that I could that we would meet again and I know you have." Separation proved too much for Grant and Malinda to bear, and the couple resolved that reunion would happen either in life or in death. These forms of religious sentiment emerged repeatedly in the letters of common whites who, even before the war, upheld a long tradition of religious devotion.[57]

Just as family honor and duty guided the roles and relationships of common whites in prewar Alabama, so too would those expectations draw them into a war that sought to create an independent nation to preserve slavery. Though with minimal investment in the institution, common whites came to see that a Confederate nation would offer the best source of protection of their family from the forces of outside invaders. Once into the throes of war, men and women leaned heavily on the material support of family, whether at home or in battle. The family offered supplies to common white soldiers who often faced a lack of vital supplies in the camps. The great emotional trials families endured took their toll on common whites, who turned to sentimental expressions of home life, relationships, and religious faith to provide the comfort needed to sustain their support for the war. As long as family provided the main crutch to weather wartime conditions, common whites continued to support the Confederate cause.

When William Moxley left for war, he knew that he left behind a despondent wife. Even after Emily's touching appeal to her husband to come home, as his absence was "the hardest trial I have ever had, by far," William remained loyal to the Confederate mission. Despite the outpouring of emotion that filled their letters, both recognized that a return to home and family offered the greatest sense of comfort. William wrote to Emily in October 1861, "I dreamed of you evry night. . . . Some times when I would open my eyes I could hardly believe but you was some where not far from me." William muted the pain of separation by holding on to the prospect of one day seeing his family again. And, in his estimation, an end to the war was the only means of achieving reunion, for, as William concluded, if "we have peace as we desire it, that I shall be as happy as a man can be on this Earth." Emily and William held fast to the hope that they would one day see each other again. Yet, as fate would have it, Emily died during childbirth, and William returned to a broken family circle.[58]

3

"This Unholy War"

Families in Crisis, 1863–65

In January of 1864, a local paper issued a call to Alabama women to use their world of domesticity to show their devotion to the Confederate cause. "It is your province," one citizen wrote to the *Alabama Beacon*, "to inaugurate the honorable system of home manufactory. While your fathers, husbands, brothers, and sons are in the field, you should be at home bravely working for their comfort." In a scolding tone, the author demanded that women "must perform some duty," as the war effort called for "more sacrifices, more honorable exertion." He rebuked those whom he perceived as failing to live up to the ideals of female sacrifice, demanding that "it is no time for sport, levity, and festivity."[1]

For common white men and women, however, there rarely existed a time of leisure to enjoy sport, levity, and festivity. On the contrary, their socioeconomic conditions prior to the war created circumstances in which work and family remained central to all aspects of their lives in their quest to thrive in an unequal world. As the war called on the loyalty of citizens, family again emerged front and center heeding those calls. Notions of family resonated beyond the private boundaries of the household and into the public realm of the state. In their conceptualization of sacrifice, they pledged themselves to a larger, metaphorical family in exchange for their care and safety. Yet, when the effects of waging a total war took a greater toll on their families than they initially anticipated, common whites began to take issue with that implied agreement. In their estimation, the patriarch of the metaphorical family, the state, proved unable to protect their loved ones. They increasingly turned those frustrations toward elites whose economic and political privilege meant that they bore less of the hardships of fighting the war. To most common whites, those of wealth and their allies were to blame for their families' being in crisis.[2]

Common whites in Alabama greeted 1863 with hope that the war would soon come to an end. The sacrifices expected of civilians and soldiers undermined the emotional and physical well-being of their families. Strains of military life left soldiers exhausted and facing grueling conditions. Their initial enthusiasm for enlisting gave way to increasing war-weariness and wondering whether remaining in the conflict was worth the consequences. Although not all soldiers lost faith in the Confederate cause, the subjects in this study certainly demonstrate a willingness to call into question the means to achieving it. To Alabama's common whites, it seemed as if the family they had sworn to protect was now in a state of peril, as news from home left them fearful for the safety of loved ones. How could they continue to protect their families by serving the Confederacy if they could not protect their kin while they fought? How could husbands and wives, mothers and fathers allow their family to keep on suffering for the cause that seemed in line more with the interests of the elites than with their own?

It became clear that if they remained committed to fighting the war, they risked the security and thus the survival of the family. This realization would make its way into the consciousness of common whites as the exigencies and deprivations of war settled into the routine of their daily lives. Calls to continue sacrificing loved ones to the front added even more hardship as the loss of much-needed male labor along with limited aid from the state weakened their already tenuous existence. The tools used to cope with the disruptions of war—connections to home, continuance of gender roles, and sentimental reflections—transformed into expressions of discontent. By 1865, common whites all but turned their backs on a war that placed their families at risk to save the interests of the elites.

For common white soldiers, their struggle to remain committed to fighting the war originated, in part, from the declining conditions in the military. The early difficulties of adjusting to camp life no longer seemed temporary. Rather, these soldiers came to see the harsh realities of that life become increasingly worse. Complaints about camp conditions were ordinary occurrences among soldiers in all stages of the war. Learning to sleep in uncomfortable quarters and eat subpar rations appeared typical adjustments. By 1863 increasing battlefield defeats, rising inflation, and diminished home-front supplies only added to their anguish. The common

Figure 3. This portrait of Henry Stokes Figures (*left*) with an unidentified young man illustrates the brotherly bonds that developed between soldiers who endured similar hardships during the war. Figures served as a private in Company F of the Fourth Alabama Infantry and later as adjutant in the Fort-Eighth Infantry. Alabama Department of Archives and History.

white soldiers in this study display a broad spectrum of responses to those conditions. Some saw the cause of their situation as the fault of the invading Union forces, while others blamed the lack of resources available to the state governments and Confederate military. Regardless of where they fell on that spectrum, all common white soldiers expressed a sense of war fatigue and genuine fear for the fate of their loved ones as cause to question the integrity of elites and their fight to protect slavery. They blamed those in power for placing an unbalanced burden on them for fighting the war and its resulting sacrifices.

Growing difficulties in procuring food provisions showed early signs of declining conditions as the war moved into 1863. Soldiers often wrote home detailing the limited food resources around them, frequently directing their frustrations toward the military charged with feeding them. In a letter to his future wife, Samuel King Vann, a young man reluctantly serving in the Nineteenth Alabama Regiment, blamed his low spirits on meager rations. "I am getting tired of this place," he explained, "unless they would feed us better. We get very scanty rations indeed." The morale of Vann and others like him depended partially on the ability of the military to provide for their basic dietary needs. He declared that "a soldier's task is a hard one, but we have to submit to it. I would not if they would give us plenty to eat, but our rations we draw are very light indeed and bad eating at that." For a young man growing into adulthood, the lack of food weighed heavily. Vann revealed that the scarcity of food "goes pretty hard with me." James Woods wrote to his love interest back home that the lack of "rashons" had tempered his enthusiasm to serve as he soon "foind out what a solger's life is." Grant Taylor likewise commented on the short food supply for soldiers. He related that they "are faring worse in the eating line now": "We only get meal enough for breakfast and dinner and sometimes we have none from one morning to the next." Yet, in most likely an attempt to ease his wife's concern over his well-being, he assured her, "We do pretty well and keep in good spirits."[3]

Oftentimes soldiers wrote home about the unbearable state of life in the military. High among their complaints were sleeping outside in the elements or in inadequate shelter. Early in the war, they limited such grumblings, perhaps to ease the anxieties of their loved ones at home. By 1863, however, a marked increase in complaints about living conditions occurred in several of their correspondences. John Gwyn repeatedly expressed his frustrations to his wife that they lacked tents while encamped in Murfreesboro, and the situation worsened after it "turned cold." He feared that if the military failed to supply them with adequate shelter, "they [would] be compelled to suffer." Common soldiers did indeed suffer through the elements while their superior officers enjoyed the comforts of a tent or the residence of a local civilian. Such unequal conditions between soldiers and elite officers amplified already-existing resentment among common white men toward those charged with providing basic care. This situation certainly got the attention of Grant Taylor. "Not more than one third of the men have even one blanket," he wrote to his wife. "Fifteen hundred convalescents that is men who have been sick and discharged from the hospitals without even a shoe to their feet and half of them half naked and the snow was six inches deep." William Riley Jones also came to see camp life as almost too much to bear. He admitted to his wife, "I avant now good newse but a plenty of bad the times is very hard her." In a January 1863 letter to his wife, Harriet, James Garrison described a similarly bleak situation, noting that "a winter blanket was wet and cold and you may know that I had a nasty time of it then you know I would like to have been in bed with you." By the spring of that year, James described the constant strain of marching from one location to another: "I have marched a heap and very hard . . . I never slept more than 2 nights in eight and you may know how a man feels under them kind of camps part of the time lying in breast works in the mud and water and then we chard back to our camps."[4]

To alleviate the stress of camp life, soldiers depended even more on the household supply line that connected them to family. From the onset of the war, common white men relied on family for material goods unavailable from the military. As the conflict moved into its third year, however, family aid became a matter of emergency in caring for the welfare of soldiers. Horace Smith, a transplant from New York to Eufala, wrote his wife asking her to "make me some cloths for I have nothing at all now." He even joked that his conditions had become so bad that "when I do come home I shall be so shabby looking I shall stay outside of town until dark." Fighting the elements in the camp, Benjamin Jackson requested a "woolen quilt" as the military failed to supply the soldiers with cover, revealing, "I have not any blanket nor can get any, so I fare bad of a cold night." W. V. Fleming recognized his dependency on home for clothing and requested shirts that would withstand his constant "wallow in the dirt." Fleming continued to ask his wife even for basic clothing required for a healthy standard of living. With his clothing depleted from wear and tear, he feared "getting bare for clothes and the weather is cool," and with the winter coming what he had was "very thin." Expressing a sense of desperation, he instructed her that if his situation blocked him from coming home for his clothing, she would have to deliver it herself. Soldiers also asked family to send food supplies if possible, as camp rations had sharply declined by 1863. James Riggs went so far as to ask his sister not only to send clothing but "to send me some edibles," including peas, onions, and other vegetables that "wont spoil" by the time he received them. As these conditions worsened over the course of the next two years, it became clear that the Confederacy's efforts to fight a total war had serious consequences for common white soldiers, leading many to question whether to continue the fight at all.[5]

Benjamin Jackson's perception of material conditions in the military changed over time. Imbued with patriotism for Confederate independence, Jackson, of Covington County, joined the Thirty-Third Alabama Infantry Regiment early in the war. Difficulties supplying soldiers appeared to him a mere inconvenience that came with the territory of camp life. Jackson requested clothing and food to offset the uncomfortable conditions as he adjusted to his new surroundings. Two years into the conflict, however, the situation had grown worse for Jackson, and his letters home reflect a changed view of how much the common soldier should bear. To Jackson, the situation seemed bleak when "there are so few provisions in this portion of the Confederacy." Food figured prominently in his growing requests for help from home; he notes in one letter, "We get beef and bread and a little bacon but it is a little. We get no vegetables at all." As the war moved into 1864, letters home continued to emphasize problems with finding sustenance. He particularly noted that at times the soldiers felt as if they never got enough to eat, even when the military offered rations. Despite his desperation, Jackson expressed some guilt about asking for food, admitting, "I feel like if people can live there I can here, if I do have to live on bread."[6]

Jackson became increasingly candid in letters home about the worsening state of camp life. He explained that the physical strains of marching and occasional combat seemed to wear down their morale. "We have had the worst marching right lately," he wrote. "We had to retreat from Wartrace. I lost everything I had and throwed it away together." With long stints marching, soldiers often discarded all but the bare essentials, to lighten their packs. For Jackson, this meant losing clothing that would otherwise protect him from the rainy elements. He explained, "We have been in a line of battle or fighting on day and night for fifteen days and it has not missed but one day but wat it rained. I have been wet for four or five days and nights at a time." Jackson further described that these marches happened "without anything to eat for three days at a time" and confessed that "it has been hard times with us and worse a coming I am afraid." The problems procuring food continued to plague Jackson throughout 1864 and into the following year. Low provisions gave way to none at all, and his letters reveal the psychological toll such deprivations exacted on soldiers. "It is hard that a poor soldier cannot get enough to eat," he finally confessed to family. Jackson's own cousin confirmed worsening conditions when describing returning soldiers from the siege at Vicksburg. He noted that the men he accompanied were "the poorest looking set of men" and that some of the soldiers "were so poor that they did not look like human beings."[7]

Thomas Smyrl likewise found 1863 a transformative year with regard to living conditions in the military. As a small farmer from Russell County, Smyrl made barely enough to support a wife and three young children prior to the war. The 1860 census listed his family as having personal property of $300, which placed him in the poorer end of the common white population. In requesting supplies from home, Smyrl placed greater demands on his family to sacrifice their meager resources. He went so far as to ask his wife to take an old blanket and "make a coat out of it and line it with wool," as relying on her efforts was "the cheapest way" to procure basic necessities. At times Smyrl noted that having little assistance from the military, the men relied on their wits to supplement what the military could not provide, including sharing food from home and building their own shelters. The beginning of 1864 brought little change in the conditions of Smyrl and his fellow soldiers. In one letter home, he remarked, "We have suffered great with barefootedness and nakedness" and that his own "pants and socks are both worn out." With the military's inability to supply its soldiers with adequate food and clothing, Smyrl and other soldiers from common families depended upon their loved ones for a crucial lifeline. By the summer of that year, Smyrl was asking his wife to "send anything to us" by way of food and clothing that she and the children could spare.[8]

The inconsistency of receiving military pay added to their growing problems with finding crucial supplies. William Riley Jones held out hope to be paid at the beginning of 1863. Yet in a letter to his wife, he seemed to lose faith when he disclosed, "Tha keep talken of payen us up to the first of this year it looks like talk is all." Joseph Wesson likewise feared that without pay he would continue to burden his family for assistance. He noted that prospects of drawing some money seemed grim, confessing, "I am out of money." Frustration over pay left many soldiers questioning their ability to remain the sole provider for their families. Writing to his wife, Benjamin Jackson admitted, "I have not received any money yet and don't know when I shall." Thinking of how he could support his family, he mentioned rumors that "we will get paid before we leave here." In that case, he contended, "I will send some home in a letter mailed in Montgomery," but warned, "I don't know when I shall get it." The rapidly declining value of Confederate currency by 1864 left many speculating whether they could draw enough money to make a difference for their families. Thomas Smyrl responded by turning to other male kin serving with him in the army. "Our rations has been very short for along while," he wrote home. "Bob and my self has spent a great deal of money on this trip and Bob has none only what I lone him." Thomas mentioned that he likewise depended on money from home and that "we haven't been paid off yet for this year." Out of fear for the state of his loved ones, he promised that if the government could pay him, "I can let you have one hundred and fifty as soon as I draw money or perhaps more than that." He concluded, however, that the prospects seemed slim at that point.[9]

As supply shortages continued throughout the remainder of the war, common white soldiers bore many of the effects. Letters from male kin described a lack of basic needs, again mainly food and clothing. James Branscomb, for instance, remarked on the lack of food in the camps when he quipped that "soldiers are a right happy people when they get enough to eat, but we have not been very happy since we've been here for grist has been scarce." In several letters to his wife, Newton Davis detailed the uncomfortable conditions made worse by the declining availability of military supplies for soldiers. More and more he came to rely on his wife Bettie's sewing skills to ease his situation. "My pants have all nearly worn out and I am nearly barefooted," he confided to her. "It is impossible to get any thing here in the way of clothing at all." The high cost of clothing tested Newton's patience when paying "sixteen dollars for a very common pair of Grey Jeans pants which would not be worth more than two dollars . . . in ordinary times." With few supplies that he could afford, he requested that she purchase and send boots and a hat as well as make shirts for him, all scarce commodities in the declining Confederate economy. When she obliged by sending shirts to Newton, she received his high praise as "a very smart and industrious wife." In some situations reliance on supplies from family provided the only means of meeting even basic necessities. Benjamin Jackson, for example, expressed his gratitude for the shoes his wife sent him, noting that he was "barefooted or nearly so."[10]

Adding to their supply frustrations, soldiers in 1863 faced rampant illnesses in the camp. Common soldiers had grown used to combating all types of ailments early in the conflict. Despite the dangers sickness posed, soldiers held fast to their faith that the military would care for its people. In addition, the cause of independence as a means to protect their family and homes offset the trials of poor health, at least in the beginning. Thomas Smyrl recognized the tenuous nature of one's health in the camps. He wrote often to his wife that illness plagued the many soldiers around him and that, by the summer of 1862, had begun to affect him. "I havent been well since I here," he wrote to his wife. " My bowels is damaged." He blamed his growing malaise on the military's inability to provide for its soldiers. Smyrl revealed that "they have taken our tents and we only are aloud one fly or sheet to 10 men," and in addition the constant physical demands of marching to new encampments compounded their health. He noted, "Part of our army will have to march and that will leave a man a one scattered a long the road and may a poor fellow will die under trees." He even made an awkward joke that a new recruit should be wary of camp life, as "he is soon a dead man." Such constant battles with sickness wore down the resolve of soldiers to endure camp conditions, and they grew critical of military leaders' inability to manage the problem. William McCullough revealed to his wife that "the health of our regiment is not vary good here I fear we will all be sick" and blamed the poor provisioning by military officials. "We have neither wood water nor meet," he wrote. The same held true for Benjamin Jackson, who feared that the military's problems with supplying soldiers with even the bare essentials left them unable to fight off illness. He observed that as able-bodied soldiers gave up the comforts of shelter for the infirm, the chances increased that more men would succumb to sickness. "There is a right smart of sickness in our regiment now," he wrote home, "and I expect will be more from leaving our houses with chimneys to them." He feared that those exposed to the elements "with but very little bedding and taking the rain and cold as it comes" would become sick.[11]

Over the course of Grant Taylor's service, he wrote constantly about rampant sickness dogging his regiment. Taylor revealed almost immediately after joining the army in the spring of 1862 that a measles outbreak created a dire situation among soldiers and depleted their numbers. He reasoned, like many of his peers, that illness came with the territory of living in the camps. The soldiers' conditions continued to decline during his first year of service. He recorded, "There have been 32 cases of measles in our company and several other cases of other sickness," and within one week three men had passed away. For Taylor, it seemed that sickness surrounded his regiment; he stated, "The measles are rageing in other companies a man dies nearly every day." The possibility of dying remained threatening as "some dangerous cases of Pneumonia and camp fever" swept through their quarters. Taylor, however, still refused to hold military leaders accountable for the soldiers' ill health. Rather, he saw it as a potential danger that came with camp life. By 1864, however, his sentiment changed, and he placed more of the blame on the military's lack of adequate shelter and nutrition for soldiers. "We make out pretty well in our cabbins," he wrote to his wife, "but if we were out of doors it does seem to me that we would freeze to death. There is a good deal of Diarrhea in camps caused I think from bad diet and having to drink ice water. For we have to use water out of the branch."[12]

Conditions among Alabama's civilians were little better. By 1863 it became clear that families that had managed to subsist in the antebellum era now struggled for daily survival. Foremost, declining supplies and increased inflation on the home front magnified class inequities for common whites. The prolonged absence of male kin and their essential labor strained the family's financial situation. Sarah Espy, for example, felt a growing sense of crisis when left with only one of her five sons at home to help her on the farm. Moving into winter that year, she became concerned with the cost of household items, such as wool, necessary to weather the season. She laid blame for the high prices on "the villainous work of speculators who are taking this time of trouble to enrich themselves" and the lack of government effort to punish those seeking to exploit the decline in supplies. Emily Moxley wrote frequently to her husband about the hardships of acquiring even the bare minimum for the family. She saw that the cause of her situation stemmed from her husband's continued absence, which forced her to seek help elsewhere. "I am dependent," she wrote, and punctuated her comment by explaining how the men of her family and community had failed to assist her in supplying her home. Emily wrote to William that she feared their family teetered on the brink of starvation, requiring her to beg for help. "You don't know how I feel to go any body else for something to eat when I never had it to do in my life," she wrote, "I have all ways had my dear Husband to provide for me . . . and now I have no one that cares for my wellfare that is about here."[13]

Union occupation in parts of Alabama added to the difficulties common white families faced in providing even the basic necessities. Worse still was the practice of Union troops to commandeer civilian food, livestock, and material possessions to help supply their armies. In a September 1863 entry in her diary, Sarah Espy recorded that soldiers had come through her community, taking everything "except for a few chickens." She remarked that the following year Union troops once again came through her community, depriving her family of a good amount of their household items and food supply. "There was a company of them," she wrote of the federal soldiers. "They fed their horses leaving the ground covered with corn and oats; and carried as much away as they could I presume." For this head of a common white household, such loss of possessions would take months, if not longer, to replenish in a time of severe inflation and lack of supplies. Espy further stressed the severity of their loss, writing that "they took nearly all the boys fine clothing . . . spurs; sheets; towels; pillow-cases; knives and forks, and all other things too tedious to mention." She concluded that the experience left her feeling "helpless as infants." In the end, Espy had no choice but to rely on her community for help, especially to provide food: "We have lost nearly everything, but we have been fortunate in having good friends." The Moxleys also spent much of the war struggling to keep their family fed and clothed. Emily and her children found themselves in dire straits exacerbated by a Union raid in their area. In one instance she wrote to William that federal soldiers had taken all the hogs except for one and that, as a result, now "left in a bad fix a bout meat."[14]

News of deteriorating home-front conditions added to common white soldiers' fears that the war now endangered their families. Distance had strained their ability to serve in their roles as economic providers and physical protectors of the family. Now, word of loved ones suffering from lack of food and facing dangers from both the Union and Confederate armies compelled many men to question whether they should stay in the war. Letters from home merely increased those concerns. Writing to her male kin, C. S. Allen sent less-than-optimistic news about her family's state. "All the news that I am in possession of is bad and is of little value." She described "the land of pleasure, peace, and plenty" as "now a land of mourning." James Garrison's letters to his wife revealed conflicting views about remaining in the military with his family's livelihood at stake. Foremost was that he believed he could do more good at home than in the military, noting to his wife, "I ought to be at home plowing this morning this is such a nice time for the business I think that it would benefit me more than being here lying about doing nothing." Garrison also seemed concerned about the disruptions that war caused to the well-being of family members and, in response, attempted to exercise authority in matters relating to his children. "I want you to send Beck to school," he wrote. "I understand there is a school going on at the school house her and Martin could be going every day tell her that I want to hear her to go to school and learn to read in that book so when I come home I want to hear her read." Of course, news of family members becoming ill or facing other hardships added to a sense of helplessness of male protectors. Joshua K. Callaway, from Dallas County, wrote frequently to his wife, Dulcinea, while serving in Twenty-Eighth Alabama Regiment. His letters brought to light the constant sense of emasculation in a soldier's inability to govern his home. For example, he wrote about his wife's ill health and his concerns: "I am very uneasy about you and long to be at home, but can not. I do hope you are well."[15]

Morale on the home front directly affected a soldier's reasons to fight. Those on the front, for example, often saw firsthand the declining conditions among the civilian population with whom they came in contact. Witnessing families suffering around them raised concerns for their own loved ones and how they too fared amid growing deprivations. William Riley Jones commented in a letter home that the civilians around him "draw rashens like the solders" and that with little provisions they looked on the brink of starvation. Such observations raised concerns for Jones about his own family. He was a small farmer from Tuscaloosa County who had left behind a pregnant wife to join Company G of the Forty-First Alabama Infantry Regiment in April of 1861. By December of that year, his wife, Fannie, gave birth to their only son, adding father to his list of family duties. William, like many common soldiers, entered the war concerned about the people he left behind. He wrote frequently about his hopes that his extended family would "bee spared from all danger that may come before thim." Yet the lack of resources and support for civilians beginning in 1863 brought him to the point of despair over the fate of those at home.

A concerned William sent word to his wife to purchase as many supplies as possible and draw aid from the government in case "you live long an I hafto stay out her long you will neede it." His entreaties for family to prepare themselves for dire circumstances stemmed from what he witnessed as he marched through hard-hit communities. "I think a bout you often times," he wrote. "I think a bout the hard times that is back thar and I am frade that some folks will suffer for the want of bread and meete an other things tha neede." He feared that the suffering he saw also visited his own household. Jones, however, lost his life in the Battle of Chickamauga in September 1863, never knowing his own family's fate.[16]

Other soldiers echoed his distressed sentiment as wartime conditions worsened. Henry Bray wrote to his mother that he dreaded the worst for his family in Montgomery and wanted her to use all available sources of aid. He asked "how yar are making out for a living and whether the governments helps you yet or not." Grant Taylor, likewise, felt guilty about purchasing items from his clothing allowance, remarking to his wife, "We are suffering badly for something to eat but if I draw any money for clothing I consider it belongs to you and I will send it to you by the first chance." He grew more anxious after hearing word that one local man tried to take provisions from his wife, and he warned her that "if he can beat you he will do it." Joseph Wesson, from Talladega County, also worried about how his family fared in his absence. He wrote to his wife, Rachel, that she would need to prepare supplies, including having "yo wheat cut" and caring for the hogs and cows. Joseph assured her that he would try to send her money but that it would be hard to get it home.[17]

The correlation between anxieties about home and remaining loyal to fighting the war seemed clear in the letters of John Cotton. At first he wrote his family expressing a desire to come home long enough to "make arrangements for another year" when it came to the farm. But, by the beginning of 1863, his view changed, wanting the war to end in order to "come home and see what you all are doing." His largest concern stemmed from whether his wife would have enough supplies without his labor on the farm, noting, "I would like to no whether you have got any body to make a crop for you." Cotton likewise worried about the mental strain of separation on his wife and advised her to stay busy visiting neighbors and to "go to meeting." He tried to keep his family's situation in perspective when admitting that "there is lots of soldiers' wives that has not much to eat." Yet he still felt that if they "had nothing to eat," he would desert the army.[18]

Common white soldiers saw the struggles of families like theirs in devastated parts of the state. And such observations led to a growing sense of conflict between their loyalty to the family and that of continuing the war. Certainly, disillusionment with war did not necessarily mean disloyalty to the Confederate cause. And few examples in this study reveal declining support for the original mission. Rather, the sacrifices involved in waging a total war that depended on the efforts of soldiers and civilians led to growing frustrations with those in control. The resolution was clear: their duty was to family, first and foremost, which now seemed in peril at the hands of state leaders.

The experience of William Thomas Jackson epitomized how uneasiness gave way to alarm as home-front conditions deteriorated. William left behind a small family that consisted of his wife, Mary Ellen, and their infant child when he enlisted in 1862. Although he seemed to adjust to camp life, he never felt at ease about how they would survive without him. One way was to rely on his father-in-law to serve as patriarch in his absence. Even with this aid from extended family, he remained concerned over how the farm, their primary source of income, would continue to thrive. At one point he asked Mary Ellen's father to hire someone to help work the land, but he never received a response. By 1863 he was increasingly worried that leaders entrusted to protect their loved ones now seemed unresponsive to matters of their survival. For one, the state government passed a tax-in-kind on civilian food sources. Another threat to family came from the military practice of impressment policies targeting home-front goods. He wrote at one point to Mary Ellen, "You stated in your letter that there was A talk of their takeing all the provisions that the people could spair." Fearing the burden of such demands on the family, he advised her, "If you have to dispose of, let them have it but be sure to have all you can get for it for I have to pay five prices for any thing I have to buy hear and when you get the money appropriate it to the paying of my debts." In one letter he admonished her for working the fields rather than depending on a hired hand to do the work. His concern, however, was more from his fear that her labor on the farm took away from much-needed domestic production and less a challenge to social conventions regarding appropriate female work. As Confederate currency devalued significantly in 1863, William again advised his wife to be wary of selling off foodstuffs vital to the home, especially as he still owed money to those in the community. "I have decided that you need not sell any more of my wheat," he wrote, "as our money has depreciated so in that country and I think you have enough of it all ready to pay me out of debt."[19]

By 1864 William clearly understood that as long as the war continued, the severity of home-front conditions would grow. And he saw productivity of the family farm as the only means to weather the storm at home. Supplies such as livestock and firewood took on greater significance in his letters home. He urged his wife, for example, to plant as much wheat and corn as possible, since "we dont know what another five or six months may bring forth." For this young father and husband, the inability to fulfill his masculine duty as provider and protector of the household caused him to worry less about the success of the Confederacy and more about the survival of his family.[20]

The hardships stemming from increased privation, rampant illness, and continued familial separation led common white soldiers to waver in their commitment to the war. By 1863 a form of war-weariness became increasingly apparent in their letters to loved ones. John Gwyn wrote to his wife that he feared that the military faced problems sustaining the conflict and wondered how long it could last. He admitted, "[I] am sorry to say as for our Country is getting in a very critical position I greatly fear that the Yankees will get the best of the war though I hope to the contrary." Grant Taylor realized that the longer he remained in the military, the more he struggled with honoring his agreement to fight. In his letters home, he began to refer to the conflict as "this cruel war." Grant's unit served in Vicksburg during the heated stalemate in the summer of 1863. After Union troops overtook the town, they paroled Grant's unit, and he returned home. A jubilant Grant believed he was on a path to restoring his emotional and physical strength surrounded by his family. The visit home, however, produced the opposite effect. The Confederate military ordered Grant to return to military service, which he purposely delayed. The taste of home fueled his frustrations with the war and brought him to question whether he should return to camp at all. He eventually went back, a demoralized and exhausted man. Growing even more weary of the war by fall of 1863, Grant refused to mince words about his disillusionment of staying in the military. He asked his wife, Malinda, "Pray for me, pray that I may be enabled to drag my weary limbs through this struggle. Sometimes I feel nearly out of heart of every living to see you again."[21]

Many men remarked about the mental stress that accompanied life as a common soldier in a protracted conflict. Benjamin Jackson swallowed his masculine pride and admitted to his wife his declining mental state. "My mind is always so torn up that I cant write anything I want to write," he wrote home. "I can hear some a groaning almost dying, some cursing, some screaming, until it distracts my mind." The loneliness resulting from continued separation from family also took its toll on soldiers. John Cotton was convinced that a trip home, even if for a short period, would help his mental state, saying, "It would do me a heap of good to start home for a few days," especially if the war continued into the summer of 1863. His frustrations over not seeing his family remained as the war moved into 1864. By this point, he was convinced that returning home to save his family outweighed his willingness to stay and fight. "I am very anxious to have . . . this unholy war ending so I can come home," Cotton wrote to his wife. "I think if I was out of this war I would be the happiest man in America almost every bady thinks the war will end soon but for my part I cant see no chance of it to end unless we go back into the Union and free the negroes." Grant Taylor, despite his growing reluctance to stay in the military, attempted to find some semblance of hope he would return home. He went so far as to admit to his wife, "I think we had just as well look the worst in the face and steel ourselves to bear still greater trials." Nonetheless, the trials of military life began to takes its toll on the soldiers' belief in that their primary duty was to remain in the conflict. William Riley Jones wrote to his wife that he did not "want to bee in nary nother Fight as long as I live" and admitted that "if I could see you I could tell you a heap that wood interest you a bout the seenes I have sen lately of one sorte or nother hard times an I fer worse a coming." And as such his life in the camps appeared a monotonous routine of enduring rain and cold, as well as sleeping on frozen ground, which increased his desire to leave camp life behind. As he surveyed conditions among the civilians he encountered, Jones believed that the war inflicted too many hardships and wished "it twill come to a clos soon."[22]

Other signs of war-weariness stemmed from the soldiers' need to process the horrors of battle with their loved ones. More and more soldiers disclosed the internal struggle between remaining in the military and the potential of dying. Samuel King Vann admitted to his future bride that he feared dying in battle. "I don't want to die just yet awhile," he wrote in 1864, "but alas, serious times with me for life is so precarious that a man ought to feel so, for in a moment he may be shot through as one poor fellow is out there on the ground crying to God for help." Yet he attempted to temper his fears with reassurance that those who do remain "are in fine spirits and can whip many a Yank yet." Others refused to be optimistic and offered more graphic depictions of wartime scenes. After witnessing a particularly horrific battle, William McCullough described to his wife scenes of death and destruction around him. "I have bin over the battle ground it is awful site to be hold. I seen 18 baried in one hold an hardly civerd up the sent is var bad there was a vary fine Hotell burnt in town nite be fore last one lady burnt up in the hous I am sorry of that . . . my dear I have thout we lived hard be fore but never tel now." In another letter to her he disclosed the conflict between wanting to remain brave and his fears over the destruction war brought. "I ant whipt my self tho you no I am a powerful man," he wrote, "but I hope I will never here another canon I am gettin vary tierd of them."[23]

The emotional and physical burdens of fighting the war led common soldiers to see that relief would come only with peace. An increasing number of soldiers spoke openly about their disillusionment with continuing the conflict. Even the young men who courted Mary Loftis abandoned their masculine bravado for a more somber tone, as they grew tired of the daily trials of camp life. Writing in February of 1863, James Pritchett reasoned that the only way to get home was for the Confederacy to negotiate an end to it all. He lamented the extended separation from home and confessed to Mary that his will to remain in the fight had worn thin. "I hope that the time is close by when this war will close," he wrote, "we can return home and see all of our folks in health and in joy the pleasure of this life a gain. . . . I am tirered of this war." D. D. Bonner began his service bragging to Mary about his willingness to sacrifice his life for the Confederacy. Yet, after a year in the army, his eagerness to sacrifice had faded into a bleak hopefulness that the war would soon be over: "I have one thing to say I want this cruel war to end." He confessed, however, that surrender mattered little, as "we are ruin any way." Gone were their patriotic words meant to encourage them to fight. Their sense of purpose to protect the Confederacy was now replaced with a desperation to return home to protect the ones left behind.[24]

William Thomas Jackson revealed the conflicted emotions of a soldier who wanted to honor his duty to the military but desired to return to his family. Writing to his wife in March of 1863, Jackson disclosed that he had become "low spirited" due to ill health and the reality that the war would continue on with no end in sight. "My health is not verry good," he admitted, "and the prospect of the war's closeing soon is getting to be verry dark and gloomy to me." He directed his rancor toward the federal government and its failure, in his estimation, to end the conflict. Jackson contemplated that "the northern Congress has made Old Lincoln dictator, has put all power in his hands. He can either carry on the war or bring it to a close and sometimes I think it will hardly close as long as he is in office." Nonetheless, Jackson concluded that regardless of who was to blame, he wanted the war to end "so I can get to come home." He composed another letter just a few days later that redirected his resentment toward the Confederacy and its insistence on remaining in the war: "Although starvation is seems like is stairing us in the face and a great many think that we will have to give it up on that account but they will never give it up as long as they can get as much as three buiscuits to a man A day." Jackson thus believed that as long as military officials supplied the bare minimum, the war would continue, at any cost to the common soldier.[25]

The sentimentalism that at one time helped common whites endure separation now provided the voice to process their mental anguish. Letters between Grant and Malinda Taylor demonstrate how, in the first two years of war, sentimental expressions of family life offered a way to mitigate the necessary disruptions to family life. They saw the home as a place of normalcy and comfort that offered a distraction from the emotional hardships. However, by 1863 the language used to reflect on family life began to reveal a growing cynicism among common whites. Malinda's letters carried the words of a heartbroken wife who blamed the war for keeping them apart. She offered very little sentiment that echoed the patriotic sacrifices expected of Confederate women but rather lamented their involvement in a conflict to which her allegiance was waning. She wrote that she had grown "tiard of this way [of] living." Malinda saturated her letters with sad images of a separated couple whose only mention of the war was for it to end so they could reunite. "I want to hear from you so bad," she confessed. "I want to see you so that when I am away from home, I hurry back hoping you air their." In another letter to Grant, Malinda reiterated that her loyalty stood not with the war but to his return home: "I am willing for peace on any turmes I had rather live on bread or meat by itself than to live the way I am living."[26]

By 1864 thoughts of home grew intensely desperate in expression and tone in the letters between Grant and Malinda. The sentimentalism that had at one time comforted them became manifestations of grief and pain. Grant regretted the time that had passed "since I knew the luxury and peace of home where I was surrounded with peace plenty, friendship love." Although scenes of family life helped sustain Grant during his service, those same scenes compounded the hardships that came to define the soldier's life. It seemed too that the brief visit home after the fall of Vicksburg served rather to diminish his spirit:

> I have studied and longed to be at home with you and the children more I believe since I came back to Mobile than in all the time since I left home last time up to the time of coming here. . . . Me thinks I see the convulsive sobs that you gave when I parted from you and hear the wild cry of Leonards childish grief . . . ringing in my ears to this day and see big tears rolling down poor little Jim['s] manly cheeks with scarcely a noise. . . . My heart is full to overflowing this evening. I could not sleep last night for thinking of you and to-day.

The Taylors' sentimentalism provided an emotional crutch to navigate a war that had separated them. Nevertheless, as common white families continued to make sacrifices for the cause, their thoughts of home amplified rather than eased their emotions, thus adding to their resentment toward the war.[27]

Other common whites went through similar changes in the use and expressions of sentimentalism. John and Mariah Cotton relied on domestic images to sustain them through their separation. Yet, as the war wore on, the couple turned to scenes of home with a sense of sadness that dampened their morale and in turn increased their resentment toward fighting on. Mariah wrote to John in the summer of 1863 that she hoped the war would end soon and they could reunite, saying that "it wood bee a day of joy to see you com home saft again" and that "if peace was made it wood be the joyfullest times that ever has ben in wood bee to me." By the beginning of 1864, John agreed with Mariah that his thoughts of home fueled his desire to abandon the war effort. "I want to come home very bad," he wrote, "for I dont want to spend all the best of my life here in this cruel and unholy war but I hope to outlive it so I can once more enjoy freedom again." As separations dragged on, idyllic scenes of home life served little comfort to soldiers, but rather fueled a desire to return to the family regardless of the war's outcome. In early 1863 William Riley Jones disclosed to his wife that he wanted nothing more than to be with her and their young son. "I wood bee glad to see him playing a round you I wood bee glad to hur him call hogs for his granmah and I wood luft to her his sweet little tong a talking," he wrote, "it twood bee a heap of satesfaction to mee to see him seting on your knees and talking to you." The same held true for William McCullough when he explained to his wife that he wanted to return home "so I cod get a drink of water o that I cod get one out of your spring this morning it wod do me more good than a good diner an that's what I hant had sens I left you." W. V. Fleming struggled to come to terms with his inability to be present to be a father to their children. In one letter home, Fleming attempted to assert his paternal influence by instructing his wife in how to teach the children to write so that they could correspond with him. He also advised his wife to "tel them to be good children . . . and prey to god to assist you in all things." For Fleming, like many of his peers, his attempts at fatherly advice did little to fill the void left by his absence from home. Gradually the separation from home weighed on the minds of common white soldiers, leading them to contemplate deserting and returning to their families needing their protection.[28]

The most compelling evidence of their wavering desire to stay came from their many attempts to leave the military through either legal or extralegal means. The most sought-after way to escape the strains of military life was to apply for a furlough. Yet this temporary release for a soldier seemed less likely by 1863. Amended conscription laws that expanded the age limit and required indefinite terms of service indicate the dwindling troop supply. Reliance on the draft likewise exposed the growing reluctance of men to voluntarily leave their families for military service. Ablebodied men rarely received furloughs, which became a point of contention for common white soldiers who worried about the fate of their families. Horace Smith wrote to his wife in May of 1863 that the only way he could get home was "by going to a Hospital." Joseph Wesson likewise advised his wife to forget his prospects of a furlough, writing that "tha is no chance" of coming home through official means. The same held true for Benjamin Jackson, who often expressed his hope that he would return home, even if temporarily, to take care of the family. By December of 1863, however, he revealed to his wife that despite his desire to come home, he doubted the prospects. "As for getting a furlough," he wrote, "I think it to be a bad chance for me." The realization of a protracted absence from home turned into feelings of anger and diminished enthusiasm for fighting. Jackson confessed to his wife, "I have ever since this war has been going on, tried to keep in good heart, till now, and I have now given up as for leaving the army. I dont know as I ever shall do that though as for fighting I shall do as little as possible."²⁹

Grant and Malinda Taylor epitomized the increased anxieties that drove soldiers to search for ways to leave the army. Declining supplies coupled with the economic exigencies of the Confederate home front left the Taylor household struggling during the war. Grant, who professed very little patriotic sentiment in joining the military, entered the war with trepidations. Foremost, he worried how his wife and family would survive the conflict without his support. The call to arms posed some early challenges to his ability to provide for his family, but his prolonged absence fueled his desire to return home. As early as spring 1862, Grant began his quest to gain a furlough home, yet he soon discovered that only those in poor health would be granted leave.. He wrote to Malinda that "there is no chance for a well man to come yet." Malinda encouraged Grant to request a furlough, even quipping, "I want you to beg like a prety boy for a ferlow." The couple held out hope for a temporary reunion into the following year. Unfortunately, Grant continued to confront the problem that all able-bodied men must remain in the camp. He wrote, "I intend to come home as soon as I can but a man must have a good excuse before he can get a furlough." Eventually, Grant received a pass home for a ten-day visit but violated the terms of his release and returned late to his company. For this husband, the need to care for his family outweighed the potential punishment for ignoring the time allowed for his furlough.³⁰

Hiring a substitute offered another legitimate way to return home. According to Confederate conscription policies, those facing the draft could hire a substitute for $300 to serve in their place. Prospects of finding a substitute, however, diminished as the number of troops went into a steady decline by 1863. Some common whites, however, were willing to pay the large fee or part with other valued resources to return home. Such sacrifices demonstrate the lengths to which they would go to leave the military. This alternative to a furlough would also allow men to leave the war with their masculine identity intact. William Riley Jones, for example, embodied much of the sentiment of those contemplating a substitute when he wrote to his wife, "I drother giv all I hav in this world than to stay her an bee exposed like I am an I now you had two if you can get any body send them as quick as you can if you dont get now body I cant blame you for it."³¹

While Grant Taylor made the formal request for a furlough, he and

Malinda constantly worked to procure a substitute. Writing in July of 1862, Malinda urged her husband to find a replacement even if it meant sacrificing all they owned: "I am willing to give the land, houses and all." Grant echoed Malinda's willingness to sacrifice their livelihood to get home to his family. The ever-increasing discussions of a substitute, even with the great financial sacrifices that it would entail, illuminated Grant's growing desire to give upon a war that he saw as the source of all their problems. "I believe that if I had a substitute here," Grant wrote to Malinda in August of 1862, "I could get to come home for twenty [days] if not more. But if you are not making corn enough we can not pay what it will cost." At one point Grant joked that perhaps the only alternative was to recruit a woman to serve in his place, since military policy dictated that soldiers receive a furlough when a recruit could take their place. Eventually he found James Riley, a man from their community, who claimed he would go in Grant's place in exchange for a yearly fee. The couple pressed Riley to serve as Grant's recruit, and they devised a plan to pay him with money and land. At one point they determined that they could offer Riley eight hundred dollars and 160 acres of land, along with all the structures on the property, if he would serve for three years. Much to their chagrin, however, Riley backed out of their agreement, and the couple continued to search for a substitute. Malinda wrote frequently pressuring Grant to seek such a route, even suggesting that he should "see if some of the young men wont swap names with you so you can come home." She persisted in her efforts to shame Grant into leaving the army, at one point writing, "My eyes is allways full of tears when I try to write to you," and, "The children says they want to see you so bad."[32]

Diminished opportunities to receive a furlough or hire a substitute led common white soldiers to contemplate extralegal means of leaving the army. Examples of military desertions emerged early in the war. For most, the practice called into question a soldier's manhood, leaving few eager to consider it. Men understood that deserting the army meant facing harsh public rebuke. Such were the heated responses to desertion in Alabama that actually revealed a disconnect between the state's aim to sustain the war and the needs of its people. In a letter to the *Selma Morning Reporter*, one citizen railed against the actions of deserters not as a sign of desperation but rather as flagrant disloyalty to the Confederate cause. The author took particular aim at the families of deserters, who he argued should receive no aid from the state, regardless of their circumstances. He detailed rumors that "wives of deserters" received public aid in Alabama under the guise of a military family in need. In particular he accused women of Bibb County and other areas of pretending to be soldiers' wives and seeking corn from the state supplies. He claimed, "We can never stop desertion, if the deserters are fed by the Government and good citizens," and that "men have sent their wives after corn and have paid their tax in kind with it when received." Such public admonishment of desertions shows that assessment of desertion tended to lean toward betrayal of masculine duty.[33]

Returning home to protect family seemed a greater call to duty than to serve the military. John Cotton exemplified this change in perception concerning desertion. He wrote to his wife, Mariah, as early as the summer of 1862 that the military authorities refused to grant passes home for common soldiers except in the case of sickness. John explained to his wife that rumors circulated that upward of fifty soldiers abandoned their brigade, stating that "our army is in a heep of confusion and mitely out of hart" as the cause of their actions. In another letter home, he assured his family that, despite their need for his help on the farm, he rejected the idea of deserting. "I think it is the worst thing that our men has ever done for the South," he wrote. "There has several of our men deserted from the battalion I want that to bee the last thing that I do." He refused to return home "without a furlow." Choosing desertion thus would mean abandoning his duty to the Confederate mission and in turn disgracing his public reputation and that of his family.[34]

However, by 1863 John pivoted in his sentiment toward abandoning the military as he contemplated the toll of war on his family. He offered little discussion of desertion at first unless to mention the actions of other men. As conditions grew worse at home, however, he began to consider desertion but quickly walked back from the notion, perhaps to protect his family's reputation. "I shant run away yet maby I will get a furlow some time or other," he wrote. "I dont want it throwed up to my children after I am dead and gone that I was a deserter from the confederate army I dont want to do anyting if I no it that will leave a stain on my posterity hereafter." Nonetheless, just a few weeks later, John changed his mind about desertion and disclosed that his devotion to his family eclipsed his loyalty to remaining in the military: "If they dont give me a furlow I will come without one." By the spring of 1864, he came to believe that a biased system of granting furloughs existed, hardening his feelings against the war and reinforcing his desire to be home. "General Johnson has passed order for no more fuloughs to be granted for the present," he revealed to his wife, "so there ant no chance now to get a furlough I would give anything in the world almost to bee at home with you."[35]

William Thomas Jackson underwent a similar transition in his views on desertion in the last two years of the war. In a letter of August 1863, he explained to his new bride that "the soldiers hear are verry much disheartened now and a great many of them are deserting and going home." The limitations set on furloughs coupled with letters from home detailing the desperation of loved ones motivated soldiers like Jackson to take drastic actions and leave their posts. He confessed that soldiers increasingly criticized Confederate leaders for failing to make peace and, in the process, ease their suffering. In his estimation if the government's efforts to end the conflict were unsuccessful, the soldiers would force the issue:

> They have waited for the war folks to make peace and they have found that they aint a going to do it and they have decided to bring it to A close themselves and I believe the war will break up just that way be desertion for I hear a great many say that they are before this winter. They will not stay hear and suffer this winter like they did last and others say that if they dont get A furlough by Christmas that they intend to take one and if they get home they dont intend to come back any more.

Nonetheless, Jackson, still filled with a sense of duty to the larger Confederate family, refused to admit that he would follow suit. As the number of deserters rose around him, he professed to his wife that if the only way he could come home was through desertion, he would never come home at all. Eventually, though, Jackson concluded that he would remain in the army "unless times get A heap worse than they have every been." At that point, he suggested, the call to duty to protect his family outweighed his duty to fight the war.[36]

Much like his peers, Benjamin Jackson grew to question why he should stay in a war that eclipsed his responsibilities to the family. Even as he remarked about soldiers deserting the army, he admitted his own inner conflict on the issue. In the summer of 1863, he wrote home that "they are deserting every day. They say they dont get enough to eat." He hints at a growing clash between his duty to the military and declining camp conditions: "We get a plenty here, such as it is but I am tired of one thing all the time." The struggle between enduring privations in the camps and preservation of the self for the sake of his family remained a common theme in his letters. By October of that year, he mentioned to his wife that the military's inability to offer adequate food made it more difficult to stay away from the family. He resolved that he would stay "as long as I can make out to get anything at all to eat." Jackson observed that among those who did desert, many tended to return to service after a brief visit home to help their loved ones. Perhaps fearing public admonishment, he continued to reassure his wife that he would avoid desertion, regardless if it could be for just a short time. Even by 1864 Jackson still contended, "If I ever come home I shall come honorably." His desire to protect his honor, however, soon gave way to a belief that his true duty remained to the survival of his family.. "The men are so badly disheartened that a good many are leaving of a night," he wrote in March of 1864, and "Those that leave call it going to protect their families, which I think is a man's duty."[37]

The choice to desert or to stay boiled down to a choice between the preservation of family and their loyalty to the Confederate cause. Choosing between the devoted husband/father and the brave, loyal soldier created a crisis of masculine identity. William McCullough wrote to his wife, Martha, in the summer of 1863 that morale among soldiers had declined to a point that they "are all out of heart and running a way every day" but hoped that perhaps the cause stemmed rather from military defeats. The connection between poor military conditions and desertions was not lost on William Riley Jones, who viewed the root cause of men leaving was poor treatment at the hands of the military. "Tha hant now body deserted in some time," he conveyed to his wife, "tho I beleave that thay will some more go if thay dont treat thim beter thay make us drill ever morning and do hevey guard dewty an half feed us." Horace Smith likewise revealed to his wife, Caroline, that he struggled with the possibility of leaving the army, citing his concerns over the family's conditions. He describes the inner conflict as "a great struggle . . . between duty and desire. . . . At times I almost get up ready to start but with a kind of despairing sigh fall back and say to myself 'wait until after the next fight.'" This struggle between masculine ideals of honor at home and those on the battlefield haunted Horace as he tried to reconcile even remaining in the military. "I was never so heartily sick and tired of the service as I am now," he revealed by May of 1863, "and if it was not for a law which requires the Brig. Gen to immediately conscript any officer who is dismissed or resigns, I think I would resign at once; but I don't care to exchange my present place for that of a

Private." Letters from home did little to resolve the conflict between duty to home and duty to the military. Grant Taylor considered desertion the only viable option after one particular correspondence from his wife in which she pleaded for him to come home. He continued to contemplate desertion in late 1864 when he saw "no chance to get a furlough" even as he battled illness. Grant blamed the denial of furloughs on the "meanness" of officers, which drove him to consider abandoning the military. "I see no chance now of ever coming home unless I run away," he wrote to Malinda. Despite his fears of being branded a coward, he admitted, "I do not know what I may be driven to."[38]

Over the course of the war, common whites grew increasingly aware that they bore a substantial burden in fighting the war. Government policies that favored interests of the elites while offering little relief on Alabama's home front created resentment among common whites toward the war's continuation. In their estimation it was time to place their families first and abandon elite interests. Joseph Wesson saw that other soldiers shared his view that the burden of fighting rested on the backs of those like him who had little reason to sacrifice the welfare of their families. "I think it is hard to leave yo and the children and give up my one life for to protect negros," he wrote. "Thar is great dissatisfaction in this part of the army and if pees ant made by the 1 day of March tha will al go home any how tha say tha wont los another crop and I will bee glad to se the day." Malinda Taylor confessed to her husband that she too believed that they faced an unfair war that called on them to sacrifice for little in return. "It looks harde and you of[f] fighting for thare property," she argued. "Some times I think you are simple for staying in the army another day. Thare are thousands deserting evry day. I am almost temted to persuade you to come home and never go back." In John Cotton's estimation, the continued suffering of common whites on the home front stemmed from the selfish desires of elites and their allies in the state and Confederate government to prolong the war by any means necessary. Writing in May of 1863, he intimated to his wife, "There is more men wanting the war to end than ever I saw they are all getting tired of it," and opined, "If the big officers were as tired of it as the pore privates it would soon end but I am afraid they will carey it on a heap longer." And, as shown in the next chapter, Alabama's leaders enacted policies that fueled common whites' fears that the war placed their families in ever-increasing danger while protecting the interests and security of the elites. In doing so the state betrayed its promise to protect the family in return for common whites' service and sacrifice.[39]

Despite the calls to continue wartime sacrifices, as evidenced in the January 1864 article of the *Alabama Beacon*, conditions among common whites on the home and military fronts had grown unbearable. Constant calls for civilians to demonstrate their patriotic support through sacrifice rang hollow by the last year of the war. While wealthier Alabamians had the means to weather the storm of war, common white families found themselves in a world of suffering. Envisioned as a metaphorical father, Alabama's government had failed its children. These were the children who, among the common white majority, shouldered the lion's share of the fight and home-front sacrifice. When their father did very little to ameliorate the situation for those starving, in need of shelter, or growing sick, he lit a fuse of social revolt, leading to a new relationship of common whites to the state. And the divide between common whites and elites grew even wider as leaders attempted to aid those in need but ultimately came up short. Still, their suffering raised the call for the state officials to respond to their demands and, in the process, shaped wartime policies regarding the home front.

4

"There Is a Great Wrong Somewhere"

The State and Family in Conflict

By 1864 the disparities between elites and common whites concerning wartime conditions drew greater public attention among Alabama's citizens. In a letter signed "Weary Pilgrim" published in the *Montgomery Daily Advertiser*, the author sounded an alarm over government policy that favored elites at the expense of common white families. Expanding draft requirements coupled with mounting numbers of exemptions placed the burden of fighting the war on the backs of men who could barely afford to leave their homes. The author pleaded with the government to take issue with a draft that "took a special pain to leave all farmers the happy privileges of either going to the front or shelling out from two to five thousand dollars for a substitute." As men left their homes to fight the war, he reasoned, it became apparent "that the toils of the farmer are not appreciated" among state leaders, leaving civilians scrambling in the state to feed their families. The "Weary Pilgrim" noted that the situation of common whites reached a state of emergency as the impressment of civilian supplies for the military without "the shadow of remuneration" left families at the mercy of the state. At that point the author reminded state leaders of their responsibility, as head of the metaphorical family, to care for those rendered dependent by wartime circumstances. He urged Alabama's leaders to "not prove recreant to duty, remember that 'tis but the price of liberty. Liberty, is that blessed boon, for empty stomachs, and broken bones, for families without a home destined ever more to roam." This appeal to the state's role of protector and provider resonated with common whites, who grew increasingly aware that survival of family meant more to them than a sustained devotion to a war that placed them in greater peril as it dragged on.[1]

Even with the Weary Pilgrim's cries for help, common whites continued to receive the message that honor existed in their ongoing sacrifices. In one example the same *Montgomery Daily Advertiser* released a letter imploring female citizens to do their part to fight against desertion and remain faithful to the cause. The piece, entitled "To the Women of Alabama and Mississippi," proclaimed that desertion signaled a form of dishonor that would force the Confederacy to "plunge into a yawning abyss of degradation, ruin, and misery, and fall like the darkened star, to rise no more." Women, the author contended, had the power to maintain the honor of their cause by remaining vigilant in their sacrifices, even those involving their loved ones. "In different ages of the world," the author wrote, "heroic and patriotic women, have sacrificed at the shrine of their country's safety and honor." He further implored women to shun any deserter by accusing him of the dishonorable action of "loafing, skulking, or hiding from duty." Yet 1864 saw a rise in desertion rates in the Confederate army. The majority deserting the army did so in response to family members' pleas for help. Many who left saw their absence as a temporary condition, intending to return to the military to complete their service. Others sought to make it a more permanent condition. The above author either was unaware of or refused to recognize those circumstances, as apparent as they were, that led soldiers to leave the army. Rather, Confederate leaders remained determined to continue the conflict at any cost to the people fighting it. The resulting expectations to remain in the war did little to sway the perceptions of common whites. On the contrary, they fueled a sense of class inequality among common whites that brought them to challenge the class structure of the state. Elite members of the population, and the state as an institution that favored their interests, became the targets of common whites' growing resentment.[2]

Common whites blamed those who held power over wartime policies for the continued privation, separation, and emotional strain that seemed to increase over time. The muted class differences familiar in antebellum Alabama gave way to rising conflicts during the war. The fact that those of wealth found ways to avoid service brought to light the unfair nature of fighting the war. Additionally, elites also possessed more economic resources to weather rising inflation and supply shortages than did their common white peers. As declining supplies reached crisis levels among common whites, they directed their frustrations toward those charged with protecting their homes and families in wartime. From the onset of fighting, Alabama's government offered aid to soldiers' families in need. State leaders, however, fell short of recognizing the fundamental problems plaguing common white households. In particular, the call to arms among Alabama's small farmers and laborers created a void in the state's workforce that left the population struggling to procure even the most basic supplies. As a result, common whites forced into dependence on government assistance came to believe that the independence they held as sacred in their prewar lives now stood in jeopardy. Those left on the home front refused to fall victim to their changing circumstances, and they defended their families from further suffering through forms of public action. Common soldiers also found help to combat conditions in the camps as the military conflict took its toll on the Confederate armies. Their physical sufferings along with the psychological effects of prolonged separation from loved ones brought them to protest remaining in the fight through the only means at their disposal: desertion. Given the totality of common whites' experiences at home and on the front, their relationship with the state ultimately took on different meaning. They rebuked the role of victim by demanding a part in shaping the political agenda of the state throughout the remainder of the war, all in the name of family.

The harsh realities of war brought divisions between the rich and poor into high relief by 1863. In a letter to a local newspaper penned by "A needy soldier's wife," the author makes clear how those from the ranks of the common whites felt overburdened by the war in ways that escaped their wealthy neighbors. The anonymous writer asked, "Can those who stay at home and enjoy their warm houses and comfortable beds stand heedlessly by and see the poor of this community suffer?" In particular, many feared the coming winter would heap extra hardships onto citizens, especially among the poorest, who had few resources to survive the harsh elements. Yet the author refrained from challenging the war altogether. On the contrary, the writer defended the cause of the war, referring to the fight as one "against a degraded and merciless foe, one full of vengeance and tyranny." The pleas to assist families during the winter stemmed from the observation that members of the community "are not able to buy wood at present prices." The author explained that even women forced to take on seamstress jobs faced wages too low to sustain their households. The soldier's wife "who has three or four helpless children depending upon her for bread, working all day, earning only the small sum of $2, when she has to pay $1 per pound for beef, and everything else in proportion, if not more," can barely survive. At the same time, the state's elites seemed to move through the war unaware, or so it seemed, of the dire economic situation on the home front. As the author contended, "It is very easy for those who live in plenty, to pass this unnoticed, but ought it be so?" One solution proposed in the letter would be for the wealthier class to pay more for suits and other clothing. In turn, those producing the items would benefit from an increase in pay that could ease their financial struggles. The author closed with a firm warning that "unless justice is dealt to the poor, here, they are bound to suffer. . . . Do not forget this."[3]

Sarah Espy came to embody the resentment predicted by "A needy soldier's wife." The entries in her diary increasingly identified the problems common whites faced while, based on her experiences, elites went through the war relatively unscathed. She first directed her criticism toward the Confederate government and the draft that called more and more male kin to the front. When they passed yet another law in September 1862 extending the age requirement to forty-five, Espy decried the policy "as shameful a one as congress ever passed." She also called into question the actions of government officials who seemed to care more about their own economic needs than about those civilians struggling to survive. "They also passed a law giving themselves $2700 a year," she wrote in August 1862, "and the greater part of the time they are at home attending their business." She predicted that such actions would lead to a potential "rebellion among ourselves at the rate of going on for the war taxes the people heavy enough." By 1863 Espy viewed the conflict as one waged more on the backs of "the workingclasses," who suffered from want of financial resources. And as federal troops neared her community, she criticized elites who could retreat from potential danger while her family's depleted resources forced them to stay and face the enemy. These class inequities roused in Espy a sentiment that those like her shouldered an unfair burden of sacrifice in the name of war. "They are well off," she wrote, "and are going to wealthy friends whereas I, and many others, have no friends and our children even barely boys, are taken from us and put into the serves. There is a great wrong somewhere."[4]

The material and emotional hardships that Lucinda Hunter experienced on the home front brought her to question why even to continue the fight. She wrote her brother expressing her discontent with seeing the conflict through after losing their youngest brother to the military front. James attempted to comfort his sister by assuring her, "The prospect does look a little gloomy, but wait a while and you will hear of another great victory from Genl Lee's army that will cheer every southern heart." Louis Branscomb, another brother, shared his sister's sentiment about the continuation of the war. "I was sorry to find you so low spirited," he wrote to her in October 1863, "but I can't blame you for you have enough to make you so. I must admit that I am in that line myself . . . I am getting like you. I am losing all my patriotism."[5]

Soldiers also recognized the unfair treatment of common whites at the hands of elites. All the suffering of the soldiers and their families, they believed, resulted from unfair conditions that seemed to favor those who held more economic and political power. They understood their sacrifices for the Confederate mission in terms of a reciprocal relationship in which common soldiers swore their loyalty in exchange for protection and security from state leaders. However, this relationship of reciprocity seemed all in vain by 1863. As resources and manpower declined, the government found the task of protecting its loyal dependents more difficult. Soldiers and their families, as a result, became cognizant of the class differences endemic in the wartime experience. And their growing resentment toward the elite classes ultimately gave them permission to turn against the war without feeling disloyal or traitorous. After all, those elites who convinced them that going to war would protect their families now threatened to endanger their welfare. Soldiers needed only to turn to the conditions in the camps and on the home front for proof that the leadership with whom they had entrusted their lives failed to live up to their end of the bargain.

Common soldiers grew increasingly hostile toward declining conditions in the camps, and they turned their frustrations toward those in charge. Soldiers understood that their service entailed a level of discomfort and privation. Yet by 1863 continued ill health compounded by poor diets and miserable living conditions led them to believe that military officials cared little for the well-being of those in the lower ranks. Thomas Smyrl recognized the disparities between the privates' experience and that of higher-ranking officials as early as the summer of 1862. After enduring bouts of sickness, he wrote to his wife that his commanding officers did little to ameliorate problems in the camps. "They are trying to kill us all," he confided. "Any how it seems like I can tell you a private soldier aint cared no more for than a sheep killing a dog." Perhaps he was merely venting frustrations over camp life in those early months of service. Yet Smyrl's anger toward his leaders over what he saw as unfair treatment hardened by

Figure 4. Many common whites became desperate for state assistance in the final year of the war. "Alabamians Receiving Rations," sketched by A. R. Waud and published in *Harper's Weekly*. Alabama Department of Archives and History.

the following year. After being denied a furlough home, for example, Smyrl was convinced that officers showed favor to fellow officers while neglecting the needs of privates. He contended that the only ones granted passes home were those with "very particular business such as business for the government" and that authorities "wont grant furloughs to but a few men and they are some particular men who have strong friends to intercede for them." J. D. Jenkins witnessed the same type of favoritism but attempted to make light of the discriminations toward low-ranking soldiers. Writing to his female love interest, Mary Loftis, Jenkins quipped, "You say that you simpathise with the soldiers. I was thinking that the mos of the young ladys looked upon the soldiers with contempt except it was an officer and then they praised him and flattered him very much. That is the way here in hell." Most soldiers, however, found little humor in the disparities between the wealthy and common whites. William Riley Jones wrote to his wife that the special privileges officers received often came at the expense of those privates suffering the most from illness or injury after a military engagement. For Jones, the only hope of relief of such unfair treatment would be to end the war: "I do hope and pray that tha wont naver bee a nother fight in America and let us returne back home in peas and happiness with our wives and children Fathers and Mothers and brothers and sisters what joyful time twood bee to us all I would give all I percess to see the time for tha ant nothing her to enoy any way but money seekers and officers who lives at thar ease." He came to see military officials and civilian elites as working together to make a profit off the backs of families like his. Jones went so far as to advise his wife to avoid selling any surplus farm goods to officials, who he feared merely sought to line their pockets. He warned her that "most of thim is Mississippiens an some fom all Stats the Rich men are driven thare . . . to Ala an I don't want nune of you to sell thim one thing."[6]

The Confederate government's changing policies by 1863 extended its authority into the personal lives of common whites, posing a greater threat to their survival. In an effort to help fund the war, for example, Confederate Congress passed a tax-in-kind requiring the collection of 10 percent of agricultural goods, such as potatoes, beans, and corn, and livestock for food processing. Such depletion of food sources led to dire consequences for common whites, especially those who remained on the home front. As McCurry demonstrates, the policy was one of the largest incursions of the government into the lives of soldiers' wives, who found the tax "an insupportable burden" that meant "the very difference between an eked-out subsistence and starvation." A good example of the strains of the policy in Alabama's families comes from the correspondence between John Cotton and his wife. He received letters from her sounding the alarm over the potential effects of the tax-in-kind in their daily existence. He responded with resentment and admitted, "I dont think it would be rite for them to press a pore mans property and him in the war." He urged his wife to sell as much as she could, rather than submit to government policy of confiscation without adequate compensation. He reasoned that "you are home and me here in the war and so many little children to support that you ort to have as much for anything you have to sell as any body else if times dont get no better."[7]

The passage of the tax-in-kind, however, seemed to undermine efforts to address food supplies for Alabama's common whites. The demands of the tax placed greater burdens on their households than on elite families who could withstand the sacrifice of supplies. Some families found ways to avoid paying the tax by limiting the production of farm goods; but such actions placed even greater stress on their households. Most common whites made the sacrifice to pay the tax and seek assistance from the state to offset the depletion of foodstuffs. In some cases counties hardest hit stopped the collection of the tax altogether. State officials did appeal to the Confederate government for a temporary suspension of the tax given the increasing number of destitute families. The Confederate government eventually recognized the dire conditions caused by the policy and in 1864 moved away from a blanket tax to one that allowed more flexibility in its collection.[8]

Still, as word spread of the government's impressment of civilian supplies, soldiers grew anxious about their ability to protect their families. William Thomas Jackson became concerned after hearing news that the government would take food supplies from their community. His wife informed him of rumblings that officials would take "provissions in the country xcept five months rations," and that she feared little would be left for the family. He agreed and directed her to hold on to as much meat as possible and, when she had to sell it, to ask for as much money as possible. The household of Kinnon Lee likewise faced added suffering as depleting supplies coupled with soaring inflation left the family seeking assistance from the government. Kinnon Lee and his wife, Mary, lived in Covington County in 1860, and the census listed his occupation as grocer, with a total of $500 personal property. When Kinnon enlisted in the war, he left the family struggling to procure financial support beyond his soldier's pay. By August of 1863, Mary turned to the government to "draw money" from the state funds allotted for "indigent families." Benjamin Jackson also saw that the declining economy along with the inability of Alabama officials to alleviate the financial strains of war left his family in need of income to survive. He wrote in March of 1864 that Confederate money had little value after observing that "in Macon and Atlanta they wont have any Confederate bill over five dollars now" and that even government bonds appeared to be as valuable as "a blank paper."[9]

The efforts of state leaders to aid common white families did little to change opinion about who was to blame for declining conditions. At home civilians suffered from lack of provisions while battling impressment of material goods from already-struggling households. On the military front, soldiers faced what they perceived as unfair treatment at the hands of the leaders they trusted. Their sense that the government failed to care for its dependents came into greater focus as families disclosed the extent of their suffering. Alabama and Confederate leaders did, in fact, attempt to exhaust as much of their resources as possible to sustain its military and civilian population. Yet the limitations of the Confederate economy along with the continuation of the war left common white families believing that their state, which they had sworn to serve, had forsaken them.

The correspondence between Thomas and Mary Smyrl demonstrates this growing acrimony toward those in power. Thomas and Mary lived on a small farm in Russell, Alabama, where they raised their three children, the youngest being three months old on the eve of the war. With little personal property and only his labor to support the family, Thomas reluctantly left his young family to serve in the Confederate military believing that the government would ensure the well-being of his loved ones. By April of 1864, however, he clearly felt differently about the ability of officials to fulfill their part of the agreement to keep their families secure. He became increasingly critical of military and government leaders whom he believed out of touch with the reality of common white households. In one letter to his wife, Thomas referred to Jefferson Davis as "his Royalty" when discussing how men who left out of desperation over their families' declining state faced court-martial for deserting the army, a punishment he deemed unjust. Adding to his bitterness was that the military fell short in its efforts to provide much-needed soldiers' pay that could be used to help their families. He wrote in July of 1864, "They owe us 6 months wages now and we haven't got any money at all scarcely." In another letter following soon after, he confided to his wife that the situation had become so dire in the camps that many of his fellow soldiers wanted to "see this desperate war come to an end."[10]

Their lack of income continued to plague the Smyrl family as the war continued with little relief in sight. At one point, Thomas grew so desperate that he instructed his wife to nurse an injured horse "back to health and sell it as it would be worth $1,000 in Confederate money." The lack of protection in the remote areas of the state also made it difficult for Thomas to offer financial aid. "I have some money that I could spare to you," he wrote Mary, "but every thing I send you some Scoundrel takes part or all of it consequently I am afraid to Mail Money to you." With little protection from state leaders, the Smyrls faced the prospect of the war tearing the family apart and leaving them destitute. Writing to Mary in November of 1864, Thomas described a bleak scene of devastation that left even some of the wealthiest in a state of destitution: "The chimneys of the most beautiful Mansions perhaps in Ala standing alone whie the houses are in ashes the negroes all teken away by the Yanks and a great many of the families who wrer once immensely rich are now as poor perhaps as you and I . . . our army is now taking nearly all they have they pay for some and take some without pay." Given such widespread poverty, he concluded, there would be little hope of financial assistance for their family. Sadly, their situation reached a dire state just one month before the war's conclusion, when Mary received news that Thomas had been killed, after a tree riddled with bullets had fallen on him. The family now faced life after the war without their primary breadwinner.[11]

The situation of Grant and Malinda Taylor provides a telling example of how common whites came to redefine their relationship with the elite power structure. Grant and Malinda lived in Tuscaloosa County with their small children. Grant farmed as well as taught school. As a non-slaveholding family, the Taylors lived a modest life with little connection to the looming conflict over slavery. Only with the first conscription law passed in 1862 did Grant enlist in the Fortieth Alabama Regiment in order to avoid the draft. Throughout the couple's correspondence, Malinda and Grant expressed at the least indifference and at the most annoyance with the interference of the Confederate cause in their personal lives. By early 1863 conditions at home worsened to the point that Malinda attempted to receive aid from the state. Grant wrote to his wife, "Put in your claim for your share of the public money for you are as much entitled to it as any of them." His biggest concern was that the military failed to provide enough money for him to send home, and he wrote Malinda that she would "have to depend on [herself] for a living." Unfortunately, the government denied the Taylor household assistance, believing that they failed to meet the state requirements to be labeled "indigent." To Grant, this rejection by the state raised questions about the fairness of public relief. "I am sorry that you cannot draw anything from the public," he wrote in April 1863. "I think there is no justice in it just because you happened to have a little money to buy provisions." Hearing rumors of favoritism in the dissemination of public assistance convinced Grant that the whole system was corrupt. He wrote to Malinda that "other families that have Negroes to work for them drew corn and I have heard Captain Willets wife drew. There is no justice in any such doings."[12]

Grant's concerns about his family's situation grew to the point that he ceased asking for supplies from home. He had become aware that families like his suffered on the home front and informed his wife that he would "rather suffer on than for you and the children to lack for meat and bread." Money became another concern of Grant, as he learned about the decreasing value of the Confederate dollar. He wrote to Malinda in early 1864 that she should be aware that the economic problems of the Confederacy would affect their livelihood. He advised her, "If you have any [money] on hand get advice what to do with it. It must be funded for bonds by the first of Apr. or there will be heavier tax on it still." By March of that year, the situation worsened for the Taylor household, and they pulled their children from school, a luxury few could afford during the war. Grant wrote to Malinda that they needed to rely more on family than on government relief, as state leaders seemed to care more for their own interests and those of the elites. He even said that she should look to another source of income, as the military failed to pay its soldiers: "I do not know what you will do for money for as I wrote you before I have not been paid since last Jan. and for clothing and wages the government owes me $200." The fall of that year, Grant's concerns worsened as he learned of government impressment of civilian food sources. He worried that if the family lost any of their supplies, they would perish at the hands of an uncaring state.[13]

As a soldier, Grant likewise blamed biased government policies for the suffering of soldiers in the camps. His own observations led him to believe that the same leaders who depended on soldiers like him to fight the war seemed little interested in their well-being. In one letter to Malinda, Grant revealed, "We are faring badly for something to eat. . . . And we do not get near bread enough. . . . I do not see how men can expect to keep an army together on such fare for we all know they could give us bread plenty." He saw the morale of soldiers as the root cause of waning support for fighting the war, noting that most men "are generally low spirited and think our cause is gone" and that few "think it worth while to fight in so hopeless a cause." For Grant, this response from soldiers came solely from their reaction to the actions of military leaders. "I do not see how a government can expect to keep an army together fed as we are," he concluded. Military officials, moreover, added to the stress of the situation by forcing soldiers to lean heavily on the household supply line. Grant asked Malinda to send "your bed cover when cold weather comes on," believing that "it will be a bad chance to get a blanket from the government." By October of 1864, the situation worsened to such a degree that Grant observed, "Many of the boys are barefooted and have to borrow pants to wear." To Grant and Malinda, that devotion to a war that threatened the security of the family, whether at home or in the military, seemed to cause nothing but heartache. At the opening of 1865, the couple could no longer sustain their motivation to support the war and focused more on mere survival.[14]

Community organizations in Alabama attempted to fill gaps in aid to struggling families. The *Selma Morning Reporter* issued an announcement about a fundraiser put on by the "ladies of Newbern" who provided supplies through one of the many soldiers' aid societies throughout the state. These women, whose elite status afforded them the time to devote to charitable work, hosted an event featuring music, tableaux, and other activities. The money raised from the event was "to be applied to the purchase of corn for the destitute families of soldiers of Alabama." Other groups directed aid to children left orphaned by the war. In 1864 wealthy citizens launched a fundraising campaign to build a state orphanage. These efforts also stemmed from the patriotic support of Alabama's elites, who wanted to aid the cause of soldiers' in need. J. M. Sutherlin, who donated $15,000 to the project, viewed his assistance as a way to pay back the men "who have left home, wife, children, all for country and liberty, to a large share of my property, which has been preserved to me at the expense of their lives." Sutherlin further emphasized that the children of fallen soldiers, left with no place to go, would "become vagabonds in society" a position he viewed as "a dangerous element in the government, a reproach to their noble sires and a curse to posterity." By creating an institution for orphans, Sutherlin ensured that they would be preserving the good of the state. Governor Watts also issued a public letter thanking Sutherlin for his contribution, which he believed should bring about the assistance of all "statesmen, the philanthropist and Christian." The institution, Watts posited, meant that "the people of Alabama not only erect a noble monument to the memory of departed heroes, but they build for themselves a temple to perpetuate their own deeds for the admiration of posterity." By November of that year, the fundraising efforts continued as calls went out from the newspapers to raise an additional $100,000 to complete the project.[15]

Appeals to the general public to continue their material sacrifices remained even as conditions in the Confederacy sank deeper into despair. Alabama's newspapers frequently published pleas for civilians to give all they could in an effort to keep the war going. State leaders and their advocates either disregarded or lacked knowledge of the already-dire conditions of the people in making such requests. In a letter to the editor in the *Selma Morning Reporter*, one author pleaded with citizens to contribute money and supplies to the regiments of soldiers from Perry and Dallas Counties. "The wants of the army in the field are numerous and ever recurring," the author proclaimed. "Clothe them and shoe them—protect them from the rude blasts of winter, and the frozen earth and drenching rains, and they will protect you from the ravages of a merciless foe, whose pathway is invariably marked by desolation." Calls for the citizens of Montgomery to help soldiers continued well into the summer of 1864: "Every necessary which they require should be sent promptly, and thereby saved many a gallant soldiers life . . . they are to be cared for when stricken down." Appeals to the community targeted women by playing upon their maternal sentiments. In a letter to the editor of the *Alabama Beacon*, dated January 8, 1864, the author emphasized the moral value of women's industry in the home in sustaining the war. "It is your province to inaugurate the honorable system of home manufactory," the author contended. "While your fathers, husbands, brothers, and sons are in the field, you should be at home bravely working for their comfort. No hand should be idle . . . the necessities and emergencies of the times demand more sacrifices, more honorable exertions." Yet, for common white women, those exertions seemed nearly impossible as they struggled for their own survival at home.[16]

In reality, continued sacrifices appeared impossible for common whites and resulted in greater demand for state assistance. In the counties of Perry and Dallas combined, the number of families seeking government aid rose from 138 in 1862 to 606 in 1864. The same held true for the capital of Confederate Alabama, Montgomery, by the summer of 1864. Records indicated that the number of families seeking assistance in the country jumped from 233 in 1862 to 710 in 1864. The *Montgomery Daily Advertiser* put out a call to citizens of the city to donate items for the soldiers, including "every necessary which they require." Civilian support, according to the article, meant nothing short of saving "a gallant soldier's life."[17]

Alabama's leaders saw their efforts to aid families in need through a paternalistic lens. They envisioned their role as protector of the much larger family of civilians who depended on them. Even Gov. John Gill Shorter emphasized the duty of state leaders to provide on "behalf of the indigent families of soldiers absent in the Confederate armies, or who may have fallen in battle, or died in the service" in addition to those disabled beyond the ability to provide for their families. Shorter urged legislators to remember the reciprocal relationship to care for civilians as their male kin, volunteer or conscript, "peril their lives and all they have and are in the defense of their bleeding country." Continuing to call on the fatherly image of the state, Shorter proclaimed that "their wives and little ones are bequeathed to our watchful care and protection." The gendered rhetoric used to conceptualize the relationship of government to the people thus placed the political elites in a position of responsibility to their dependents. Failure to fulfill that responsibility would mean risking the loyalty of common whites toward the state's elite power structure.[18]

In fact, Alabama's government offered public aid to families in need and continued to do so throughout the course of the war. Each year, officials broadened the public assistance program to address worsening conditions in the state. Legislators passed a total of $11,633,000 in public aid, much of which came more in the form of supplies and less in direct payments. The first year, the amount paid remained relatively low. In 1862, however, the legislature approved $2,000,000 funded by a twenty-five-cent tax along with contributions from each individual county. The number of families requiring aid reached 8,156 that year. By 1864 the total number of families in need of aid grew to 35,393, the majority of which came from the ranks of common whites.[19]

This provision of aid began with the creation of a system for ascertaining who would need funds and how to distribute them. During the first regular session of the General Assembly of Alabama in 1861, leaders passed an act "to provide a fund for the Aid of Indigent Families of Volunteers absent in the Army." The government portioned each county into precincts or beats, usually consisting of ten to twelve in the smaller counties and twenty-five to thirty in the more populated areas. Beat agents oversaw collecting information such as names, number of family members, cause of their economic conditions, and type and amount of aid needed. The agents also gathered evidence of the number of material items in the home and the mental and physical state of each family member. In most cases families receiving aid did so primarily in the form of provisions. The agent then reported his findings back to the county probate judge, who would, along with the commissioners, determine which families would receive aid and set the amount. In the first year of the war, this assistance targeted solely families of volunteers as well as men who had left service due to an illness or injury that kept them from supporting their families. The program also provided aid to widows and orphaned children of volunteers who died in service. Other efforts to assist the poorer socioeconomic sectors of the state came in the form of exemptions from poll taxes and allowing counties to use surplus finds from their treasuries. Such policies excluded Unionist sympathizers and families of soldiers who hired substitutes, stipulations intending to reinforce Confederate allegiance and penalize the disloyal.[20]

By the second year of the war, Alabama legislators took steps to increase assistance to poor families. The General Assembly passed an act exempting a designated amount of property of volunteers and widows of deceased soldiers from taxation. They changed the language from "volunteers" to "soldiers" to reflect the shift in the number of conscripted troops after the Confederacy initiated its first draft in 1862. State leaders recognized that conscription forced more men from common white households into service thus leaving families searching for means of support. On November 12, 1862, legislators passed an act that specified that any excess funds from the tax to help poor families would go the general fund of the state treasury and be earmarked for use in providing additional aid. The state appropriated two million dollars in aid for families of soldiers in the form of providing supplies and other forms of payment. State leaders, however, continued to withhold aid to those considered traitors to the cause and extended the practice to include deserters. Only the true volunteer or the conscripted soldier, in their estimation, deserved aid in return for their loyalty to the Confederate cause.[21]

State officials continued to increase assistance in the face of growing inflation and declining supplies. In its 1863 session, the General Assembly appropriated one million dollars "for the support of the indigent families of soldiers" who served in the army, again excluding substitutes. They noted that if the state lacked the money, then the governor could use treasury notes to fund the aid. They also passed protections against anyone who attempted to exploit the system or misuse the funds. Extending their efforts to reach more citizens, officials offered more aid to families of former soldiers who became disabled or had died in service to the military. Legislators again increased the amount of aid to families, peaking at three million dollars in 1864. However, this time they allowed aid to families of substitutes "except in the cases where the substitute received more than fifteen hundred dollars for becoming a substitute." Doing so distinguished between those attempting to profit from the war and those serving out of a sense of duty. Still, state leaders attempted some level of equity in providing aid in an effort to curtail the declining conditions among more of the population.[22]

Alabama's leaders also sought other forms of aid to civilians. Perhaps in a show of solidarity with its citizens, the General Assembly, on December 8, 1863, approved an act to contribute "the carpets of the State of Alabama for the use of private soldiers from Alabama in the Confederate Service." More than likely, however, legislators passed the act as a way to salvage their public image in the face of growing criticisms. Additional acts addressed providing poor families aid in the form of low-cost cotton yarn and other materials difficult to purchase in the state. Alabama's leaders likewise addressed the need for medical aid to the population. They approved legislation providing payment for medicines "not exceeding the market price or usual charge" to needy families of soldiers from the state. State officials even went so far as to pass legislation to provide an artificial leg to "every maimed indigent soldier of Alabama."[23]

Government leaders also sought to provide aid to common whites when it came to the state's salt reserves. Salt served as a main form of meat preservation and, as such, took on greater importance amid declining food sources. Even as early as 1862, families could foresee the necessity of keeping salt on hand, given the military's demands for its own supply. Henry Bostic advised his family in February that if they failed to find their own source of it, to turn to a family member for help. Grant Taylor likewise saw that "salt is mighty scarce here at 14 dollars per sack." He warned his wife to keep as much of the precious commodity for herself as possible and sell the rest to render a small profit. "Watch every chance you can get to get some salt," he wrote Malinda. "God only knows wat you are to do if times do not change before next winter." Such fear about a potential shortage became a reality in Alabama in 1862. Before the war the state had few problems suppling citizens with an abundance of salt at a cheap cost of one dollar a bushel. Yet the Union's blockade of major ports, along with rising demands, shot the price of salt up to twenty dollars a bushel by 1862. Alabama's leaders stepped in to find alternative sources of salt while keeping as much of it as possible in the state for its residents. The state commissioner overseeing the supply traveled throughout communities to observe salt production, and Governor Shorter relinquished state reserves to the general public.[24]

Alabama's leaders took steps to address inequities in the distribution of salt to civilians. In a message to the state legislature on October 27, 1862, Governor Shorter addressed the problems of speculators and "extortioners," as he termed them, who raised prices of salt beyond the means of a common white household. Officials passed legislation hoping to equalize the distribution of salt, especially to those hardest hit by declining supplies. In December 1863 legislators approved a motion "to supply the wants of indigent families of soldiers from this [Alabama] State." Such actions, however, focused narrowly on families of soldiers serving in the military rather than creating a blanket policy for all of the state's families in need, regardless of their loyalties. As specified, state officials determined the "respective wants" of families who had male kin in the service, disregarding substitutes and deserters. Further legislation entrusted commissioners to "engage in the manufacture of salt for the use of indigent families of their counties." By October 1864 they likewise attempted a system to make salt accessible to all families by voting favorably to "equalize the price of salt to the indigent families of soldiers." State leaders made every effort to provide the citizenry with salt, but the war ultimately slowed their ability to produce and distribute it effectively.[25]

Alabama legislators also attempted to protect citizens from the effects of military impressment or destruction of their supplies. During the 1863 session of the General Assembly, they raised the issue of citizens targeted by Union and Confederate armies for confiscation of goods, especially food supplies. They set up a fund of $500,000 to aid "persons" left destitute "by the seizure, waste or destruction of their means of subsistence by the public enemy" but also at the hands of Confederate forces. This assistance, however, excluded those who moved to the state after 1863, as well as anyone considered "disloyal to the Confederate government" or its military. A year later state leaders strengthened efforts to protect citizens from the effects of confiscation by targeting those who abused such military practices. They approved legislation that would allow officials "to prevent the oppression of the people of Alabama by the illegal execution of the impressment laws of the Confederate States," by imposing jail time for those who conducted unauthorized seizure of civilian supplies. These actions of state leaders to address gaps in public aid certainly fell in line with their agreement to protect the people from the extreme effects of war. Yet they remained unable or unwilling to recognize the systemic problem of the state's depleted labor supply in areas of agricultural production and other trades necessary to the economic health of common whites.[26]

Government officials also attempted to deal with the growing concern about safety on the home front. The attacks on local communities at the hands of raiders, many of whom came from the ranks of deserters, added to the exigencies of common white households in the state. Anticipating the need to offer protection to civilians, Governor Shorter issued a proclamation on May 12, 1862, calling for the creation of local militia: "I propose to organize a State Guard, to be composed on the entire white male population, capable of bearing arms, not subject to conscription, who will, for that purpose, unite in the formation of Volunteer Companies and tender their services to me. We have reached the point in this struggle for independence, when every man who can fight, must become a soldier." The governor's organization of a home guard reaffirmed the state's role as paternal guardian of its citizens. And, as attacks on local communities increased, more appeals for such protection made their way to the governor's office. In the case of the Piney Woods region, historian Tommy Craig Brown contends that the raiding of local communities gradually increased over time "but evolved slowly beginning with relatively small numbers of 'tories' and conscription evaders in 1862," and ended with violent attacks in the last year of the war. The escalation of assaults on local homes and neighborhoods existed in other areas throughout the state as well. Josiah Jones pleaded to Governor Watts to remove the commandant in charge of guarding his community in Covington County, who, in his view, failed in his duties. He asked the governor to replace the commandant with someone more competent to deal with "deserters and outlyers" who raided local homes. He argued that the county suffered at the hands of criminals and that "there is nothing to eat and not much to steal." He went so far as to call the current commandant a "good for nothing sort of man with small brain and no energy at all" who refused to use local guards to deal with the issue. For Jones, the notion that any man who shirked his duty to protect the community meant he should be removed from office. Thus, in an effort to keep people safe, especially as raiders plagued Alabama communities left vulnerable to attacks, Jones looked to the state for action.[27]

Despite the efforts of state officials to help them, common whites believed that they faced an unbalanced government system that favored elites. Fueling their resentment was who was placed in charge of managing civilian aid. Most of those assigned these posts came from the ranks of the elites whose service to the government exempted them from the military. And those in charge came from what appeared as a fraternity of elites consisting of probate judges, commissioners, and special agents whose main role involved determining those most worthy of aid. In essence they served as a type of "missionary," intending to go into the communities of common whites and distribute assistance at their discretion. Such a relationship served only to cast a stark light on the differences between common whites and elites, as well as on the contrasts between those suffering and those who rode out the war exempted from service. In a letter to the *Selma Morning Reporter* in 1864, one citizen accused the state of failing to provide aid fairly. He cited his own county, where assistance "has been very meagre and inadequate; and in some instances hardly appreciable." The author blamed an unfair system headed by "those to whom the duty of disposing of the appropriation is assigned are negligent or unfaithful." He concluded that those in charge would do more good by volunteering for the army and leaving their posts for "men over the military age."[28]

The issue of exemptions from service added to perceptions of unequal treatment due to elite privilege. Changes in the conscription law to lengthen the term of service and extend the age limitations demonstrate the Confederacy's desperation to supply troops. By the end of 1863, the government eliminated the use of substitutes and the next year ordered that all men who had a substitute enlist or be drafted. Yet problems with finding able-bodied soldiers still existed, and in 1864 they increased the age range of those subject to the draft to qualified men between seventeen and fifty. Still, the extensive number of exemptions played a role in keeping wealthier citizens out of the army in two distinct ways. First, many applications to avoid service illustrate the class biases embedded in draft policies. Men from the elite ranks had the resources and connections to take positions in the government that excused them from the military. Second, the governor's office received thousands of applications asking for exemptions that cited special circumstances outside of government office, many of which were granted. All together, this system implied that if one could find a position of power or necessity to the Confederacy, one could avoid service, leaving the bulk of common white males to fill the army. As a result, those common whites who applied for exemptions with the governor's office received a higher rate of rejection.

The examples of men granted release from service uncover a preference for those who served the elite interests of the state. Foremost, the governor often exempted those elected or appointed to offices, which meant that anyone with political and economic clout could utilize their power to avoid service. Justices of the peace, constables, jailers, mail carriers, and court clerks were among many of the positions cited as justifiably exempt. Those petitioners took care to emphasize the necessity of their positions in keeping their residents safe and filling much-needed roles for the community. Other petitions show the willingness of the governor to grant exemptions based on the interests of the planter class. As early as March 1862, Governor Shorter allowed exemptions of overseers when it appeared that leaving a plantation without management of enslaved individuals would render the white community vulnerable to potential social unrest. One planter sent the governor a telegram asking him to exempt the overseer who cared for his plantation. "My overseer W. B. Calhoun," he wrote, "has joined a Company for the war—can you not send me order releasing him from his enlistment?" And he emphasized that he would have to "make some arrangement to take care of my negroes." Shorter granted the request. Similar appeals came into the governor's office throughout the course of the war. One female petitioner submitted an application asking that Shorter exempt her overseer. She claimed, "I have no one to attend to the business of the plantation. There will be no white person that I can put on the place." In April of 1862, Mrs. P. E. Collins asked that James Nunnalee, the son of one of their plantation owners, be released from service, as he would be the only male in the area who could protect the community. As a plantation mistress from Cahaba, Collins stated that "the ladies of the neighborhood" felt vulnerable in the plantation district and asked that Nunnalee take charge to protect them. Appealing to the fatherly role of the governor toward his people, she wrote, "You are our temporal head," and noted that with the white men away at war, "We are in a very unprotected condition." She argued that Nunnalee proved a "rigid disciplinarian" with enslaved men and women and was thus an asset to the whites of her community. Yet, as these early examples demonstrate, Alabama's elites used the weight of their power to minimize disruptions to their socioeconomic interests. Obviously, such an approach came from the idea that some sort of local policing was necessary in the wake of white men leaving for military service, though clearly the petitions favoring the interests of the planter minority meant that the state would draw more from the ranks of common whites to fight the war.[29]

Concerns about plantations left without white authority over the enslaved prompted the Confederate Congress to add the "twenty-slave" exemption law to the Conscription Act in October 1862. This policy intended to serve the interests of all whites in the state significantly favored elite families, who then could use the law liberally to protect their livelihood. In September of 1864, W. J. Sterling submitted a petition claiming that as an overseer he needed to remain at home to manage over 150 enslaved individuals. Mr. Alvis likewise cited that as the only white male in charge of a Marengo County plantation, he needed an exemption. Joseph Knight, a plantation owner, argued that with only three field hands, he needed to stay out of the military to help protect the community. He also called on the gendered rhetoric of paternal duty in making his case for exemption. Knight noted that he took care of his widowed daughter's farm as well as his own plantation but that two of his sons and his son-in-law all died "in the service of the country" and that his wife, their four small children, his daughter, and her children all depended on him for support. J. F. Pickett took a different approach to his petition. He proposed that as superintendent over the plantations in Pike County, he needed to remain at home to oversee 150 enslaved people during harvest season. Another petition, from William Clark, asked for an exemption because he supervised a local salt works that utilized slave labor. He noted that the "manufacture of salt for the indigent families" rendered him necessary to remain at home and manage the production. Clark added that leaving enslaved individuals to function independently at the salt works would, in his estimation, hurt the state, as they were "consuming the provisions of the county, and doing comparatively nothing."[30]

Those of wealth also applied for exemptions based on their role in providing charitable aid to the poor. R. C. Goodman appealed to the governor for an exemption on the grounds that he took care of "a family of a poor soldier which have been almost entirely dependent on him for aid and support." Whether these people claiming to serve the welfare of the poor actually made a difference proves difficult to discern. In June of 1864, Jackson Raly appealed to the governor for an exemption because he served as the superintendent of the "Poor House" that was the only means of welfare for the community. Applicants oftentimes cited multiple reasons for an exemption in an effort to prove their presence at home as "indispensable." In his petition to Governor Watts, Mr. Smith, as listed on the document, claimed that he not only served as justice of the peace but also assisted in the distribution of supplies to poor families in the Midway community. Watts approved his petition.[31]

Although the state considered the economic benefits of exempting elites, it appeared less likely to consider the same for common whites. Those men who applied often cited their employment in trades or professions that offered essential services to their communities. The governor's office in some cases recognized that some occupations needed to remain filled to support the destabilized economy and supply the population. In March of 1864, a petition from George Hale of Tallapoosa County requested an exemption from militia duty on "the grounds that he is a wool carder, and one of the proprietors of a wool and cotton factory" and that the community depended on him to keep the factory going. A petition submitted to Governor Watts on behalf of R. C. Goodman likewise emphasized his contributions to the state; he "produced a considerable surplus of provisions" that he "let the government have cheerfully."[32]

Still, common whites receiving exemptions based on their employment proved less likely as the war demanded more men to serve in the military. They had little choice but to appeal to the governor, given that exemption clauses to the draft failed to address their situation. The state, in turn, scrutinized their applications and granted exemptions only when extraordinary circumstances could be proven. A. J. Griffin, for example, requested an exemption from service, as he was the only doctor in his small community in Shelby County. In addition, he noted that he made an important contribution to the economy as he "engaged in manufacturing spinning wheels and reels." Governor Shorter, however, denied the request, leaving the community without a physician and a source of much-needed tools for farm production. A petition to Governor Watts on behalf of Sam Shepard also met with similar results. As a resident of Tallapoosa, Shepard had the backing of many from his community, who signed the petition. They claimed that they needed this mechanic "to stay at home for the good of this community," which was "entirely dependent on him for soporting the interests of indgent familys of those in the war for there country." Trying to strengthen his case for exemption, the petitioners added, "He is a man of feeble hilth" and therefore would do more good at home than in the military. Even those who directly contributed to the support of the state faced denial of their petitions, such as George Lane from Mobile. As a miller Lane provided a necessary service "in grinding the corn used in distilling the alcohol and whiskey" that, according to the petition, he was "contracted to furnish the State of Alabama." Vital roles for poorer farming communities, such as blacksmiths, likewise did little to move state leaders to advance exemption petitions. In an application from Hickory Flat in Chambers County, residents asked the governor to release William Littlefield from service so they could have more than one blacksmith in the area. They reasoned that "one blacksmith is not enough for the work of said place and its patrons" and contended that most of the people of Hickory Flat came from "moderate circumstances dependent on a public blacksmith for their work." An exemption request on behalf of a man from Dale County who owned a sugar mill likewise exemplified the state's willingness to send common whites into the army rather than allow them to labor at home for the benefit of the community. Petitioners argued that many residents depended on his mill and that if he went into the military, "a large number of needy and worthy family will be wholly unable to have their cane ground." Attempting to bolster his claims for exemption, they reasoned that "your petitioner being a poor man with no assistance except his wife and two small children" would "be more service to the country at home attending his mill." Unfortunately, the governor's office denied their request. As these petitions prove, while Alabama's leaders offered aid to families in need, they continued to act in ways that undermined the labor interests of common whites, forcing them into a state of dependence.[33]

Even citing masculine duty to the family as cause to avoid service carried little weight in the governor's decision. In a November 1863 petition to Governor Shorter, community members pleaded with him to allow a local shoemaker to remain out of the army. They reasoned that if he were called away to service, his family would suffer from the loss of his income. In an effort to strengthen their application, the petitioners detailed his sacrifices for the Confederate cause, mentioning that he had "five brothers in the Confederate States Army and at an early period of the war his two brothers in law volunteered." Adding to his image as sole provider, the application included that "he moved both their families on his land" and took care of them as well as his mother-in-law, a widow, and that if called away for service, he would leave "four families—all of them females left without a protector." The petition of Thomas Pulliam, of Talladega County, highlighted his role as a mechanic who produced and repaired wagons in the area but focused more on his familial role. It mentioned that he had a wife, four children, and a mother-in-law with her own two girls and one boy that depended on his labor for support. Additionally, the petitioners reminded the state of his sacrifice by noting that one of his family members "died in service," and another remained at home "due to being wounded in battle."[34]

The governor's office also rejected applications in which common whites claimed financial hardships or fear of lawlessness on the home front. In a petition on behalf of Rodden Hodges, from St. Clair County, community members appealed to the sympathy of Governor Shorter to allow Hodges to remain with his family. They noted that he had less than $4,000 in assets, five daughters, and one small son. Hodges had paid a substitute to serve in his place, but part of the fee remained unpaid, leaving him susceptible to the draft. The petitioners argued that the father and husband needed to remain "with his family and protecting and providing for them," and that, for a subsistence farmer, paying the substitute proved "a much greater sacrifice." The petition included a section that implored the governor to allow Hodges to remain at home based on the fear of his family being "exposed to outlaws and robbers." Allen Herring also petitioned for exemption from the state militia based on his role as family protector and community provider. Since his sixteen-year-old son already served as a substitute in the Confederate army, he reasoned that he, as a father and a farmer, would do more for the "public interest" by remaining at home. Furthering his claims, he recorded that over the course of a year, Herring had "made about four hundred bushels of corn." But perhaps even more telling was that Herring gave particular attention to the financial strains of caring for his daughter-in-law and young grandchild. His appeal to the sense of masculine duty shared by southern white men, as in most other cases, did little to advance his cause. In a similar case, Anna King asked Governor Watts to exempt her neighbor's son from service, as he by 1864 was the only remaining male in their community. King stated that her neighbor needed her son home, as she had two daughters that could "give her but little aid, as they find it a difficult matter to cloth and feed them." Again the familiar narrative of masculine protector to female dependents proved an insufficient cause for exemption. Although family served as the central argument for fighting the war, it appeared to provide little weight when granting petitions to protect them from its consequences. More so, their rejections fueled the sense that the state valued the economic contributions of elites over saving common whites from a state of crisis.[35]

Adding further to the state's biases in who bore the burden of fighting the war, Alabama's leaders created a policy of releasing common whites serving prison sentences to offset the diminishment of Confederate troops. Such actions demonstrate government's desperation to fill the ranks of the military by exploiting the circumstances of incarcerated common whites. The year 1863 saw a new trend of prisoners in the state's penal system applying for release in exchange for their military service. These men held out hope that joining the fight would bring them one step closer to reuniting with their families. Yet, for many of these men, their continued absence from the home proved a greater burden to their families. Numbers of letters passed through Governor Shorter's office pleading for early release to serve, and he granted the majority of those requests. Using the language and symbols of masculine duty to protect the family as well as to serve the larger Confederate family, prisoners sought a new path to freedom by risking their lives to fight in the war. Many of these prisoners called on members of the community to offer letters of support to emphasize that they possessed a form of masculine honor required of a loyal soldier. In a letter dated October 14, 1863, John McGuire, who faced a five-year sentence for forgery, wrote to the governor asking to be released in order to serve in the Confederacy. In his petition, he reasoned, "I am prompted to make an appeal to your Excellency for my freedom which if you will grant, I promise your Excellency to go forth to the rescue of our bleeding country and there serve faithfully as a soldier." He even stated that the presiding judge in his case could verify his willingness to serve in the army. McGuire received clemency on October 22, 1863, and subsequently left to join the military. Although the scarcity of criminal court records leaves little information on the crimes that these prisoners committed, we do know that they include those convicted of crimes as serious as murder. William Gibson, for example, sought assistance from a prison official to verify his character as a potential soldier. Gibson arrived at the Alabama penitentiary on May 23, 1857, after being convicted of second-degree murder. Sentenced to fifteen years, he saw the war as an opportunity to avoid serving out the remainder of his time as early as 1862. The prison official declared that "his conduct has been exceptionable" and that "the release of said Gibson would not endanger the public welfare."[36]

The case of William Bowden further illustrates the narrative used to justify the release of prisoners to serve in the Confederate army. Sentenced to ten years for murder in 1859, Bowden saw the war as an opportunity for freedom. Calling on notions of masculine duty to protect his family during the wartime crisis, those who supported Bowden's release described him as an upstanding citizen who was more victim than perpetrator of criminal activity. George W. Coleman, a neighbor and friend, argued that Bowden acted in self-defense against James Yancy, the man whom Bowden killed. After verbal threats to Bowden's life, his only option was to kill Yancy, according to Coleman's testimony. "Threats were communicated," Coleman contended, after which Bowden armed himself with a pistol that he used eventually in self-defense. Coleman added that members of their community could attest to Bowden's character and that Yancy was a threatening man. An additional document that included twenty-nine signatures from citizens of Barbour County, where the defendant lived prior to his conviction, testified to his good standing. The signers argued that Bowden left behind a "helpless family" and that given the condition of their home county along with time served, he should receive the Governor's pardon. Additional petitions went forward with several more signatures again attesting to the good character of Bowden and that, upon his release, being "a strong able bodied man under age of forty will make a good soldier." By August 15, 1863, Governor Shorter granted the pardon on the contingency that Bowden would be released to the Confederate army.[37]

Turning to convicts in prison likewise revealed continued class biases in fighting the war as they drew from another pool of common whites rather than turn to the manpower of elites. Shorter pardoned Daniel Lewis, Pat Carroll, and Leonidas Brown, all convicted for different crimes, on the contingency that they serve in the Confederate Army. Both Lewis and Carroll served three years of a six-year sentence when released from prison. Brown, of Barbour County, entered the penitentiary for larceny to serve four years. According to the recommendation of the board of inspectors for the prison, all three men demonstrated good conduct and would make a better contribution to the state by serving in the military. Thomas and Madison Wheeler faced a different situation, in which the community rallied around the two men who had been mistakenly accused of killing a man. The Wheelers, from Cherokee County, got into an altercation with a man with whom they had been drinking. A fight ensued, leaving the man injured and the Wheelers presuming that they had killed him. When they went on trial, the court accepted that the man had perished in the fight, but after their conviction officials discovered the man very much alive and living in Georgia. The board of inspectors writing on behalf of Thomas and Madison cited that the men had served a sufficient five years and should be released to support "their indigent families." Forty-one members of their community signed a petition attesting that the men would do much more good out of prison and in the Confederate army. Governor Shorter agreed and pardoned the men on the condition that rather than going home to care for their families, they would enter the military. Other inmates made similar pleas for release, citing their willingness to risk their lives in the war instead of returning home to their families.[38]

The bizarre case of William McCormick illuminates the extent to which the state would go to draw soldiers from the ranks of prisoners. McCormick and his wife, Mary, submitted a petition for his release. He received a ten-year sentence for a "Crime against Nature" after he sexually assaulted his stepdaughter while drunk. Mary asserted in her statement that William "was intoxicated, so much so that he did not know what he was about." She claimed that she turned him in to the authorities "under the influence of passion and resentment" but later regretted it. Mary pleaded with the governor to release William, stressing that they had three children to support that had "to depend upon her daily labor and the price of provisions are so high and labor so scarce . . . in consequence of the war and public troubles that she has to strain every never to procure food for them." Adding to the financial strain of only one income, Mary mentioned, four of her sons who had once helped the family now served in the military, leaving her destitute. Mary carefully evoked the imagery of her dependency on William as head of the family to make a case for his release, arguing that "her small children are deprived of their means of support by the continued imprisonment of her husband and the absence of her sons in the service of their country." Governor Shorter granted McCormick clemency in July 1863 with the promise that he would enter the military. Rather than allow him to return home to provide for the family, the governor believed his service in the military trumped the needs of the household.[39]

The crisis on the home front brought on by severe privation, continued separation, and government policies favoring elites led common whites to demand action. And in protesting their treatment, they redefined their relationship to the state. The most visible form of protest came in the form of bread riots in the port city of Mobile. Declining supplies in the city became a powder-keg issue that eventually erupted in violence led primarily by the wives of common white soldiers. McCurry contends that women in cities where such riots erupted viewed themselves as suffering due to "systematic, not personal, injustice" primarily as it related to "policy that was literally consuming their substance." Their willingness to take their anger to the streets was a response to wartime policies that pushed common whites to their limit. And their public demands for relief "registered, contested, and reshaped the insupportable demands of the wartime state."[40]

The same held true for the women of Mobile. The city served as a major thoroughfare for goods coming into and out of the Confederacy. Yet the blockade of major ports and river ways, under the Anaconda Plan initiated by the federal military early in the war, created an immediate shortage of goods and impeded the export of cotton and other items out of the state. In his study of Confederate Mobile, Arthur W. Bergeron Jr. explains that the rising costs of basic goods in the city created a crisis among common whites. The cost of flour, for example, went from $45 a barrel to a staggering $400 by early 1865. The growing population of migrants from the rural areas seeking work and refuge, along with Confederate soldiers stationed in the city, also placed greater demands on already-dwindling supplies. This situation created tensions among the population that manifested in growing divisions between common whites, especially women, and elites. Many of these women sought jobs and other means of support while their loved ones fought in the military. The pressures of low pay, rising populations, shortages of supplies, and increasing inflation, however, proved too much to bear. Like many others, they placed their hopes on state leaders and their relief efforts. The city attempted to augment state aid by offering its own public assistance. Civilians from the wealthy ranks, for example, created the Mobile Supply Association, charged with purchasing supplies from their own funds and selling them to the population at cost rather than inflate the price. Even the Confederate government stepped in, when Col. Lucius B. Northup, who served as the commissary general and led the Subsistence Department, created a program for each Confederate state to offer a program for the collection of supplies as well as to store and distribute them to the people.[41]

But it was the state that served as the main supplier of direct aid. The rising demands for assistance coupled with the declining economic conditions in Alabama made it difficult to keep pace with demands. As a result, efforts to aid the needy proved insufficient, especially among women whose husbands and other male kin were off fighting the war. The number of families seeking government aid went from 668 in 1862 to 2,674 in 1864. Typically, the counties also contributed as much as possible to the supplies to offset the cost for the state. By 1864, however, Mobile reported that the county could not offer any additional supplies, and city officials requested $2,000,000 from the state coffers alone. Between those years, the situation grew tense in the city, with newspapers reporting dire circumstances with little effort of the military or government to help.[42]

The military policies of commanding officers appeared to common whites as a primary cause of their suffering. In particular, they directed their hostilities toward Gen. John Pemberton, the Confederate commander stationed in Mississippi near Vicksburg in 1863. Pemberton needed supplies to help sustain his army in Mississippi and issued a command prohibiting supplies to be shipped out of the state. Mobile's mayor R. H. Slough and Governor Shorter pleaded that Pemberton suspend the command, but he refused. Maj. Gen. Samuel B. Buckner, commander of the District of the Gulf, responded to Pemberton's refusals by issuing an order to disallow the shipment of supplies and impressed other goods from speculators. Yet the conflict between the military leaders and the state added fuel to the fire, and the ones to suffer were the poor. The *Mobile Tribune* reported that citizens were reduced to sneaking supplies into Mobile via the Mississippi River. A headline read "Gen. Pemberton Beat" and retold how a citizen used crafty means to procure supplies via the Mississippi River. "The story is as follows: A gentleman wanting meat, purchased it up the road; but knowing that it would be confiscated if found, he procured a common pine box about six feet long, made to resemble a coffin, such as are commonly used to transport the dead. He filled this box with good sound bacon, which he found at reasonable prices in Mississippi, and then marked his dead body thus: John Shoat, 32d Ala, Regiment, Mobile, Ala." Such actions, according to the article, resulted from the belief that Pemberton was intent on "trying to starve out the city of Mobile" by refusing to send down food that they believed was "lying in the warehouses rotting."[43]

The Ladies' Military Aid Society urged Governor Shorter to provide assistance to those among the poorest in the city. In April of 1863, Adelaide V. Chaudron, secretary of the organization, wrote the governor thanking him for sending them dried fruit to distribute to the needy of the city. She noted in her letter to him that shortages were the result not only of enemy interference but also that from the state. "Fruit (like everything else)," she wrote, "is very rare, in this unhappy town, blockaded alike by friends and foes." Yet she carefully praised the governor for his efforts: "Our State will always look back with pride & fondness upon the days of your Excellency's wise & paternalistic government." Calling on the language of dependents seeking the necessary protection from their father, Chaudron wrote again to Shorter asking him to do what he could to help: "We know dear Sir, how troublesome we are, but we also know, how paternally our Governor regards his people." Her letter to the governor, dated

May 1, 1863, asked for "factory thread" so that they could provide clothing for families of soldiers. Yet such efforts of civilians did little to ameliorate their hardships.[44]

The situation reached a fever pitch when, in September of 1863, riots broke out in Mobile in which primarily women took to the streets demanding "Bread or Blood." Similar riots took place in major cities throughout the Confederacy where supplies ran short and populations boomed. The most infamous was the Richmond Bread Riot, which erupted among the poor populating the Confederate capital city. Much as in Mobile when the government failed to intervene on behalf of common whites while elites fared better, emotions exploded into protests that spilled into the streets. The *New York Times* reported that what appeared as a riot in the city was led by women who saw no recourse but to bring their issues to the public stage. According to an eyewitness account: "The women of Mobile, rendered desperate by their sufferings, met in large numbers on the Spring Hill road, with banners on which were printed such devices as 'Bread or Blood,' on one side, and 'Bread and Peace' on the other, and armed with knives and hatchets, and marched down Dauphine street, breaking open the stores in their progress, and taking for their use such articles of food and clothing as they were in urgent need of. It was, in fact, a most formidable riot by a long-suffering and desperate population." The commanding officer in the city ordered the Seventeenth Alabama Regiment to stop the crowds; however, by the eyewitness account, they refused to do so, possibly feeling a sense of solidarity with them. Eventually the protestors dispersed based on promises that their demands for assistance would be met. Nonetheless, as reported, disturbances broke out again later in the evening, but through lack of evidence there was little report on the outcome. Mayor Slough did address the situation by setting up an emergency organization known as the Special Relief Committee to collect and disperse money and supplies. The city, however, continued to suffer from depleting resources throughout the remainder of the war.[45]

As common white families struggled amid declining conditions on the home front, their resolve to see the war carry on began to wane. By 1863 it was clear that both civilians and soldiers of modest means shouldered most of the burdens sustaining the conflict. Unable to weather the economic and emotional trials, they turned to state leaders who promised safety and security in exchange to their loyalty to the cause. Those leaders, however, whether knowingly or not, underestimated the extent of hardships common whites endured. Their policies that they intended to combat the declining conditions for common whites provided little relief. And at times state leaders tended to favor the economic interests of the elites at common whites' expense. Families suffered from strict conscription laws that separated families, government impressment of civilian supplies, and dangers of both armies invading their communities. Depleted supplies coupled with the failure of the Confederate economy to create the basis of a strong fiscal system to support a new national structure, created a situation in which common whites suffered the most. As a result, they came to ignore the calls to remain loyal to the war in the interest of their families. It seemed to many that while fighting an enemy coming from outside the South, they faced a greater threat within their own backyard. Class disparities that became more pronounced during the war placed the state on the course for greater conflict between common whites and the elite power structure. When the war came to a close, the relationship between the classes was left broken. And, when the state moved into the period of Reconstruction, the apparent inequalities led to a sense of injustice among the common whites, who fared little better in the postwar period.

5

"Oh! How Changed Everything Has Become"

Families in the Postwar State

In 1865 John W. Brown returned from service in the Confederate army to discover his wife missing. Having conceived a child with another man, Ellen J. Vandasdel Brown moved out of their residence in Pike County, Missouri, abandoning their marriage. John subsequently moved to Perry County, Alabama, where he began formal divorce proceedings. The couple had married in 1861 with all hope of beginning a new family once he returned from his command in Cockrell's Brigade. In the throes of petitioning for a divorce, during which his wife was mysteriously absent, Brown pointed to his veteran's status to justify severing matrimonial ties. For Brown, his wife's willingness to transgress ideas of "proper" female behavior while he served nobly the cause of Confederate independence was enough to claim power within the Alabama courts. Even Brown's employer, John Bates of Perry County, echoed this sentiment when he proclaimed, "He [Brown] is as virtuous a man as I know and as esteemed by those who know him," and trumpeted that, having met Brown during his military service, believed his "character then was as good as any man's in Alabama." His testimony revealed that, as with many common whites, efforts to sustain the family's integrity continued to guide his actions even in the postwar period. According to court testimony, Brown had successfully performed his manly duty on the battlefield while his spouse failed in her role as a pure and submissive wife on the home front. Such declarations, he believed, seemed necessary as he moved toward rebuilding his life after the war.[1]

John W. Brown's case seemed the exception rather than the norm for his socioeconomic group. Yet his case exemplifies the desire of common whites to return to a better life in postwar Alabama. After four years of separation, physical adversity, and economic downturns, the search for normalcy shaped their family and home life after the war. Unfortunately, that quest to restore order proved challenging as the state struggled to regain its economic footing after emancipation and defeat. Once again, the demands of common whites for protection from state leaders gave them the power to shape policies concerning public aid. The state attempted to address issues of food supply, rising taxes, and job opportunities for common whites through various aid programs. But Alabama's government, facing new postwar concerns, lacked the resources needed to meet those demands. By the 1870s, moreover, state leaders started to turn their attention away from the needs of common whites to focus more on rebuilding and refashioning the economic landscape, restoring state political power of ex-Confederates, and navigating the transition from slavery to freedom. This shift in the state agenda then placed more pressure on local communities to provide aid to common white families in need. As a result, common whites once again seemed at odds with state leaders who seemed to care more for the economic, social, and political interests of elites than for the protection of their struggling families. Common whites' sense of abandonment at the hands of state leaders during the war continued into the Reconstruction era, leaving many to feel as if the familial social contract they had forged with the elite power structure once again had failed to materialize.

Common whites barely weathered the storm of war, only to emerge on the other side faced with mounting obstacles. During the war, policies that favored elites at the expense of common whites redefined their relationship with the state. Government impressment of civilian supplies along with the state's tax-in-kind policy placed common whites in a state of crisis. Destruction of crops at the hands of Union and Confederate troops further depleted the food supply in the state, and common white families suffered the most from it. Moreover, conscription laws took much-needed farm and skilled labor away from their families, leaving them vulnerable to economic destitution and unsafe conditions. After the war the state confronted a mounting crisis. Homes left ruined by the ravages of war, destroyed crops, and depleted livestock meant common whites endured diminished food supplies and little economic means to purchase scant provisions. Instability resulting from mob activities in postwar communities also forced common white Alabamians to seek protection for their families.

Along with the bleak postwar landscape, the state suffered from crop failures in 1865 and 1866 that added to the distress of common whites who depended on their farms for sustenance. At the same time state leaders attempted to provide assistance to common whites, they made decisions that at times seemed to contradict those efforts. In particular, taxes imposed by the federal and state governments intended to help with recovery crippled much of Alabama's small, landowning farmers. Unable to pay the taxes, they lost their land, and many moved into the status of tenant farmer. Gone was the independence that land ownership afforded them before the war. It seemed as if Confederate defeat came at a greater cost to common whites, who struggled to situate themselves in the emerging New South.

Common whites continued to assert a voice in the state's relief agenda by relying once again on a paternalistic narrative. Immediately after the war, the state shifted its focus from supplying the soldiers' families to providing aid to a greater number of Alabamians. Government policies addressed the population of men and women, both whites and African Americans, who felt the full weight of poverty in the postwar period. Along with the Freedmen's Bureau, the state offered relief to a larger number of needy households. These efforts came as a result of the direct and indirect demands of those in need who sought action from their state leaders. Common whites especially injected themselves into the political agenda of postwar Alabama by turning to the state for relief. Their dependency on government leaders to act in accordance with their "fatherly" duty meant common whites demanded a presence in the emerging debates over the direction of the state primarily between 1865 and 1870, after which policy interests began to pivot away from the concerns of needy families.[2]

As the conflict ended, common white families turned to the prospect of returning to life as normal. For some, however, the death of loved ones meant redefining normalcy in a postwar state. As early as 1862, William Moxley received the untimely news that his wife, Emily, died while giving birth to their child. For William, returning to his home a widower would mean a reorientation of household responsibilities that forced him to rely on extended female kin for assistance. Death also cast a dark cloud on the Branscomb family household when, by late summer of 1864, Louis was killed in battle. As the brothers returned from battle, they felt a void within their kinship relations. In addition to the emotional toll of losing their brother, the loss of his labor forced greater burdens on the family as they sought to recover. Although the sons of Sarah Espy who survived the war

Figure 5. "Scenes in Cotton Land—the Home of the Poor White," from *Frank Leslie's Illustrated Newspaper*, October 7, 1871. Poor whites found the postwar years especially difficult, as critical assistance became less of a priority for state leaders. Alabama Department of Archives and History.

returned home, they carried with them the physical and emotional scars of their experience. Espy's son Marcelleous, for example, spent time in a federal prison camp, to be released only a month before the close of the war. When he returned home, it was clear to Espy that the conditions her young son had endured left him in a state of poor health. Yet after families reunited the hope of rebuilding life after Confederate defeat provided a way to refocus their energies. Now the concerns of recovery would occupy their daily lives.[3]

At the same time families confronted a broken household, they attempted to resume life as they knew it before the conflict commenced. For the most part, the postwar period meant a return to the familiar gender roles that had provided them with a sense of equality and power in the antebellum period. The hope of coming home to restore their prewar lives proved difficult amid economic deprivation and loss of life. Men and women wanted to resume their prewar lives, but the war had taken its toll. Despite having lost his wife in childbirth, William Moxley eventually remarried. He, along with his family, relocated to Texas, where he resumed his practice as a physician. Grant and Malinda Taylor also turned inward to the family, hoping to settle into a comfortable domestic routine. The couple extended their family by having three more children. They also resumed their devotion to their church culture, especially after Grant helped found a Baptist church in Greene County, Alabama, to which the couple moved in the 1870s. John S. Jones likewise saw the routine of family life as a way to move on from the chaos of war. After his son died in service to the Confederate military, John remained in contact with his daughter-in-law, writing to her often, even after he relocated to Texas and she stayed in Tuscaloosa. Resuming life as normal meant focusing on his farm to support his extended kin. In one letter he boasted of a fifteen-acre cotton crop that he hoped would yield some success. In addition, John wrote about returning to church life for his faith but also as a social outlet, noting that he lived "close by the meetin hous" where he attended to hear "fine singin hear twist a month." Family, however, remained central to John, especially regarding his grandson whom he feared he would no longer see given the distance between them. Still, for John as well as for the Moxleys and Taylors, going back to something resembling their prewar lives, particularly the roles and rituals of family, became the source of comfort amid the uncertainty of the postwar South.[4]

The same held true for Eliza Fielding, from Limestone County, who focused more on returning to daily concerns of a young, single woman. Fielding resided with her mother and several siblings on a modest farm on the eve of the Civil War. With about $5,000 in personal and real property, the family lived a relatively comfortable life before the war. Fielding entered her teenage years when the war commenced. By the end of the conflict, Fielding had matured into her twenties, ready to marry and start a family of her own. The instability of Alabama's postwar social and economic landscape, however, made her quest for marriage and motherhood even more difficult. Rather, she turned to the mundane routine of household production to fill her time, which provided a source of normalcy. She started a diary in 1866 in which she documented her daily activities following the war. Filling it with details about household chores, family relations, church life, and potential courtships, Fielding demonstrated the extent to which white Alabamians wanted to put the war behind them and resume their regular lives. Work figured prominently as a constant theme of her daily activities and reflected the necessity of female labor in sustaining the household. Writing in January of 1866, she bragged, "[I] have acted man an woman both to day. Spun nearly six cuts, got dinner, milked, cut wood, brought water, helped Jack shell corn since supper, been knitting on my shawl tonight." But, as a single woman in the throes of her courtship years, Fielding also intimated her hopes to one day marry one of her potential suitors in her community. On Valentine's Day of 1866, she described her many friends who intended to marry within the year, leaving her to ponder her own marital fate. "I believe every body is going to marry except myself an one or two more," she wrote. "I am afraid if I don't look sharp they will be gone up too. The first thing I know I won't know nothing but will be left alone to moarn my fate." Her church activities and religious faith gave her a feeling of getting back to normal life. She went to great lengths to detail church attendance and the social outlet that it provided her. Fielding's diary, with little mention of the turbulent atmosphere of postwar Alabama, revealed that she wanted nothing more than to lead the life of a typical female youth.[5]

For others, the disruptions following surrender took on a different meaning as Alabama faced the realities of a defeat and emancipation. Margaret Gillis wrote in her diary in October of 1865, "Oh! How changed everything has become. . . . so much darker has it become. The Yankees have triumphed and we are now a downtrodden and oppressed people." Even more revealing was the scant commentary on the demise of slavery and its consequences for the South's social order. Rather, white southerners believed that Confederate surrender coupled with emancipation would bring about social chaos at the expense of their safety. As Gillis reflected, in the days immediately following defeat:

> The negroes were constantly running to us telling us tales of barbarity and cruelty, such as stripping the women to find their valuables and whipping them, and other things more barbarious. Oh! What a miserable week. We were hourly expecting them here, but thank the good Lord they never came, although within a few miles of us all the time. We could look out at anytime of night and see the flames of burning buildings. Then came the awful news that we were subjugated, and our President in the hands of the enemy, and he is still a prisoner, his fate doubtful. Our property destroyed, negroes freed, and no law or order. This is the present state of affairs.

The idea of vulnerable women left at the mercy of former enslaved people and their vengeful Union allies became a common trope among former

Confederates seeking to justify a return to white supremacy. At the heart of that justification lay the gendered rhetoric of white womanhood in need of protection by the "best men" of the state, which would gain broader acceptance as Reconstruction ran its course.[6]

Some looked to the potential of vice president and Tennessean Andrew Johnson to bring order to the postwar South by showing sympathy to former Confederates. After Abraham Lincoln's assassination, Reconstruction seemed at a crossroads as Radical Republicans vied for greater influence on the process while Johnson resumed a milder approach already under way. Johnson, however, proved less interested in following the course of Radical Republicans, who wanted to dismantle the former elite power structure and extend civil rights to former enslaved men and women. Alabama's common whites took interest in such debates over the requirements for southern states to return s to the Union. Martin Gateway Milligan, a Presbyterian minister from Gadsden, attempted to balance his pessimistic views of Reconstruction with his hopes that Johnson would protect white southerners from what he perceived as threats against social order. His grim outlook on the political landscape came from what he perceived as an effort of Republicans to advance racial equality at the expense of white privilege in Alabama. He wrote to one friend that such efforts emerged from a partnership between "Tories and a set of corrupt designing men to low and mean to have a place among decent white men," and in his estimation had "no apserations such as white men have but seek in a stealthy manner the degredation and ruin of the white man, willing to sacrifice him to elevate the negroe." For Milligan, however, some hope to combat racial equality came with Johnson's plans for Reconstruction, more lenient than those of Radical Republicans, as long as the president "trys to suppor the Constitution of the once United States." Milligan, like the majority of common whites, absorbed the prewar ideas of racial ordering and feared the effects of emancipation in the postwar era. In his view the dismantling of the racial hierarchy and the rise of the Republicans in Alabama spelled doom for the state. "Will we ever have a good government again," he asked. "I am beginning to think that if we do blood will have to run more freely than ever known in the history of this continent." Milligan's sentiments reflected the widespread alarm of former Confederates that Republican efforts to empower freedmen and women with civil rights meant losing their own place in the sociopolitical landscape.[7]

Common whites' concerns over emancipation did more to align them with elites seeking to regain power in postwar Alabama. The emergence of the Ku Klux Klan shows the concerted efforts of former Confederates to fight the influence of Republicans and the effects of African American suffrage. Additionally, its primary purpose was "the maintenance or restoration of white supremacy in every walk of life." The Klan that originated in Pulaski, Tennessee, in 1866 morphed from fraternal organization into a terrorist wing of the Democratic Party, intending to fight against the Radical Republican agenda. Its membership and organization mimicked that of the Confederate army, with elites serving in higher commands, while common white men served as infantry-like soldiers who conducted most of the terrorism. Just as elites connected the ideals of liberty to support for the Confederacy during the war, they refashioned the same narrative to serve their postwar campaign to regain power. The elite minority had manipulated, cajoled, and even forced common whites to separate themselves from enslaved and free people of color in the antebellum era. Notions of protecting liberty from outside invaders bent on destroying their "way of life" provided the narrative for common whites to join forces in fighting the war. Those same concepts of liberty endangered provided once again the rallying cry for common whites to join forces. Their membership in the Klan became a means to protect their freedom and preserve the racial order in the South. For elites, however, their alliance with common whites served a different purpose. It created one path to reestablishing the prewar status quo.[8]

Government leaders in the state, on the other hand, concentrated on transforming Alabama's economic structure. Gov. Robert M. Patton, elected in 1865, focused on luring business interests into the state as a way to turn the financial tide. He concentrated on restoring the economic health of the state, first by rebuilding much-needed institutions, such as expanding the public school system, reforming prisons to utilize convict labor, and restoring the state university after the war. But addressing the needs of the common whites, especially those suffering from the postwar economic crisis, served, in part, as motivation to lure industries into the state. Industrial jobs would offer an alternative to farming and provide especially poorer whites hopes of a stable income. Development of railroads also appeared a beacon of hope in creating economic diversity in the state. The resulting growth of towns and businesses that railroad interests encouraged posed an opportunity to draw people away from the farm and into other financial sectors. Regardless of these efforts to diversify, farming still remained the most sought-after source of income among common whites. And state leaders hoped that common whites, along with freedmen and women, would move to farms and plantations, filling the labor gap left after the end of slavery. Such optimism for economic change for the state resonated among the white population despite ongoing economic destitution.⁹

Newspapers trumpeted the positive message of economic development in the state and encouraged citizens to embrace such changes. Immediately following the war, newspapers reported on the economic and material devastation in war-torn Alabama. And most placed the locus of control in rebounding from the conflict on the shoulders of the citizenry. One author in the *Livingston Journal* proclaimed that if the citizens of Alabama wanted to recover from "the changes brought about by the war," then they would have to make the change themselves. The article included observations on the state of communities as places of "neglected homesteads and uncultivated fields . . . seen on every side." Even areas of fertile farmlands that "put forth and gr[e]w and flourishe[d]" now produced only "the thorn and thistle." The author urged Livingston residents to "turn back again to the natural resources" to bring about prosperity. The call for "vigorous, energetic, manly effort" to rebuild the region touched on the gendered ideals of masculine prosperity through industry and self-reliance so familiar to nineteenth-century Alabamians.¹⁰

Other newspapers echoed such sentiments with articles featuring the development of manufacturing and railroads following the war. Championing the agenda of government leaders, journalists offered commentary on the benefits of industrial interests and how they could rebuild a more prosperous state. One article in an April 1866 edition of the *Union Springs Times* noted the advantages of a railroad that connected "Pensacola with Montgomery" and that many citizens supported the "moneyed men, at home and abroad," whose wealth provided "the capital required." Just a couple of months later, another article appeared to serve as a recruitment pitch to potential investors in the town of Union Springs. The author contended that the real achievements in the small town came from the growing number of mechanics and blacksmiths, as well as those who ran other businesses that "would resound once more with the music of the artisan's saw and hammer." The author mentioned that investors would likewise benefit from the farming enterprises of the area, as they boasted of being "the centre of one of the best farming sections in eastern Alabama." Regardless of their interests, the author maintained, "an enterprising man can find . . . an inviting field which promises rich returns for well-directed energy and perseverance." In an October 1866 article in the *Union Springs Times*, the author reiterated the need to diversify the state economy and encouraged citizens with wealth to invest in their own industries rather than rely on outside manufacturers. He noted that investors should "turn their attention to another channel of industry—manufacturing" that would offer many "advantages" to those wanted to process their own cotton.[11]

The editors of the *Gadsden Times* likewise touted the progress of their city in hopes of luring investors into the area. In a July 1867 article, one author turned to the development of schools and churches as a sign of prosperity after the war, citing the construction of two new churches and the establishment of the "Male and Female Seminary" as evidence. A number of articles in the three years following the war highlighted new construction and population growth to showcase how Gadsden remained a vibrant city that enticed new residents to move to the area. "Within the last month," an author wrote, "new houses have gone up. . . . The same amount goes up regularly nearly every month." The author reasoned that new construction stemmed from the population "increasing rapidly" and that "trade of the place is widening and expanding." As if to promise the reader a guaranteed success story if they invested in Gadsden, the writer concluded that "everybody, in business, that we know of, is getting rich." The song of prosperity that carried through the state promised Alabamians a better life. Yet this better life came at a price that the common white majority, still fighting to recover from the war, could rarely afford. As a result, they found few alternatives to the struggling existence on the farm or the substandard wages of factory labor.[12]

Four years of war left Alabama's economic and physical landscape in a state of flux. Families torn apart by death confronted the task of rebuilding their lives and returning to a sense of normalcy. Common whites also saw the destruction of their farms, leaving them with few economic resources on which to survive the postwar period. In 1865 provisional governor Lewis E. Parsons issued a proclamation on the state of postwar Alabama that recognized the state of ruin in which citizens found themselves and the problems with restoring order and stability in their communities. "A very large proportion of our material wealth has been exhausted," he declared, "our fields are laid waste, our towns and cities, our railroads and bridges, our schools and colleges, many of our private dwellings and public edifices are in ruins." More significantly, Parsons acknowledged the emotional toll that war exacted on the intimate lives of his citizens when he noted that "silence and desolation reign where once stood the comfortable home which resounded with the joyous laugh of childhood and innocence." The war, he concluded, not only took the material comforts from Alabamians but also stripped the emotional security of families who endured "untold sufferings." True to his paternalistic role as head of the state, Parsons paid particular attention to the suffering of those he saw as most vulnerable: "our women and children and the aged and helpless of our land."[13]

After Confederate surrender, incidences of disorder and crime exacerbated common whites' already precarious circumstances. In a letter to President Johnson, Parsons painted a bleak picture of the postwar state, emphasizing the need to restore order. Criminal activity certainly plagued families, with little protection by authorities. But for Parsons, blame for the unstable conditions rested more with the people after the war than on the policies and practices of state leaders. The moral failing of returning soldiers, according to Parsons, contributed the most to the crime that threatened social order. He argued that a portion of soldiers returned with "the habits of improvidence induced by protracted and in many cases undisciplined and unrestrained camp life." Such habits led a man to commit "many deeds of wild lawlessness, engendered and encouraged by a laxity of morals, the almost invariable accompaniments of war." In Parsons's estimation, the only means to securing order from well-armed criminals was to permit sheriffs to "provide a sufficient number of deputy's to be well armed from the purpose of executing the process committed to them and preserving the public peace within their respective communities." The answer to restoring order was an armed population, rather than addressing systemic issues, such as poverty, that could cause one to commit criminal acts. And, all around the state, evidence emerged that Alabama's common whites faced an economic crisis that placed many in a state of such desperation.[14]

New concepts of gender ideals emerged in this context to help reconceptualize the racial and class order in the postwar state. Elites in the former Confederate states looked to the home and family as a means to regain their elevated place in the social order, allowing them to claim political power once again. As historian Laura Edwards contends, this new domestic ideal came from a mixture of "liberal ideology and northern consumer culture." The ideal wife and mother displayed a type of domestic virtue through her ability to create a home as a haven safe from the ills of the outside world while serving the needs of all family members. The true duty of a woman was to create, in essence, a domestic retreat valued for its material trappings and comfortable lifestyle. On the contrary, the masculine conception of the "best man" was that of provider and protector who secured the financial resources to meet the financial needs of the home. He helped raise the family to a higher standard of living that justified their elevated position within the social order of the post–Civil War South. They saw these ideals of womanhood and manhood as the example with which to gauge all others around them. Those who failed to live up to those standards did so because of a moral failing on their part; this ignored the systemic poverty resulting from inadequate state policies. These new postwar gender prescriptions thus aided elite whites in resuming their power in the years following the war. Conversely, common whites and freedmen and women stood outside these new definitions of the ideal man and woman. As Edwards demonstrates, they "lacked the means necessary to live up to elite white standards." Even so, the new domestic ideology failed to resonate among common whites and African Americans. Instead, they constructed gender expectations based on "social ties and mutual responsibilities, not physical structure and material possessions."[15]

Common whites and African Americans created postwar gender ideals that fit their socioeconomic needs and, in doing so, empowered them to shape government policies in postwar Alabama. Their conceptions of manhood and womanhood, however, varied by race, as emancipation created a unique set of circumstances for freedmen and women apart from common whites. Both groups constructed notions of proper gender roles that met the immediate needs of the family. Notions of womanhood emerged from the fear of poverty and what that would entail for their families. Focusing on their daily survival became the driving force shaping their domestic lives. Women subordinated themselves to the male head of the household, abiding by the patriarchal framework of the southern social order, but their focus on providing basic necessities such as food and clothing dictated their day-to-day existence. On the other hand, men relied on personal freedom and independence to define manhood in the postwar era. Being able to provide for one's family without depending on aid, and personal liberty from laboring for others, became the primary gauge of one's masculinity. Although freedmen and women shared these gender concepts with common whites, the situation in which these concepts emerged was vastly different from that of common whites. Freedmen and women created their ideas of manhood and womanhood within the context of transitioning from slavery to freedom, something foreign to all whites. Still, these gender ideals, set apart from those of elites, provided the means by which common whites could raise their own voice of protest and demand that the state once again construct a postwar agenda that included their demands.[16]

Common whites, dependent on their farms for sustenance, encountered a failing economy made worse in the wake of wartime destruction. Crop failures occurring in 1865 and 1866 led to catastrophic food shortages that brought many families near starvation. As a result, the lack of foodstuffs generated by farming placed greater burdens on the state to offer relief. A government committee formed to address the issue reported that in 1865 nearly 130,000 whites identified as destitute. Lack of credit coupled with taxation requirements forced families to remain in a state of poverty and dependent on aid. Emigration out of the state offered one solution as people hoped to find better prospects in neighboring states or outside the region altogether. The general condition of Alabama's postwar economy also motivated common whites to migrate to other areas of the state, seeking some alternative in the plantation districts. Those in the mountain district of northern Alabama and the southeastern portions of the Wiregrass region moved into areas they saw as having more-fertile ground and better farming prospects. Even with migration, common whites in those regions struggled to rebound after the war due to inflation, devalued currency, and lack of food supplies. Moreover, these areas of the state harbored most of the Unionist population, who experienced discrimination in the state's wartime government policies. Identified as traitors, they received little of the aid offered to common whites until later in the war. After the conflict they continued to face an uphill battle in trying to regain their economic footing. For the population of common whites, regardless of their allegiances during the war, moving to towns within the state offered employment as laborers but with meager compensation. Most continued to find that their prospects remained in the farming sector. Common whites with no credit or savings found the only alternative was to rent land. Even those who had owned land in prewar Alabama watched their economic prospects diminish after the war. Unable to afford the taxes imposed at the state and federal levels, farmers exchanged their status as independent landowners to dependent tenant farmers. Other factors such as natural disasters affecting crops, depletion of farm labor due to the war's death toll, and the insecurity of market prices for cotton and other crops exacerbated the crisis facing common whites.[17]

The dark clouds of impoverishment that hovered over common whites in the years following surrender became their impetus to demand a place in Alabama's postwar policies. Once again they saw the state government as the larger protector of Alabama's families and turned to its leaders for relief. With some families on the brink of starvation, many common whites faced dire circumstances. They wanted to return to their normal lives after the war, but the residual effects of the conflict felt in the years to follow coupled with new postwar economic hardships made it difficult to come back to life as usual. Instead, many faced conditions that left them dependent on the state to keep them from starvation. Their dependency, however, actually became a source of power for common whites to shape the political landscape in Alabama in the years between 1865 and the early 1870s. As during their wartime protests, the family formed the rhetorical basis for that power. Their demands for relief to protect their loved ones garnered enough attention to influence the government's agenda in the first few years after the war.

State leaders first responded to the immediate crisis by creating a program to administer provisions. Distribution of foodstuffs, primarily corn and bacon, required a bureaucratic apparatus in order to reach all families affected by wartime conditions. In March 1865, state leaders created the Committee on Destitution to survey the extent of the postwar crisis. After recording conditions among the state's impoverished, they transformed the committee into an office of Commissioner for the Destitute that same year. The governor appointed Marcus Cruikshank as its head, and legislators appropriated $500,000 for supplies. But as the commission was late to start, the Freedmen's Bureau stepped in as the main provider of supplies until the beginning of 1866. Other state efforts consisted of acts passed in the General Assembly to fill any deficiencies in the program. In particular, the state would work with county commissioners in the process of transporting and dispensing provisions. Additional actions by the assembly ensured that those claiming need would produce some proof of their status and demonstrate "to the best of his or her ability, [that they use] every proper exertion to support himself, herself, or family." The General Assembly that met in 1866 maintained assistance into the following year by appropriating additional funds for relief and granting the governor more authority over the program. According to an act passed in that session, the governor could use funds at his discretion for the needy as well as appoint agents to help with disseminating provisions. Still, Cruikshank, as the state commissioner, worked closely with Gen. Wager Swayne, head of the Freedmen's Bureau in Alabama, to dispense food supplies throughout the state. The governor's office working in tandem with the commission and the bureau certainly appeared as if the demands of common whites determined, at least in the few years after the war, the direction of the state's postwar agenda. In fact, historians conclude that more whites received aid in Alabama than did freedmen and women after the war.[18]

Certainly, immediately following the war, common whites in Alabama gained the attention of government officials. Their initial efforts to access the needs of families brought to light the full extent of the problems facing the population. Reports of men, women, and children left destitute by the war and with barely any means of support revealed just how much relief common whites would demand from the state. The government once again turned to the narrative of protecting the family when responding to the pressure to offer relief. Field agents, for example, used the language of dependency to push the issue that many families lacked a capable male head of the household to act as provider and protector. In the example of Coosa County, several households reported living on the brink of starvation because of the death of the male head. In other case, families reported the presence of an adult male but also that he was unable to support the family due to injuries sustained during military service. Agent A. E. Pase reported one situation in which four children under the ages of ten resided in a household with no adult male to "woke for them." In the case of Henry Harrell, the field agent likewise listed him as wounded from military service, with six total in the family and "no one to woke for him and family and destitute of subsistence." Another family, consisting of three orphaned children all under the age of ten, also claimed they had "no one to woke for them," including no extended kin. Several other reports cited homes with widows whose husbands perished in the war. Other cases described fathers and husbands willing to provide for their dependents but unable to due to when they returned from the military. The cases of Patrick Smith, Eps Brown, and J. C. Palmer, for instance, represented the many men who served but, after surrender, failed to return home in time to plant a crop for harvest. Smith, with a family of seven, was wounded and unable to get back home in time "to make a support," while Brown's long journey home after he was discharged from the army kept him from harvesting enough crop that would "make a support" for his family of six. Palmer, also with a large family to provide for, likewise returned by May, too late to produce a crop able to sustain the household.[19]

As the commission launched its program in 1866, Cruikshank and other officials took heed of the crisis and shaped their policies accordingly. In his March 1866 report to Governor Patton, the commissioner revealed that they needed to increase the amount of provisions due to the rising number of families in need of food. He mentioned that despite requesting more assistance from the federal government, his office received nothing and thus needed the state to help with the deficit. To make matters worse, he reported to the governor in 1867 that poor crops from previous years were depleted, leaving families without access to food sources. Despite these issues with the state's food supply, Cruikshank cited that for the months of March and April of that year, they, along with help from the Freedmen's Bureau, provided some level of relief by distributing 45,000 bushels of corn and 100,000 pounds of bacon. The northern counties received a good portion of the aid dispersed to families, but Mobile County topped the list with 3,100 pounds of bacon and 1,400 bushels of corn. Still, all counties in the state received some assistance, however modest, in the early months of 1867. Cruikshank sounded the alarm the following year that supplies had dwindled even further. At the same time, the need for relief to Alabama's common whites started to fade from the government's agenda. Cruikshank himself started to gradually pivot away from the assistance program. He reported later that year that as crops rebounded, so too did the state's food supplies increase. This trend led him to question whether his office should even continue into 1869. Nonetheless, common whites continued to send pleas for relief aid throughout the existence of Cruikshank's office, even as state leaders began to look optimistically at future conditions in Alabama.[20]

In their many requests for help, common whites leaned heavily on their postwar gender ideals that focused primarily on the family's survival. Julia Miller, for example, wrote to Governor Patton in November 1867 asking if he could spare some money to send to a responsible male who could oversee the distribution of the funds to aid her family. She based her request on her situation that as an infirm woman left without a male protector, she needed the government to save the family from starvation. "All the dependence I had," Miller wrote, "fell in the late war a kind father and two noble and affectionate brothers they were taken away." Pleading for help beyond the mere distribution of bacon and corn, she said, "I am left alone in this cold and unfriendly world without one friend lame and no health." She sought supplemental aid from the governor's office by portraying herself as the weak female dependent absent a male presence to protect the family. Furthermore, asking that money go directly to a male supervisor rather than directly to Miller herself appealed to the paternalistic relationship common whites forged with the state. Similar appeals came from other communities in need of relief. In a letter in May of 1867, a citizen of Conecuh County asked Governor Patton to provide more corn for the "indigent orphans and widows" in his community, whom he described as defenseless to protect themselves in the absence of a male provider. C. Womble likewise described related concerns for citizens unable to fend for themselves. He noted that the lack of supplies drove citizens in his community to the point of "begging for bread."[21]

Benjamin Frank Rea emphasized the paternalistic responsibility of the state to vulnerable dependents when seeking aid for families in crisis. Writing to Governor Patton in July of 1868, Rea, a physician in Lafayette, disclosed that he submitted requests for meat and corn on behalf of struggling families but that not enough came in their shipment. He argued that the citizens depended on provisions from the government and that any decrease in relief could mean possible starvation. "There are many who are entirely destitute of corn and meat and nothing to buy it with," he wrote. Based on his observations as a community doctor, he identified the widows as among the most vulnerable to destitution. He raised the idea that the governor held a fatherlike duty to those dependent on aid, writing that "many of them who have larger families of your children have worked in the field all the year with plow and hoe and some of them are at this time sick and unable to work." Rea likewise punctuated his argument by noting that many others tried to provide for themselves but with little success. "Others work in the fields for wages which do not give them enough for a full subsistence," he wrote, "and they tell me they or their children never have enough to eat and I never see anything in their houses more perhaps than a small piece of meat and a little meal. Yet they never lose a day out of the field when anyone else can work." He concluded that while the government offered some provisions, the relief "could not reach half the cases" and that the people of his community had become dependent on state aid.[22]

These concerns over distribution eventually became politicized, as questions of corruption and partisan favor arose within the commission to aid destitute families. In some instances, citizens accused distribution agents of providing more aid to areas in which former Confederates resided than to areas populated by Unionists. Yet, in planning for relief in its 1865 session, the General Assembly passed an act to plan out the process of distribution that ideally avoided such favoritism. The courts of county commissioners would "contract and pay" for the transporting of supplies by the US government to their respective counties "for the needy and indigent families." Essentially, the counties would be responsible for the hauling and transport of supplies coming from outside the South, rather than leaving it in the hands of the state. Still, problems with the commission emerged as early as 1866, in the program's infancy. The assistance ended in October of that year due to widespread corruption and abuse of power when it came to distribution. The number of impoverished citizens reached such a high level that President Johnson intervened and allowed Alabama to continue the relief program, granting $40,000 for corn and bacon for three more months. Cruikshank's office continued to function throughout 1867 and 1868 but still confronted accusations of unfair treatment. Perhaps political gain played more of a role in accusations of favoritism. Some evidence indicates that those requesting additional aid used the idea of currying voter favor to gain approval. The probate judge of Marengo County, for example, wrote to Governor Patton in June of 1868 asking for $200 in funds or provisions to supply "some indigent persons" in his county. He alluded to the potential for nurturing voter support if he approved the funds or supplies, noting that "you will confer a great favor on our county and some of its indigent suffering people." Politics undoubtedly played some role in the decisions of Governor Patton and the commission, but other issues factored into the difficulties in supplying aid to families.[23]

For instance, race figured into decisions of aid distribution. Cruikshank instructed his agents that all destitute citizens, including poor African Americans, would receive supplies. Yet, as historian Wayne Flynt posits, "he maintained an age-old American inclination to distinguish between the needy who were deemed worthy of help and those who were not." As state leaders confronted the transition from slave to free labor and the desire to return former enslaved men and women to the plantations, an inherit bias existed concerning who would be allowed to claim dependency on the government for aid. Those African American families who determined the course of freedom through pursuing education, adhering to traditional family roles, and dictating the terms of their labor found themselves at odds with the state. Namely, government leaders believed that freedmen and women's efforts to demonstrate agency precluded them from claiming dependency. As a result, Cruikshank and other officials supplied more provisions to common white than to African American families.[24]

Other causes of poor distribution arose more from issues of mere geography and funding than from partisan concerns. Some argued that those residing in the northern portion of the state, areas known for Unionist support, experienced the most problems with receiving aid. Yet an examination of state records indicates that these counties struggled due to logistical and financial problems with distribution due to their locale. Early in Cruikshank's tenure, he encountered issues in assessing the extent of the crisis and procuring enough supplies to aid families. In Cruikshank's March 7, 1866, report to Governor Patton, he revealed that his commission depended greatly on the efforts of probate judges and agents in the counties, rather than on his own staff, to determine the needs of the population. In fact, months into his role as commissioner, he wrote to Governor Patton that "there is a large portion of the state that your commissioner has not yet visited," blaming snowy weather hindering parts of his route. Agents working in the field attempted to inform Cruikshank of the demands of their respective counties, emphasizing that the "quantity of rations apportioned them is insufficient to meet the needs of the destitute." Not realizing the depth of impoverishment and the crisis-level situation pervading the state, Cruikshank appealed to the governor for increased aid. "There is no probability of being able to secure an increase of the supply for the state from the General Government," he reported and requested that the governor make up the shortfall from the state's own provisions.[25]

Foreshadowing the problems that became the bane of his efforts, Cruikshank identified the counties struggling the most and made them a priority. County agents in especially impoverished areas situated in the mountainous areas of northern Alabama and the Piney Woods region of the state lacked the funds to transport supplies into their isolated communities. In a warning to the governor, Cruikshank concluded that "destitution in the State . . . is rather increasing than diminishing and will probably continue to increase" throughout the spring of 1866. He offered a glimmer of hope with the pending wheat harvest in the summer but cautioned that the state needed to provide much more. It seemed, according to Cruikshank, that demands of common whites to ensure their families' survival would continue to determine the direction of Alabama's assistance program.[26]

Agents in the field indicated that, given the economic climate of postwar Alabama, the largest obstacle to distributing aid was transportation costs. Pike County commissioners, for example, wrote directly to Governor Patton requesting some monetary aid to transport supplies to their residents. They feared the governor knew little of the "alarming destitution and want in this county" and cited that "many women and children will starve unless relief can be had." They procured the supplies but lacked the money to move them out of Montgomery. Since the governor had the discretionary funds to offer supplemental aid, per the direction of the General Assembly, he allotted $125 to the commissioners specifically for transportation costs. The *Union Springs Times* raised the issue of distribution in an editorial published in 1866 entitled "Starvation in Alabama." Although the author singled out Marshall County as a place where "great destitution prevails," he also recognized that the same held true for many counties throughout the state. The reason, the author suggested, lay in their location in areas "remote from depots" and therefore "unable to obtain even a limited supply of rations each month." Raising alarm, the article concluded with a plea for clergy of the state to offer relief, citing critical delays in receiving supplies. Even in areas in the Black Belt region, such as Selma, an antebellum market town during the cotton boom, there appeared hindrances in distributing supplies. Complaints in those areas came primarily from a belief that the southern counties received greater aid than their communities. C. S. England, writing on behalf of Selma residents, for example, brought to the governor's attention the unevenness with which the government moved aid throughout the state. He claimed that "all the shipments that is made goes to South Ala," and an inadequate number to the citizens of Selma.[27]

Geographical obstacles due to Alabama's sometimes treacherous terrain played a key role in the slow movement of supplies. The mountainous regions of northern Alabama, coupled with their distance from major train depots where supplies arrived, made it costly and cumbersome to move provisions as needed. Louis Wyeth wrote to Governor Patton in April of 1866 that the situation in Marshall County had reached such a level of emergency that he had received word that three people "died near this place from starvation." He wrote that nearly three thousand people needed relief, in particular the many "starving women, children, and infirm men" unable to take care of themselves. Certainly historians concur that the amount of provisions distributed to the northern mountain region of the state in 1867 "seems to suggest that destitution was more long-lasting among mountain dwellers who were unable to grow crops or find employment than it was among residents of the Blackbelt plantation districts." Cruikshank confronted issues with distributing supplies, especially deep into counties isolated from the major transportation hubs in the state. And the demand to supply bulk items to those remote areas on a monthly basis made matters worse.[28]

Letters from residents within these isolated areas poured into the governor's office throughout the years of 1867 and 1868. Most of the correspondence reveals the difficulties in trying to transport supplies to destitute families. The cost to move supplies still hindered the state's program to offer aid. Those common whites who had trusted the state as their protector during the war now demanded that leaders deal with theses issues to save families. A letter from a Tuscumbia resident, for example, requested that the governor pay for the freight to transport corn the state purchased but had not used. Even in areas heavily populated by former wartime Unionists, citizens felt compelled to ask the state to move supplies swiftly. In a letter coming from Winston County, a well-known Unionist community, J. M. Warren played on the sympathies of the governor, perhaps in an effort to demonstrate the worthiness of helping the residents once considered "Tories" in Confederate Alabama. He wrote that the people of Winston lived in "destitute circumstances" and would be "grateful for the support." Warren portrayed those in need as doing all they could to "provide for the present and future." And that "with a little more help and the blessings of health . . . they will in the future be all safe."[29]

Other requests out of northern Alabama supported the idea that citizens felt they needed to prove they too belonged to the "deserving" poor. In a letter dated May 25, 1867, a citizen from Leighton in Colbert County, situated in the northwest corner of the state, wrote to Governor Patton that "numbers of good poor people are trying to make a crop on bread and short allowances." He noted that they needed corn that thus far had gone to neighboring Tuscumbia but not his community. The author asked what would render the white families in Leighton worthy of finally receiving aid. He concluded that the women and children all worked to support themselves and therefore relied on their own "industry" to make a crop, rather than sit idle and solely dependent on aid. Bringing the point of worthiness to its end, the author raised the issue of loyalty, noting that those in need came from the "widows whose sons died in the army." For these reasons, the author contended, the state should reward the families of Leighton that had done more than enough to justify receiving aid.[30]

When the efforts of the state fell short of aiding its citizens, local communities stepped into the void. For example, those who suffered from mental or physical scars of war that rendered them entirely dependent on the state seemed the most vulnerable. Those citizens had no choice but to enter one of the state's poorhouses. Alabama's leaders, however, avoided creating a widespread program to address the severely indigent and left the responsibility of constructing and maintaining poorhouses on the local level. For instance, in Mobile, with its larger population and greater demands for relief, wealthier citizens took on the philanthropic mission of helping the poor. The Sheltering Arms program began as an organization to help Mobile's destitute families. Their mission began solely as one to assist poor mothers who needed a place to take their children while they worked outside the home. Recognizing the demands of the city's poor, the Sheltering Arms women expanded the program under the direction of Mrs. Tarlton Woodhall. The directors, she reported, realized that they "found the mother herself seeking protection, when sick, destitute and unable to work" but also broadened their program to include destitute men as well. The female directors reasoned that their efforts provided protection to vulnerable women and men subject to exploitation in the larger city of Mobile. In her summary of the organization's purpose, Woodhall explained that "they found the lonely country girl exposed to the danger of the streets, unfortunate laboring man needing the grasp of a friendly hand to snatch him from the brink of destruction." As their work grew in scope, they called on the elites of the city to donate money. An 1868 open letter to the community from the directors proclaimed that as "an institution in this city that affords relief to destitute persons of all ages, classes and denominations," their work warranted financial sacrifices. They appealed to the familial ideals of providing support in soliciting aid from particularly the planters, asking them to "come forward" and donate "anything in the way of corn, meat, potatoes, cow feed, &e." Sheltering Arms was but one example of the many relief societies that peppered the state. And certainly government leaders recognized its vital role in relief on the local level.[31]

The government acknowledged the necessity of county relief to the point of pledging monetary support for these efforts. In his report to General Patton in early 1868, Cruikshank enthused that his office distributed $1,000 to various relief societies in the state. Government aid also filtered into the health care structures in the state. Cruikshank noted that while the state lacked the supplies by 1868 to continue support for the destitute, some federal aid remained in place to support the hospitals in operation. As the commission to aid destitute families wound down, the government ramped up its actions to secure other means of protecting the poor. The 1868 Alabama constitution, passed by the Republicans at the helm, granted the state government the power to offer support to counties for the "maintenance of the poor." Government efforts to keep up such aid fell short, as they lacked a procedural plan for implementing assistance. As a result, the main focus of their policy was on establishing homes for the poor. These poorhouses or almshouses, either directed by a superintendent or serviced out to a private individual, did little to alleviate poverty in the counties. As historian Wayne Flynt notes, the county systems put in place "led to corruption and wretched care of indigents, especially as facilities became antiquated and supervision lax." One resident of Gadsden noted that a large amount of funding went toward maintaining the poorhouse in the town. He quipped that "the number of paupers in the poor house of our county is either large or the keeper receives a good salary." Within the span of a few months, nearly $600 went toward the "maintenance of the poor of the county," which came under some suspicion upon accusations that the director of the facility embezzled funds.[32]

Common whites returned from the war hoping to rebuild from the physical and emotional devastations wrought by war. While they sought to resume life as normal, they confronted a postwar Alabama that would once again force them to endure great hardships. Failed crops that brought many near to starvation fueled a sense of crisis that the state, as the caretaker of the people, would have to address. In the years following the conflict, state leaders in coordination with county agents initiated a full-scale program for aid. That program, while launched by the state, emerged from the needs of the common whites. They in essence demanded that their leaders address their conditions, thus occupying a portion of the postwar political agenda in Alabama. Yet by the 1870s state leaders turned their energies away from a relief program to seek other means of recouping the economic health of Alabama. The dual hope of a reformed agricultural landscape and industrial development occupied the attention of government officials, who viewed such efforts as the best way to help bring about change. As the state moved into another decade, it also became clear that the changing tide of partisan politics would overshadow the demands for widespread public assistance. Former Confederates launched a campaign to wrest control of the state from Republican leadership that turned attention away from the demands of common whites. Efforts to limit the civil rights gained by African Americans in the state and reestablish white supremacy eclipsed any other agenda that could improve the conditions of its struggling citizens. By the end of Reconstruction, common whites found a new political, social, and economic landscape in Alabama that would send them on a path to redefining their place in and relationship to the state.

Conclusion

As Alabama moved into a new century, its common whites looked to the future with measured optimism. Family remained the central focus moving forward in their efforts to rebuild their lives. The roles and relationships within the household offered a return to the normalcy that they craved in the postwar period. And they continued to see the state as a significant resource in ensuring the sanctity and protection of their families. Yet the resumption of Democratic rule and white supremacy throughout the South after the end of Reconstruction meant that common whites faded, at least in part, from the agenda of state leaders. With the resumption of one-party Democratic rule and the passage of a new state constitution in 1901, Alabama leaders rolled back many advancements made by the previous Republican legislature. In particular, they limited state and local governments from financing internal improvements as well as reduced funding for education and eliminated the board of education, all investments from which common whites would have benefited. The new constitution all but solidified their fate in the state. A series of suffrage requirements aimed to counter the Fifteenth Amendment, which expanded the franchise to African American men, came at a cost to common whites. The passage of several voting restrictions, such as the poll tax, signaled a willingness of state leaders to sacrifice the voices of common whites, especially those living at or below the poverty line. Out of the 232,821 whites able to participate in the 1900 elections, only 191,492 qualified to vote in 1903. However, as historian Glenn Feldman contends, rather than join with African Americans to protest disfranchisement through a shared socioeconomic identity, common whites united with their elite counterparts along racial lines, all in the name of white supremacy.[1]

Despite these limitations to their political agency, common whites found new opportunities to redefine themselves in the twentieth century. A transition from subsistence to commercial farming expanded the agricultural interests in the state, and the influx of new industries brought much-needed alternatives to farming. The extension of mining interests along with the steel and iron industries likewise diversified labor opportunities. Farming did remain a stalwart of the common whites' economic support, and tenant farming and sharecropping allowed them to continue working the land even when they did not own it. This economic landscape sometimes failed to produce the financial uplift they desired, as farmers and laborers confronted wage discrimination, unfair credit systems, and soaring debt. Common whites, however, found the voice of advocacy through the Populist Party and Progressive Era movements that swept through the region. Their messages of empowerment encouraged common whites and their political allies to demand that state leaders address their concerns over a broad range of issues from employment to education, to housing and health care, all in the name of protecting and empowering their families in the New South.[2]

Common whites found a source of power motivated by the private world of family. From their earliest presence in the state, they laid claim to the same notions of honor and familial responsibility typically associated with the elite population. The frontier conditions of early Alabama coupled with the racial hierarchy resulting from slavery helped to mute class differences in a way that gave common whites a sense of equality. In such an atmosphere, they claimed the same rights to defend their reputation, which became evident in Alabama's courts. More significantly, their willingness to stand publicly in defense of their reputation shaped localized laws in ways that empowered common whites. As the events of secession and war disrupted their daily existence, family provided a way for them to navigate the changes that lay ahead. Common whites who supported the Confederacy understood its mission in terms of protecting their liberty from the threat posed by a Republican government and its abolitionist allies. And their families, first and foremost, served as the primary reason to defend against those threats. Going into the war, common whites envisioned the larger Confederacy in terms of a family, and state leadership as a figurative head of family charged with taking care of its people in exchange for their loyalty. As a result, they came to see their relationship with the state as reciprocal. So long as the war imposed limited challenges to family life, common whites would continue to remain in harmony with the elites who drove the Confederate mission. They saw their sacrifices as necessary and manageable until the reality of a protracted conflict came into focus.

By 1863 the narrative of going to war in defense of family seemed to ring hollow to common whites, who began to see the conflict as a threat to homes and loved ones. They grew critical of the war, yet not to the point of abandoning the cause altogether. Rather, for common whites, their wartime experience transformed the nature of their relationship to Alabama's government, as they grew increasingly dissatisfied with those who benefited the most from defending slavery. Their frustrations fueled tensions between the common white majority and the planter minority, especially as wartime conditions endangered families. Hardships in the military camps as well as rising prices and declining resources at home began to take a toll on common whites' relationship to the state. One needed merely to look across the home-front population to see the number of elites who invoked exemption clauses, a luxury few common whites could claim.

The efforts of politicians to address the dire straits common whites faced seemed to fall short of meeting the basic needs of individuals on the home and battle fronts. Material items such as food, cloth, and salt grew scarce, and inflation ravaged the state's economy, making it hard to purchase such necessities. Little assistance coupled with the continued call to sacrifice both their material goods and their family members led common whites to begin to see the war as an unnecessary threat. Focusing once again on the notions of gendered duty within the family, men and women waged personal and public protests that ultimately shaped the political agenda, especially within the state. Widespread desertion from the military, resistance to military policies on the home front, and even public demonstrations of protest revealed the lengths to which common whites sought to empower themselves. Gone was the willingness to work together for a common cause; rather, the class tensions muted in the antebellum era came to a head during the war. And common whites found themselves at odds with the state that had once sworn to protect their families.

The agency of common whites continued into the years immediately following Confederate surrender. Most everyone desired to return to some semblance of their prewar lives. They searched for ways to rebuild from the destruction of Alabama's physical landscape and to heal the emotional wounds left by the death of loved ones. Unfortunately, they faced yet another crisis after the war that stemmed from continued food shortages, civil unrest, and growing poverty. Returning to life as usual therefore moved slowly for common whites, who confronted serious economic obstacles. They once again called on the symbolism of family to demand their leaders protect their loved ones from this growing postwar crisis. Common whites returned to a familiar narrative of paternalistic duty in pressuring the state for aid. Their petitions and letters showed that they viewed government officials as having a responsibility to their people and called on them to serve their dependents. As a result, common whites created a space for themselves in the postwar political agenda by challenging government leaders to come to their rescue. Up until the 1870s, Alabama's leadership passed policies addressing the economic and material crisis facing the state. Yet their approach offered merely a temporary solution, as state leaders failed to address the root problems of poverty in the state while refocusing their agenda. They put more energy into encouraging investment in the state's industrial development and commercial farming interests by the 1870s. In addition, the Democratic campaign to oust the Republican government, curtail African American civil rights, and resurrect white supremacy deflected attention away from any efforts to address the circumstances of common white families.

Despite the limitations of their socioeconomic class, common whites created a space for themselves in nineteenth-century Alabama. Although not always promising to ensure upward mobility or economic security, the masculine and feminine identities situated within the family allowed common whites to stand equally with their elite counterparts. They claimed the same dignity and honor as a man or woman that shaped elite culture while creating a sense of self unique to their socioeconomic class. Their fierce protection of familial reputation and liberty provided a source of power in the antebellum period and gave them cause to enter the ranks of Confederates without much reservation. This same devotion to family likewise provided reason to find fault with their government leaders and ultimately redefine their relationship to the state. With the failure of their fathers to care for their charges, common whites raised their voices all in the name of family.

Notes

INTRODUCTION

1. 1860 Population Schedule U.S. Bureau of the Census, Manuscript Census Schedules, Eighth (1860) Census; James P. Garrison to Harriet E. Garrison, May 22, June 11, 1862, May 18, May 9, 1863, James P. Garrison Confederate Letters 1862–63, Stuart A. Rose Manuscript, Archive, Rare Book Library (hereafter MARBL), Emory University, Atlanta, Georgia. I have chosen to retain misspellings and grammatical errors in the unedited primary sources, as it helps illuminate the distinctiveness of common whites from the elite counterparts and aids in telling their story from their vantage point.

2. May 18, 9, 1863, James P. Garrison Confederate Letters 1862–63.

3. Frank Lawrence Owsley, *Plain Folk of the Old South* (Baton Rouge: Louisiana State University Press, 1949); Samuel C. Hyde, ed., *Plain Folk of the South Revisited* (Baton Rouge: Louisiana State University Press, 1997), viii, x; Carl R. Osthaus, "The Work Ethic of the Plain Folk: Labor and Religion in the Old South," *Journal of Southern History* 70 (November 2004), 747, 752; William Harris, *Plain Folk and Gentry in a Slave Society: White Liberty and Black Slavery in Augusta's Hinterlands* (Middletown, CT: Wesleyan University Press, 1985); Bruce Collins, *White Society in the Antebellum South* (New York: Longman, 1985).

4. Charles C. Bolton, *Poor Whites of the Antebellum South: Tenants and Laborers in Central North Carolina and Northeast Mississippi* (Durham: Duke University Press, 1994); Bolton and Scott P. Culclasure, *The Confessions of Edward Isham: A Poor White Life of the Old South* (Athens: University of Georgia Press, 1998); Jeff Forret, *Race Relations at the Margins: Slaves and Poor Whites in the Antebellum Southern Countryside* (Baton Rouge: Louisiana State University Press, 2006); Keri Leigh Merritt, *Masterless Men: Poor Whites and Slavery in the Antebellum South* (Cambridge: Cambridge University Press, 2017).

5. Bill Cecil-Fronsman, *Common Whites: Class and Culture in Antebellum North Carolina* (Lexington: University Press of Kentucky, 1992), 1, 3.

6. Understanding a soldier's resiliency to remain in the fight starts with the more general studies from James M. McPherson, *For Cause and Comrades: Why Men Fought in the Civil War* (New York: Oxford University Press, 1997); and Joseph Allen Frank, *With Ballot and Bayonet: The Political Socialization of American Civil War Soldiers* (Athens: University of Georgia Press, 1998). Other historians look more specifically at how Confederate soldiers remained devoted to the fight despite mounting social divisions and dissent that threatened to undermine the war effort. Those studies include Gary Gallagher, *The Confederate War: How Popular Will, Nationalism, and Military Strategy Could Not Stave Off Defeat* (Cambridge: Harvard University Press, 1997); Wiley Sword, *Southern Invincibility: A History of the Confederate Heart* (New York: St. Martin's Press, 1999); Aaron Shehan-Dean, *Why Confederates Fought: Family and Nation in Civil War Virginia* (Chapel Hill: University of North Carolina Press, 2007); and Jason Phillips, *Diehard Rebels: The Confederate Culture of Invincibility* (Athens: University of Georgia Press, 2007).

7. More recent studies of common whites in the Civil War have started to move the discussion toward the centrality of family. See Bolton, *Poor Whites of the Antebellum South*; and

Stephanie McCurry, *Masters of Small Worlds: Yeomen Households, Gender Relations, and the Political Culture of the Antebellum South Carolina Low Country* (New York: Oxford University Press, 1995). Studies relating to the Civil War era tend to focus on reasons why they fought and sources of dissent as wartime conditions worsened. Such studies include Mark V. Wetherington's *Plain Folk's Fight: The Civil War and Reconstruction in Piney Woods Georgia* (Chapel Hill: University of North Carolina Press, 2005); and David Williams, Teresa Crisp Williams, and David Carlson, *Plain Folk in a Rich Man's War: Class and Dissent in Confederate Georgia* (Gainesville: University Press of Florida, 2002).

8. Malcolm McMillan, *The Disintegration of a Confederate State: Three Governors and Alabama's Wartime Home Front, 1861–1865* (Macon, GA: Mercer University Press, 1986); Christopher Lyle McIlwain, *Civil War Alabama* (Tuscaloosa: University of Alabama Press, 2016); Wayne Flynt, *Poor but Proud: Alabama's Poor Whites* (Tuscaloosa: University of Alabama Press, 1989); Bessie Martin, *A Rich Man's War, a Poor Man's Fight: Desertion of Alabama Troops from the Confederate Army* (Tuscaloosa: University of Alabama Press, 2003); Tommy Craig Brown, *Deep in the Piney Woods: Southeastern Alabama from Statehood to the Civil War, 1800–1865* (Tuscaloosa: University of Alabama Press, 2018); Margaret M. Storey, *Loyalty and Loss: Alabama's Unionists in the Civil War and Reconstruction* (Baton Rouge: Louisiana State University Press, 2004).

9. Thomas Perkins Abernathy, *The Formative Period in Alabama, 1815–1828* (Tuscaloosa: University of Alabama Press, 1965), 170, 178; William Rogers, Robert David Ward, Leah Rawls Atkins, and Wayne Flynt, *Alabama: The History of a Deep South State* (Tuscaloosa: University of Alabama Press, 1994), 113.

10. Flynt, *Poor but Proud*, 12, 15–16, 27–28; Harry P. Owens and James J. Cooke, eds., *The Old South in the Crucible of War* (Jackson: University Press of Mississippi, 1983), 21–22.

11. Abernathy, *Formative Period in Alabama*, 178; Rogers et al., *Alabama*, 150–60.

12. Abernathy, *Formative Period in Alabama*, 178; Rogers et al., *Alabama*, 150–60.

13. John C. Inscoe and Robert C. Kenzer, eds., *Enemies of the Country: New Perspectives on Unionists in the Civil War South* (Athens: University of Georgia Press, 2001); Storey, *Loyalty and Loss*, 1–17, 21, 56–86.

14. Merritt, *Masterless Men*, 143–78; Owens and Cooke, *Old South in the Crucible of War*, 22.

15. Anna M. Gayle Fry, *Memories of Old Cahaba* (Publishing House of the M. E. Church, South, 1908); W. G. Robertson, *Recollections of the Early Settlers of Montgomery County and Their Families* (Montgomery: Excelsior Print, 1892); Owens and Cooke, *Old South in the Crucible of War*, 224–25; Merritt, *Masterless Men*.

16. Stephen W. Berry II, *All That Makes a Man: Love and Ambition in the Civil War South* (New York: Oxford University Press, 2003); Stephanie McCurry, *Confederate Reckoning: Power and Politics in the Civil War South* (Cambridge: Harvard University Press, 2010), 17–18, 25. My efforts to piece together the connection between war and masculinity began with Bell Irvine Wiley, *The Life of Johnny Reb: The Common Soldier of the Confederacy* (Indianapolis: Bobbs-Merrill, 1943); Reid Mitchell, *Civil War Soldiers* (New York: Viking Press, 1988); Shehan-Dean, *Why Confederates Fought*; James J. Broomall, *Private Confederacies: The Emotional Worlds of Southern Men as Citizens and Soldiers* (Chapel Hill: University of North Carolina Press, 2019). I likewise turn to the long list of secondary studies to uncover the origins and manifestations of white women's support for the Confederacy: George Rable, *Civil Wars: Women and the Crisis of Southern Nationalism* (Urbana: University of Illinois Press, 1989); LeeAnn Whites, *Civil War as a Crisis in Gender: Augusta, Georgia, 1860–1890* (Athens: University of Georgia Press, 1995); Drew Gilpin Faust, *Mothers of Invention: Women of the Slaveholding South* (Chapel Hill: University of North Carolina Press, 1996); LeeAnn Whites and Alecia P. Long, *Occupied Women: Gender, Military Occupation, and the American Civil War* (Baton Rouge: Louisiana State University

Press, 2009); Lisa Tendrich Frank and LeeAnn Whites, eds. *Household at War: How Americans Lived and Fought the Civil War* (Athens: University of Georgia Press, 2020); Thomas F. Curran, *Women Making War: Female Confederate Prisoners and Union Military Justice* (Carbondale: Southern Illinois University Press, 2020).

17. McCurry, *Confederate Reckoning*, 4, 134, 136–37; Owens and Cooke, *Old South in the Crucible of War*, 24–25; Brown, *Deep in the Piney Woods*, 138–66.

Chapter 1

1. Walter Brownlow Posey, ed., "Alabama in the 1830s: As Recorded by British Travellers," *Birmingham-Southern College Bulletin* 31, no. 4 (December 1938): 11–12.

2. Thomas Perkins Abernathy, *Formative Period in Alabama, 1815–1828*, 170, 178; Rogers et al., *Alabama*, 113.

3. Rogers et al., *Alabama*, xxi, 6–8.

4. Rogers et al., *Alabama*, 54–55, 57, 58–59; Harvey H. Jackson, "Time, Frontier, and the Alabama Black Belt: Searching for W. J. Cash's Planter," *Alabama Review* 44, no. 4 (October 1991), 248.

5. Rogers et al., *Alabama*, 69; Flynt, *Poor but Proud*, ix; Abernathy, *Formative Period in Alabama*, 162.

6. Flynt, *Poor but Proud*, 6–7.

7. Flynt, *Poor but Proud*, 7–9.

8. Harvey H. Jackson Jr. and Harvey H. Jackson III, eds., "Moving to Alabama: The Joel Spigener-William Oliver Letters, 1833–1834," *Alabama Review* 48, no. 1 (January 1995): 18–23, 26; Flynt, *Poor but Proud*, 13–14.

9. Abernathy, *Formative Period in Alabama*, 163; Posey, "Alabama in the 1830s," 8, 33.

10. Jackson, "Time, Frontier, and the Alabama Black Belt," 254–58; Frederick Law Olmsted, *The Cotton Kingdom: A Traveller's Observations on Cotton and Slavery in the American Slave States* (New York: Mason Brothers, 1861), 100–101; Posey, "Alabama in the 1830s," 27.

11. Jackson, "Time, Frontier, and the Alabama Black Belt," 249–51; George Evans Brewer, *History of Coosa County, Alabama* (Greenville, SC: Southern Historical Press, 1996), 128–29.

12. Eugene Schwaab, ed., *Travels in the Old South: Selected Periodicals of the Times*, vol. 1 (Lexington: University Press of Kentucky, 1973), 198, 201; Olmsted, *Cotton Kingdom*, 101; Posey, "Alabama in the 1830s," 7; Brewer, *History of Coosa County*, 128, 163.

13. Owsley, *Plain Folk of the Old South*; Eugene Genovese, *Roll, Jordan, Roll: The World the Slaves Made* (New York: Vintage Books, 1976); Bill Cecil-Fronsman, *Common Whites*, 5–6.

14. Owens and Cooke, *Old South in the Crucible of War*, 22; Brown, *Deep in the Piney Woods*, 38, 45–46.

15. Merritt, *Masterless Men*, 4, 6, 179–215.

16. Abernathy, *Formative Period in Alabama*, 164.

17. Flynt, *Poor but Proud*, 12–15; Abernathy, *Formative Period in Alabama*, 164; Mary Neeley, "Painful Circumstances: Glimpses of the Alabama Penitentiary" *Alabama Review* 44, no. 1 (January 1991): 3–7; Petition on behalf of Joseph Turnbull, Jackson County, Petition on behalf of Langley and Gilbert, Mobile County, Pardons, Paroles, and Clemency Files, Alabama Governor, 1821–1825, Alabama Department of Archives and History (hereafter ADAH), Montgomery, Alabama.

18. Bertram Wyatt-Brown, *Honor and Violence in the Old South* (New York: Oxford University Press, 1986); Merritt, *Masterless Men*, 141, 142.

19. Scott Culclasure argues that the petition of inmates for parole, pardon, or clemency depended, in part, on the support of their community. Successful petitions to the

government on behalf of condemned men tended to vilify the victim and revered the character of the prisoner. Charles C. Bolton and Scott P. Culclasure, eds., *Confessions of Edward Isham*, 71–84; Petition on behalf of [illegible first name] Hammonds, Clarke County, Petition on behalf of Thomas Adams, Lauderdale County, Petition on behalf of Daniel West, Tuscaloosa County, Pardons, Paroles, and Clemency Files, Alabama Governor, 1821–1825, ADAH.

20. Petition on behalf of James [no last name in the record], Lawrence County, Pardons, Paroles, and Clemency Files, Alabama Governor, 1821–1825, ADAH.

21. Jackson and Jackson, "Moving to Alabama," 29–30, 26–29; February 4, 1860, Margaret Josephine Miles Gillis Diary, SPR 5, ADAH.

22. May 2, July 13, 1860, Sarah Rousseau Espy Diary, SPR 2, ADAH.

23. Osthaus, "Work Ethic of the Plain Folk:," 747; Kenneth Johnson, "White Married Women in Antebellum Alabama," *Alabama Review* 43, no. 1 (January 1990): 13–17.

24. Brewer, *History of Coosa County, Alabama*, 129–30, 135.

25. Abernathy, *Formative Period in Alabama*, 162–63.

26. Schwaab, *Travels in the Old South*, 200–201; Margaret Pace Farmer, "The Plain Folk of Old Pike County," *Alabama Review* 33, no. 2 (April 1980), 90; Jackson and Jackson, "Moving to Alabama," 29–30.

27. Craig Thompson Friend and Anya Jabour, eds., *Family Values in the Old South* (Gainesville: University Press of Florida, 2010), 1–8.

28. Laura F. Edwards, *The People and Their Peace: Legal Culture and the Transformation of Inequality in the Post-revolutionary South* (Chapel Hill: University of North Carolina Press, 2009), 3–4, 171; Loren Schweninger, *Families in Crisis in the Old South: Divorce, Slavery, and the Law* (Chapel Hill: University of North Carolina Press, 2012), 18–20, 47–52.

29. Allison Dorothy Fredette, *Marriage on the Border: Love, Mutuality, and Divorce in the Upper South during the Civil War* (Lexington: University Press of Kentucky, 2020), 5, 57.

30. Edwards, *People and Their Peace*, 169.

31. *Egbert Crossman vs. Nancy Crossman*, Minutes, 1848–1868, Chancery Court, Wilcox County, ADAH.

32. *Egbert Crossman vs. Nancy Crossman*, Minutes, 1848–1868, Chancery Court, Wilcox County, ADAH.

33. *Malcome A. McKinnon vs. Sarah M. McKinnon*, Bill of Divorce, Final Record, Chancery Court, Talladega County, LG 4701, ADAH.

34. Bolton and Culclasure, *Confessions of Edward Isham*, 9.

35. *Campbell Jefferson vs. Lydia Margaret Jefferson*, Bill of Divorce, Talladega County, LG 4701, ADAH; *James Franklin vs. Nancy E. Franklin*, Bill of Divorce, Talladega County, LG 4701, ADAH.

36. *James W. Johnson vs. Mary Ann Eliza Johnson*, Final Record, Chancery Court, Russell County, LG 005238, ADAH.

37. *James Clark vs. Nancy Clark*, Chancery Court, Perry County, LGM 249, ADAH.

38. *Byrd B. Forsyth vs. Mary A. Forsyth*, Final Record, Chancery Court, Russell County, LG005238, ADAH.

39. *Robert M. Gibson vs. Elizabeth Gibson*, Final Record, Chancery Court, Russell County, LG 005238, ADAH; US Bureau of the Census, Manuscript Census Schedules, Seventh (1850).

40. *Robert M. Gibson vs. Elizabeth Gibson*, Final Record, Chancery Court, Russell County, LG 005238, ADAH; U.S. Bureau of the Census, Manuscript Census Schedules, Seventh (1850).

41. *David White vs. Jemimah White*, Bill of Divorce, Wilcox County, LG 4012–4069, ADAH.

42. Edwards, *People and Their Peace*, 171–72.

43. Schweninger, *Families in Crisis in the Old South*, 15; *Ann M. Brown vs. Morgan G. Brown*, Bill of Divorce, Wilcox County, LG 4012–4069, ADAH. Several historians examine the issue of domestic abuse and the limits of patriarchal power as recognized by southern courts. For example, see Bertram Wyatt-Brown, *Southern Honor: Ethics and Behavior in the Old South* (New York: Oxford University Press, 1983); and Laura F. Edwards, "Law, Domestic Violence, and the Limits of Patriarchal Authority in the Antebellum South," *Journal of Southern History* 65, no. 4 (1999): 733–70.

44. *Ann M. Brown vs. Morgan G. Brown*, Bill of Divorce, Wilcox County, LG 4012–4069, ADAH.

45. Schweninger, *Families in Crisis in the Old South*, 48; *Mary A. Collier vs. Augustus Collier*, Chancery Court, Perry County, LGM 249, ADAH.

46. *Mahala (Chandler) Mansell vs. John Mansell*, Chancery Court, Bibb County, LG004698, ADAH.

47. *Mahala (Chandler) Mansell vs. John Mansell*, Chancery Court, Bibb County, LG004698, ADAH.

48. *Zelpha Reach vs. Jeremiah Reach*, Minutes 1843–1853, Chancery Court, Bibb County, LG004698, ADAH.

49. *Zelpha Reach vs. Jeremiah Reach*, Minutes 1843–1853, Chancery Court, Bibb County, LG004698, ADAH.

50. Schweninger, *Families in Crisis in the Old South*, 47–52; Bolton and Culclasure, eds., *Confessions of Edward Isham*, 39–41; *Spencer Johnson vs. Huldah Johnson*, Minutes 1843–1853, Chancery Court, Bibb County, LG004698, ADAH.

51. *Amanda Dortch vs. James Dortch* and *Zelpha Reach vs. Jeremiah Reach*, Minutes 1843–1853, Chancery Court, Bibb County, LG004698, ADAH.

52. *Margaret Jane Dye by Henry Click vs. Weldon Dye*, Final Record, Chancery Court, Talladega County, LG4701, ADAH.

53. *Margaret Jane Dye by Henry Click vs. Weldon Dye*, Final Record, Chancery Court Talladega County, LG4701, ADAH.

54. *Margaret Jane Dye by Henry Click vs. Weldon Dye*, Final Record, Chancery Court, Talladega County, LG4701, ADAH.

55. *Margaret Jane Dye by Henry Click vs. Weldon Dye*, Final Record, Chancery Court, Talladega County, LG4701, ADAH.

56. Edwards, *People and Their Peace*, 173; *Antonello A. Green vs. James A. Green*, Minutes, 1848–1868, Chancery Court, Wilcox County, ADAH; *Elizabeth Holloway vs. Washington Holloway*, Chancery Court, Perry County, ADAH; *Eliza Osborne vs. Francis Osborne*, Final Record, LG 005238, Chancery Court, Russell County, ADAH.

57. *Guilford Olive vs. Isabella Olive*, Final Record, LG 005238, Chancery Court, Russell County, ADAH; *Eiva Jenkins vs. Edwin Jenkins*, Minutes, 1848–1868, Chancery Court, Wilcox County, ADAH.

CHAPTER 2

1. Thomas Cutrer, ed., *Oh, What a Loansome Time I Had: The Civil War Letters of Major William Morel Moxley, Eighteenth Alabama Infantry and Emily Beck Moxley* (Tuscaloosa: University of Alabama Press, 2002), 1–6, 22.

2. Cutrer, *Oh, What a Loansome Time I Had*, 25, 41–42, 72.

3. May 2, July 2–6, and July 13, 1860, Sarah Rousseau Espy Diary.

4. U.S. Bureau of the Census, Manuscript Census Schedules, Eighth (1860) Census; U.S. Bureau of the Census, Slave Schedule (1860); April 28, October 14, and December 3, 1860, February 4, 1861, Zillah Haynie Brandon Diaries, SPR262, ADAH.

5. Alto Loftin Jackson, ed., *So Mourns the Dove: Letters of a Confederate Infantryman and His Family* (New York: Exposition Press, 1965), 13–14, 16, 17.

6. August 11 and September 4, 1860, Sarah Rousseau Espy Diary; August 21, 1861, Zillah Haynie Brandon Diaries.

7. Jackson, *So Mourns the Dove*, 15, 34; Lucille Griffith, ed., *Yours Till Death: Civil War Letters of John W. Cotton* (Tuscaloosa: University of Alabama Press, 1951) 3–4; William McCullough to Martha McCullough, February 17, 1862, McCullough Family Letters, SPR 198, ADAH.

8. Michael Holmes to Ned Holmes, September 7, 1861, Michael Holmes Civil War Letter, SPR 664, ADAH.

9. W. Cooper to Jmo. H. Harris, Esq., May 10, 1861, Civil War and Reconstruction Files, SG011139, folder 003, ADAH; Proclamation by Governor Gill Shorter, May 12, 1862, Civil War and Reconstruction Files, SG011138, folder 009, ADAH; *Montgomery Weekly Mail*, July 11, 1862, Civil War and Reconstruction Files, SG01119, folder 003, ADAH.

10. Wiley, *Life of Johnny Reb*; Mitchell, *Civil War Soldiers*; McPherson, *For Cause and Comrades*, 22–29; Aaron Sheehan-Dean, *Why Confederates Fought: Family and Nation in Civil War Virginia* (Chapel Hill: University of North Carolina Press, 2007); James Zachariah Branscomb to Lucinda Branscomb Hunter, January 24, 1861, Branscomb Family Letters, LPR195, ADAH.

11. James Zachariah Branscomb to Louis Branscomb, February 27, 1862; James Zachariah Branscomb to Lucinda Branscomb Hunter, January 11, 1863, January 22, 1864; James Zachariah Branscomb to Louis Branscomb, February 27, 1862; James Zachariah Branscomb to Lucinda Branscomb Hunter, July 27, 1861, all in Branscomb Family Letters, ADAH; Cutrer, *Oh, What a Loansome Time I Had*, 26.

12. D. D. Bonner to Mary Loftis, October 16, 1862, Mary Allin Loftis Letters, LPR 184, ADAH; John Davenport to Mary Jane Davenport, August 20, December 22, 1862, John F. Davenport Civil War Letters, SPR 426, ADAH.

13. August 21, 1861, Zillah Haynie Brandon Diaries; Elizabeth Danielly to Frances Danielly, n.d., circa 1862, Pearson and Danielly Family Papers.

14. Griffith, *Yours till Death*, 14, 4; Frances Danielly to Elizabeth Danielly, November 8, 1861, Pearson and Danielly Family Papers, SPR 842, ADAH.

15. Frances Danielly to Elizabeth Danielly, December 25, 1862, Pearson Danielly Family Papers; Ann K. Blomquist and Robert A. Taylor, eds., *This Cruel War: The Civil War Letters of Grant and Malinda Taylor, 1862–1865* (Macon, GA: Mercer University Press, 2000), 106; Robert Williams to Mittie Williams, July 2, 1864, Robert Williams Civil War Letters, SPR 109, ADAH.

16. Henry Bray to Marian Davis, February 19, November 4, Henry Bray Civil War Letters, Box 26, range A, section 1, ADAH.

17. Henry Bray to Devotion P. Bray, May 17, July 3, 1862, Henry Bray Civil War Letters.

18. March 19, 1860, Sarah Rousseau Espy Diary; August 21, 1861, Zillah Haynie Brandon Diaries; Jackson, *So Mourns the Dove*, 19, 17–18.

19. LeeAnn Whites, "Written on the Heart: Soldiers' Letters, the Household Supply Line and Relational War," in *Household War: How Americans Lived and Fought the Civil War*, ed. Lisa Tendrich and LeeAnn Whites, 118–133 (Athens: University of Georgia Press, 2020), 119.

20. Paula Baker, "Domestication of Politics: Women and American Political Society" *American Historical Review* 89 (June 1984): 620–47; Cynthia Kierner, *Beyond the Household: Women's Place in the Early South, 1700–1835* (Ithaca: Cornell University Press, 1998), 2; Faust, *Mothers of Invention*, 5–7; Catherine Clinton, *The Other Civil War: American Women in the Nineteenth Century* (New York: Hill and Wang, 1984), 81–82.

21. Flynt, *Poor but Proud*, 198; September 27, 1861, Sarah Rousseau Espy Diary; James Zachariah Branscomb to Lucinda Branscomb Hunter, August 24, 1861, Branscomb Family Letters; May 5, 1861, Margaret Josephine Miles Gillis Diary; D. D. Bonner to Mary Loftis, January 22, 1863, Mary Allin Loftis Letters.

22. Whites, "Written on the Heart," 121; James Jackson to Jinnie Jackson, July 10, 1861, James W. Jackson Letters, SPR 51, ADAH; US Bureau of the Census, Manuscript Census Schedules, Eight (1860) Census; William Riley Jones to Mary Frances Jones, August 14, 1862, William Riley Jones Papers, SPR 721, ADAH; Frances Danielly to Elizabeth Danielly, September 29, 1861, Pearson and Danielly Family Papers; Joseph Wesson to Rachel, January 20, 1863, Joseph E. Wesson Civil War Letters, SPR 1044, ADAH; Jackson, *So Mourns the Dove*, 45.

23. Thomas Owen to Reuben Owen, September 2, 1862, Thomas Owen Civil War Letter, SPR 14, ADAH; Blomquist and Taylor, eds., *This Cruel War*, 20, 19; Wayne Wood and Mary Virginia Jackson, eds., *Kiss Sweet Little Lillah for Me: Civil War Letters of William Thomas Jackson* (Birmingham: Ebsco Media, 2000), 7, 9, 28.

24. Cornelius Wright to Willis and Susan Wright, November 27, 1861, Cornelius Wright Letter, SPR 941, ADAH; Griffith, *Yours till Death*, 3; Henry Bray to Marian Davis Bray, February 19, 1862, Henry Bray Civil War Letters; Cornelius Wright to Willis and Susan Wright, November 27, 1861, Cornelius Wright Letter; W. V. Fleming to Margaret Fleming, W. V. Fleming Civil War Letters, SPR 509, ADAH.

25. Jackson, *So Mourns the Dove*, 17, 25, 27.

26. Frances Danielly to Elizabeth Danielly, September 29, October 11, 1861, Pearson and Danielly Family Papers; D. G. Holcombe to Martha McCullough, November 19, 1861, McCullough Family Letters; Thomas Owen to Reuben Owen, September 2, n.d., Thomas R. Owen Civil War Letter; H. S. Strom to Mary Loftis, January 21, 1862, Mary Allin Loftis Letters.

27. D. G. Holcombe to Martha McCullough, November 19, 1861, McCullough Family Letters; D. D. Bonner to Mary Loftis, October 1, 1862, James W. Moore to Mary Loftis, July 28, 1862, Mary Allin Loftis Letters; Jackson, *So Mourns the Dove*, 30, 61; Blomquist and Taylor, eds., *This Cruel War*, 64.

28. Frances Danielly to Elizabeth Danielly, October 11, November 8, 1861, Pearson and Danielly Family Papers; Thomas Smyrl to Mary Jane Smyrl, July 29, 1863, Thomas Smyrl Civil War Letters, SPR 382, ADAH; Griffith, *Yours till Death*, 11; Henry Bray to Marian Davis, July 3, 1862, Henry Bray Civil War Letters; William Riley Jones to Fannie Jones, September 5, 6, 1862, William Riley Jones Papers; Leonard Land to Darling and Eliza Land, November 12, 1862, Leonard Land Letters, SPR 867, ADAH.

29. Henry Bray to Marian Davis, July 3, 1862, Henry Bray Civil War Letters; Wood and Jackson, eds., *Kiss Sweet Little Lillah*, 8, 9; Kinnon Lee to Mary Lee, August 23, 1862, Kinnon Lee Civil War Letters, SPR 568, ADAH; Frances Danielly to Elizabeth Danielly, January 4, 1863, Pearson and Danielly Family Papers.

30. Kinnon Lee to Mary Lee, August 5, 1863, Kinnon Lee Civil War Letters; John F. Davenport to Mary Jane Davenport, September 1, December 22, 1862, John F. Davenport Civil War Letters; Thomas Smyrl to Mary Jane Smyrl, September 15, December 1, 1862,

Thomas Smyrl Civil War Letters; William McCullough to Martha McCullough, February 17, 1862, McCullough Family Letters.

31. Wood and Jackson, eds., *Kiss Sweet Little Lillah*, 1–7, 18.

32. Wood and Jackson, eds., *Kiss Sweet Little Lillah*, 22, 26, 12, 18.

33. Griffith, *Yours till Death*, 1, 2, 5, 6, 33, 35, 73.

34. Griffith, *Yours till Death*, 17, 63; Blomquist and Taylor, eds., *This Cruel War*, 22, 10.

35. William Riley Jones to Fannie Jones, June 29, 1863, William Riley Jones Papers; Jackson, *So Mourns the Dove*, 19; Jane Brooks Lindsey to Elijah Lindsey, October 11, 1864, Jane Brooks Lindsey Civil War Letter, SPR 383, ADAH.

36. Elizabeth Danielly to Frances Danielly, April 29, 1863, Pearson and Danielly Family Papers; Blomquist and Taylor, eds., *This Cruel War*, 35–36.

37. Blomquist and Taylor, eds., *This Cruel War*, 238, 230; John Floyd Gwyn to Placide Gwyn, September 22, 1862, John Floyd Gwyn Civil War Letters, SPR 953, ADAH; Jackson, *So Mourns the Dove*, 44;; Kinnon Lee to Mary Lee, September 23, 1862, Kinnon Lee Civil War Letters; Henry Bostic to Elizabeth Bostic, February 1, 6 1862, Bostic Family Papers, SPR 785, ADAH.

38. Cutrer, *Oh, What a Loansome Time I Had*, 23.

39. Cutrer, *Oh, What a Loansome Time I Had*, 33, 36, 42, 43, 47, 52, 83, 91.

40. Henry Bray to Devotion P. Bray, February 19, 1862, Henry Bray Civil War Letters; W. C. McCullough to Martha McCullough, February 17, 1862, McCullough Family Letters; Jackson, *So Mourns the Dove*, 21, 42.

41. Cutrer, *Oh, What a Loansome Time I Had*, 44, 61; Wood and Jackson, eds., *Kiss Sweet Little Lillah*, 50.

42. Blomquist and Taylor, eds., *This Cruel War*, 324.

43. Frances Danielly to Elizabeth Danielly, April 29, 1863, Pearson and Danielly Family Papers; John Davenport to Mary Jane Davenport, September 1, December 22, 1862, John F. Davenport Civil War Letters; William Hobson to Mary Ann Hobson, April 14, 1862, William Hobson Civil War Letter, SPR 737, ADAH.

44. Henry Bray to Marian Davis, January 29, 1862, Henry Bray Civil War Letters.

45. December 31, 1863, Sarah Rousseau Espy Diary; Blomquist and Taylor, eds., *This Cruel War*, 31; Marian Davis to Henry Bray, May 17, 1864, Henry Bray Civil War Letters.

46. James Zachariah Branscomb to Eliza Branscomb, September 11, 1861, James Zachariah Branscomb to Lucinda Branscomb Hunter, July 27, 1861, April [no date], 1863, Branscomb Family Letters; Blomquist and Taylor, eds., *This Cruel War*, 125; William Riley Jones to Fannie Jones, n.d., William Riley Jones Papers.

47. James Zachariah Branscomb to Lucinda Branscomb Hunter, November 17, 1863, January 22, 1864, John Wesley Branscomb to Lucinda Branscomb Hunter, September 17, 1864, Branscomb Family Letters; William Riley Jones to Fannie Jones, September 14 and 28, 1862, William Riley Jones Papers; Henry Bray to Dolly Bray, July 3, 1862, Henry Bray Civil War Letters.

48. William Riley Jones to Fannie, August 19, 1862, William Riley Jones Papers; Frances Danielly to Elizabeth Danielly, n.d., Pearson and Danielly Family Papers; W. V. Fleming to Mary Fleming, August 22, 1864, W. V. Fleming Civil War Letters; Joseph Wesson to Rachel Wesson, January 7, 1863, Joseph E. Wesson Civil War Letters; Griffith, *Yours till Death*, 64; Blomquist and Taylor, eds., *This Cruel War*, 18, 23.

49. Cutrer, *Oh, What a Loansome Time I Had*, 29.

50. Henry Bostic to Elizabeth Bostic, February 1, 1862, Bostic Family Papers; Thomas Smyrl to Mary Smyrl, October 17, 1863, Thomas Smyrl Civil War Letters; Blomquist and

Taylor, eds., *This Cruel War*, 152; Griffith, *Yours till Death*, 9; Samuel King Vann to Nancy Neel, November 18, 1863, "Most Lovely Lizzie: Love Letters to a Young Confederate Soldier," SPR 228, ADAH; James W. Woods to Mary Allin Loftis, May 22, 1862, Mary Allin Loftis Letters; John Davenport to Mary Jane Davenport, n.d., John F. Davenport Civil War Letters.

51. James Zachariah Branscomb to Lucinda Branscomb Hunter, December 17, 1861, January 1, 1863; Samuel King Vann to Nancy Elizabeth Neel, February 27, March 21, 1864, "Most Lovely Lizzie."

52. C. H. Bonner to Mary Allin Loftis, January 1, 1862, H. S. Strom to Mary Allin Loftis, January 4, 1862, G. Davis to Mary Allin Loftis, Mary Allen Loftis Letters.

53. Newton Davis to Elizabeth Davis, March 11, 1864, March 28, 1863, Newton N. Davis Papers; James Garrison to Harriet Garrison, April 22, 1863, James P. Garrison Confederate Letters, 1862–1863, MARBL; Newton Davis to Elizabeth Davis, July 9, 1862, Newton N. Davis Papers; Jackson, *So Mourns the Dove*, 17; James Crowder to Elmira Crowder, July 8, 1861, James Preston Crowder Papers, MARBL.

54. Wood and Jackson, eds., *Kiss Sweet Little Lillah*, 21, 28; Jackson, *So Mourns the Dove*, 33, 53.

55. January 19, June 3, 1864, Sarah Rousseau Espy Diary; Cutrer, *Oh, What a Loansome Time I Had*, 23, 128; June 7, August 7, 1862, Zillah Haynie Brandon Diaries.

56. McPherson, *For Cause and Comrades*, 63–71; Jackson, *So Mourns the Dove*, 27, 32, 34; William Riley Jones to Mary Frances Jones, August 19, 1862, William Riley Jones Papers.

57. Blomquist and Taylor, eds., *This Cruel War*, 5, 11, 29, 60.

58. Cutrer, *Oh, What a Loansome Time I Had*, 29, 41, 72.

CHAPTER 3

1. January 8, 1864, *Alabama Beacon*, Alabama Department of Archives and History public information subject files, 1901–ongoing, SG011155, folder 2, Government Records Collections, ADAH.

2. January 8, 1864, *Alabama Beacon*, Alabama Department of Archives and History public information subject files, 1901--ongoing, SG011155, folder 2, Government Records Collections, ADAH.

3. Samuel King Vann to Nancy Elizabeth Neel, November 18, 1864, October 3, 1864, "Most Lovely Lizzie"; James W. Woods to Mary Allan Loftis, July 28, 1862, Mary Allin Loftis Letters; Blomquist and Taylor, eds., *This Cruel War*, 164.

4. John Gwyn to Placide Gwyn, October 10, 1862, John Floyd Gwyn Civil War Letters; Blomquist and Taylor, eds., *This Cruel War*, 119; William Riley Jones to Mary Frances Jones, March 6, 1863, William Riley Jones Papers; Cutrer, *Oh, What a Loansome Time I Had*, 84.

5. Horace Mortimer Smith to Caroline Graves Smith, May 24, 1863, Horace Mortimer Smith Civil War Letter, SPR 943, ADAH; Jackson, *So Mourns the Dove*, 74–75; W. V. Fleming to Margaret Fleming, August 22, October 20, November 1, 1864, W. V. Fleming Civil War Letters; James Riggs to Sister, July 18, 1864, James R. Riggs Civil War Letters, SPR 710.

6. Jackson, *So Mourns the Dove*, 35, 40, 59, 70, 77.

7. Jackson, *So Mourns the Dove*, 55, 57, 66.

8. US Bureau of the Census, Manuscript Census Schedules, Eighth (1860) Census; Thomas Smyrl to Mary Jane Smryl, September 5, December 1, 1863, January 1, July 13, 1864, Thomas Smyrl Civil War Letters.

9. William Riley Jones to Mary Frances Jones, January 24, 1863, William Riley Jones Papers; Joseph Wesson to Rachel, January 20, 1863, Joseph E. Wesson Civil War Letters;

Jackson, *So Mourns the Dove*, 35; Thomas Smyrl to Mary Jane Smyrl, November 20, 1864, Thomas Smyrl Civil War Letters.

10. James Branscomb to Lucinda Branscomb, October 22, 1863, Branscomb Family Letters; Newton Davis to Bettie, July 29, October 29, 1863, Newton N. Davis Papers; Jackson, *So Mourns the Dove*, 73.

11. Thomas Smyrl to Mary Jane Smyrl, June 27, 1862, Thomas Smyrl Civil War Letters; William McCullough to Martha McCullough, June 23, 1863, McCullough Family Letters; Jackson, *So Mourns the Dove*, 80.

12. Blomquist and Taylor, eds., *This Cruel War*, 12, 19, 25, 139, 213.

13. September 5, 1862, Sarah Rousseau Espy Diary; Cutrer, *Oh, What a Loansome Time I Had*, 30, 83.

14. September 2, 1863, November 2, 1864, December 31, 1864, June 3, 1864, August 4, 1864, Sarah Rousseau Espy Diary; Cutrer, *Oh, What a Loansome Time I Had*, 124.

15. C. S. Allen to Milas Garrison, January 1, 1863, James P. Garrison to Harriet Garrison, May 18, 1863, James P. Garrison Confederate Letters, 1862–1863; Judith Lee Hallock, *The Civil War Letters of Joshua K. Callaway* (Athens: University of Georgia Press, 2014), 77.

16. William Riley Jones to Mary Frances Jones, n.d. circa 1863, December 21, 1862, April 2, June 13, 1863, William Riley Jones Papers.

17. Henry Bray to Marian Davis, June 13, 1862, Henry Bray Civil War Letters; Blomquist and Taylor, *This Cruel War*, eds., 209, 235; Joseph Wesson to Rachel, February 1, 1863, Joseph E. Wesson Civil War Letters.

18. Griffith, *Yours till Death*, 30, 43, 47, 60.

19. Wood and Jackson, eds., *Kiss Sweet Little Lillah for Me*, 31–32, 34, 37, 47, 52.

20. Wood and Jackson, eds., *Kiss Sweet Little Lillah for Me*, 65.

21. John Gwyn to Placide Gwyn, May 1, 1863, John Floyd Gwyn Civil War Letters; Blomquist and Taylor, eds., *This Cruel War*, 175, 183, 186.

22. Jackson, *So Mourns the Dove*, 39; Griffith, *Yours till Death*, 66, 122; Blomquist and Taylor, eds., *This Cruel War*, 179; William Riley Jones to Fannie Jones, February 7, n.d., April 2, 1863, William Riley Jones Papers.

23. Samuel King Vann to Nancy Neel, Aug. 17 and 25, 1863, "Most Lovely Lizzie"; William McCullough to Martha McCullough, June 11, July 24, 1863, McCullough Family Letters.

24. James Pritchett to Mary Loftis, February 6, 1863, D. D. Bonner to Mary Loftis, August 15, 1863, Mary Allin Loftis Letters.

25. Wood and Jackson, eds., *Kiss Sweet Little Lillah for Me*, 30, 30–31.

26. Blomquist and Taylor, eds., *This Cruel War*, 20, 27, 49.

27. Blomquist and Taylor, eds., *This Cruel War*, 116–17, 289–90.

28. Griffith, *Yours till Death*, 77, 128; William Riley Jones to Fannie Jones, February 9, July 24, 1863, William Riley Jones Papers; W. V. Fleming to Mary Fleming, September 14, 1864, W. V. Fleming Civil War Letters.

29. Horace Smith to Carolina Graves Smith, May 24, 1863, Horace Mortimer Smith Civil War Letter; Joseph Wesson to Rachel Wesson, January 20, 1863, Joseph E. Wesson Civil War Letters; Jackson, *So Mourns the Dove*, 74, 80.

30. Blomquist and Taylor, eds., *This Cruel War*, 11, 21, 13, 66, 94.

31. William Riley Jones to Fannie Jones, February 18, 1863, William Riley Jones Papers.

32. Blomquist and Taylor, eds., *This Cruel War*, 57, 59, 62, 64, 70, 72, 73, 80.

33. *Selma Morning Reporter*, April 22, 1864.

34. Griffith, *Yours till Death*, 7, 36, 38–39, 63.

35. Griffith, *Yours till Death*, 65, 72, 104.

36. Wood and Jackson, eds., *Kiss Sweet Little Lillah for Me*, 46, 49–50.

37. Jackson, *So Mourns the Dove*, 29, 53, 68, 71, 77, 80.

38. William McCullough to Martha McCullough, July 24, 1863, McCullough Family Letters; William Riley Jones to Fannie Jones, August 12, 20, 1863, William Riley Jones Papers; Horace Mortimer Smith to Caroline Graves Smith, May 24, 1863, Horace Mortimer Smith Civil War Letter; Blomquist and Taylor, eds., *This Cruel War*, 310.

39. Joseph Wesson to Rachel Wesson, February 1, 1863, Joseph E. Wesson Civil War Letters; Blomquist and Taylor, eds., *This Cruel War*, 308; Griffith, *Yours till Death*, 66.

Chapter 4

1. *Montgomery Daily Advertiser*, October 11, 1864, Civil War and Reconstruction Files, SG011138, folder 10, ADAH.

2. *Montgomery Daily Advertiser*, March 5, 1865, Civil War and Reconstruction Files, SG011139, folder 1.

3. October 14, 1863, "An Appeal for the Poor," author unknown, SG011154, folder 12, Government Records Collections.

4. August 15, 1862, December 18, 1863, Sarah Rousseau Espy Diary.

5. James Zachariah Branscomb to Lucinda Branscomb Hunter, August 7, 1863; Louis Branscomb to Lucinda Branscomb Hunter, October 25, 1863.

6. Thomas Smyrl to Mary Jane Smyrl, July 7, 1862, October 24, 1863, Thomas Smyrl Civil War Letters; J. D. Jenkins to Mary Loftis, February 24, 1864, Mary Allin Loftis Letters; William Riley Jones to Fannie Jones, March 24, July 5, 1863, William Riley Jones Papers.

7. McCurry, *Confederate Reckoning*, 167–68; Griffith, *Yours till Death*, 56.

8. Brown, *Deep in the Piney Woods*, 140–41; McCurry, *Confederate Reckoning*, 137.

9. US Bureau of the Census, Manuscript Census Schedules, Eighth (1860) Census; Wood and Jackson, eds., *Kiss Sweet Little Lillah for Me*, 34; Kinnon Lee to Mary, August 5, 1863, Kinnon Lee Civil War Letters; Jackson, *So Mourns the Dove*, 80.

10. Thomas Smyrl to Mary, April 15, July 13 and 25, 1864, Thomas Smyrl Civil War Letters.

11. Thomas Smyrl to Mary, August 5, December 7, November 20, 1864; R. R. Smyrl to Rebecca and Mary Smyrl, March 10, 1865, both Thomas Smyrl Civil War Letters.

12. Blomquist and Taylor, eds., *This Cruel War*, viii–x, 160, 177, 210, 228.

13. Blomquist and Taylor, eds., *This Cruel War*, 231, 241, 264–65, 284.

14. Blomquist and Taylor, eds., *This Cruel War*, 195, 205, 207–208, 271, 283–84, 294, 327.

15. June 22, 1864, *Selma Morning Reporter*, SG011154, folder 12, Government Records Collections; May 4, 1864, J. M. Sutherlin to T. H. Watts and T. H. Watts to J. M. Sutherlin, *Selma Morning Reporter*; "The Orphan's Home for the State of Alabama," *Sunday Mississippian*, SG011154, folder 12, Government Records Collection.

16. *Selma Morning Reporter*, March 4, 1864; *Montgomery Daily Advertiser*, June 5, 1864; *Alabama Beacon*, January 8, 1864, all Civil War and Reconstruction Files, SG011155, folder 2.

17. "Indigent Families in Alabama during the Period of the War between the States, 1861–1866," Alabama Governor military volunteer family assistance reports, 1861–1866, Government Records Collections, ADAH; June 5, 1864, *Montgomery Daily Advertiser*, SG011155, folder 2, Government Records Collections; "Indigent Families in Alabama during the Period of the War between the States, 1861–1866," Alabama Governor military volunteer family assistance reports, 1861–1866, Government Records Collections, ADAH.

18. *Journal of the Called Session, 1862 and the Second Regular Annual Session of the House of Representatives of the State of Alabama*, Montgomery, Alabama, ADAH.

19. "Indigent Families in Alabama during the Period of the War between the States, 1861–1866," Alabama Governor military volunteer family assistance reports, 1861–1866, Government Records Collections, ADAH.

20. "Indigent Families in Alabama during the Period of the War between the States, 1861–1866," Alabama Governor military volunteer family assistance reports, 1861–1866, Government Records Collections, ADAH; *Acts of the Second Called Session, 1861, and the First Regular Annual Session of the General Assembly of Alabama, Held in the City of Montgomery, Commencing on the 28th Day of October and Second Monday in November 1861* (Montgomery: Montgomery Advertiser Book and Job Office, 1861).

21. *Acts of the Second Called Session, 1862, and of the First Regular Annual Session of the General Assembly of Alabama*.

22. *Acts of the Called Session, 1863, and the Third Regular Annual Session of the General Assembly of Alabama*; *Acts of the Called Sessions, 1864, of the General Assembly of Alabama*.

23. *Acts of the Called Session, 1863, and the Third Regular Annual Session of the General Assembly of Alabama*; *Acts of the Called Sessions, 1864, of the General Assembly of Alabama*.

24. Henry Bostic to his family, February 7, 1862, Bostic Family Papers; Blomquist and Taylor, eds., *This Cruel War*, 13, 21, 29; Brown, *Deep in the Piney Woods*, 135–36.

25. *Journal of the Called Session, 1862 and the Second Regular Annual Session of the House of Representatives of the State of Alabama*, Montgomery, Alabama, ADAH; *Acts of the Second Called Session, 1862, and of the First Regular Annual Session of the General Assembly of Alabama, Held in the City of Montgomery, Commencing on the 27th Day of October and Second Monday in November 1862* (Montgomery: Montgomery Advertiser Book and Job Office, 1862); *Acts of the Called Session, 1863, and the Third Regular Annual Session of the General Assembly of Alabama, Held in the City of Montgomery Commencing on the 17th Day of August and the 2nd Monday in November 1863* (Montgomery: Saffold and Figures, State Printers, 1863); *Acts of the Called Sessions, 1864, of the General Assembly of Alabama Held in the City of Montgomery, Commencing on the Twenty-Seventh Day of September, 1864* (Montgomery: Saffold and Figures, State Printers, 1864).

26. *Acts of the Called Session, 1863, and the Third Regular Annual Session of the General Assembly of Alabama*; *Acts of the Called Sessions, 1864, of the General Assembly of Alabama*.

27. Proclamation by Governor John Gill Shorter, Civil War and Reconstruction Files, SG11138, folder 009; Brown, *Deep in the Piney Woods*, 141; Alabama Governor applications for military service exemptions, 1863–1864, Government Records Collections, SG16063, granted.

28. "Support of Indigent Families, Etc., 1861–1865," Alabama Governor military volunteer family assistance reports, 1861–1866, ADAH; May 7, 1864, *Selma Morning Reporter*, SG 011139, folder 003, Government Records Collections.

29. March 17, September 2, 1862, Civil War and Reconstruction Files, SG01138, folder 10.

30. Alabama Governor applications for military service exemptions, 1863–1864, Government Records Collections, SG16063, granted.

31. Alabama Governor applications for military service exemptions, 1863–1864, Government Records Collections, SG16063, granted.

32. Alabama Governor applications for military service exemptions, 1863–1864, Government Records Collections, SG16063, granted.

33. Alabama Governor applications for military service exemptions, 1863–1864, Government Records Collections, SG 16063, not granted; Brown, *Deep in the Piney Woods*, 117–25.

34. Alabama Governor applications for military service exemptions, 1863–1864, Government Records Collections, SG 16063, not granted.

35. Alabama Governor applications for military service exemptions, 1863–1864, Government Records Collections, SG 16063, not granted.

36. John McGuire to Governor John Gill Shorter, October 14, 1864, unknown author/recipient, August 7, 1862, SG 24882, reel 15, Governor Records.

37. May 11, 1863, Petition to Governor John Gill Shorter, Pardon of William Bowden, SG 24882, reel 15, Governor Records.

38. Robert Davis Ward and William Warren Rogers, *Alabama's Response to the Penitentiary Movement, 1829–1865* (Gainesville: University Press of Florida, 2003), 115–16, 119; Alabama Governor (1861–1863: Shorter), Pardons, paroles, and clemency files, SG 6484, folder 1 and 2, ADAH.

39. Alabama Governor (1861–1863: Shorter), Pardons, paroles, and clemency files, SG 6484, folder 2, ADAH.

40. McCurry, *Confederate Reckoning*, 167, 178.

41. Arthur W. Bergeron Jr., *Confederate Mobile* (Baton Rouge: Louisiana State University Press, 1991), 99, 100–101.

42. "Indigent Families in Alabama during the Period of the War between the States, 1861–1866," Alabama Governor military volunteer family assistance reports, 1861–1866, Government Records Collections, ADAH.

43. Bergeron, *Confederate Mobile*, 99–101; March 8, 1863, *Montgomery Daily Advertiser*, reprinted from the *Mobile Tribune*, SG 011139, folder 003.

44. Adelaide V. Chaudron to Governor John Gill Shorter, April 7, May 1, 1863, SG011155, folder 1, Government Records, ADAH.

45. Flynt, *Poor but Proud*, 38–39, 47; Rogers et al., *Alabama*, 209; *New York Times*, October 1, 1863; Bergeron, *Confederate Mobile*, 101–102; *Report on Indigent Families*, Public Information subject files, Civil War and Reconstruction Misc., SG 17 131, folder 18, ADAH.

CHAPTER 5

1. Kenneth W. Noe, ed., *The Yellowhammer War: Civil War and Reconstruction in Alabama* (Tuscaloosa: University of Alabama Press, 2013), 107–8; *John W. Brown vs. Ellen J. Brown*, Bill of Divorce, Perry County, LGM 249, Reel 21, ADAH.

2. Gregory Downs, in his study of postwar North Carolina, first posited the argument that the war shifted dependence from a negative political definition to one that allowed men and women to determine the postwar landscape. Gregory P. Downs, *Declarations of Dependence: The Long Reconstruction of Popular Politics in the South, 1861–1908* (Chapel Hill: University of North Carolina Press, 2011).

3. Cutrer, *Oh, What a Loansome Time I Had*, 136–37; John Wesley Branscomb to Lucinda Branscomb Hunter, August 5, 1864, Branscomb Family Letters; March 21, 1865, Sarah Rousseau Espy Diary. For studies of non-elites after the war, see Wetherington's *Plain Folk's Fight* and Williams et al., *Plain Folk in a Rich Man's War*. Historians examining the efforts of all southerners to rebuild the economic and social structure of their communities amid the climate of Reconstruction include Michael Perman, *Reunion without Compromise: The South and Reconstruction, 1865–1868* (New York: Cambridge University Press, 1973); and Steven Hahn, *The Roots of Southern Populism: Yeomen Farmers and the Transformation of the Georgia Upcountry* (New York: Oxford University Press, 1983).

4. Cutrer, *Oh, What a Loansome Time I Had*, 158–59; Blomquist and Taylor, *This Cruel War*, eds., 331; John S. Jones to Frances (Fannie) and Elizabeth Jones, June 7, 1872, William Riley Jones Papers.

5. US Bureau of the Census, Manuscript Census Schedules, Eighth (1860) Censuses;

Eliza Fielding Diary, January 9, February 14, May 28, October 19, 1866, SPR 389, ADAH.

6. October 22, 1865, Margaret Josephine Miles Gillis Diary.

7. M. G. Milligan to Brother Gooch, February 11, 1867, M. G. Milligan Letter, 1867, SPR 970, ADAH.

8. Allen Trelease, *White Terror: The Ku Klux Klan Conspiracy and Southern Reconstruction* (New York: Harper and Row, 1972), xv–xlviii; Laura F. Edwards, *Gendered Strife and Confusion: The Political Culture of Reconstruction* (Urbana: University of Illinois Press, 1997), xii, 173.

9. Michael W. Fitzgerald, *Reconstruction in Alabama: From Civil War to Redemption in the Cotton South* (Baton Rouge: Louisiana State University Press, 2017), 91–92; Flynt, *Poor but Proud*, 54–55, 59; Robert Gilmour, "The Other Emancipation: Studies in the Society and Economy of Alabama Whites during Reconstruction" (PhD diss., Johns Hopkins University, 1972), 72, 82–92.

10. *Livingston Journal*, November 18, 1865.

11. *Union Springs Times*, April 18, August 22, October 3, 1866.

12. *Gadsden Times*, July 3, 1867, November 11, 1868.

13. "Proclamation of Governor Lewis E. Parsons," Civil War and Reconstruction Files SG011154, folder 008.

14. To Andrew Johnson from Governor Lewis E. Parsons, October 2, 1865, Alabama Governor (1865: Parsons) administrative files, 1864–1865, ADAH.

15. Edwards, *Gendered Strife and Confusion*, 20.

16. Edwards, *Gendered Strife and Confusion*, 146–47, 148, 153, 162, 169–70.

17. Fitzgerald, *Reconstruction in Alabama*, 80; Gilmour, "Other Emancipation," 56–57, 72; Flynt, *Poor but Proud*, 52, 63.

18. Flynt, *Poor but Proud*, 52; Gilmour, "Other Emancipation," 67–68; *Acts of the Session of 1865–6 of the General Assembly of Alabama, Held in the City of Montgomery, Commencing on the 3rd Monday in November 1865* (Montgomery: Reid and Screws, State Printers, 1866); *Acts of the Session of 1866–7 of the General Assembly of Alabama, Held in the City of Montgomery, Commencing on the Second Monday in November 1866* (Montgomery: Reid and Screws, State Printers, 1867); Fitzgerald, *Reconstruction in Alabama*, 91.

19. Alabama Governor military volunteer family assistance reports, 1861–1866, Coosa County, Government Records Collections, ADAH.

20. Alabama Governor (1865–1868: Patton), administrative files, 1867 Supplies for Destitute Administrative Files, SG023024, folder 21, ADAH.

21. Alabama Governor (1865–1868: Patton), administrative files, 1867 Supplies for Destitute Administrative Files, SG023024, folder 21, ADAH.

22. Alabama Governor (1865–1868: Patton), administrative files, 1867 Supplies for Destitute Administrative Files, SG023024, folder 21, ADAH.

23. Michael W. Fitzgerald, "Radical Republicanism and the White Yeomanry during Alabama Reconstruction, 1865–1868," *Journal of Southern History* 54, no. 4 (November 1988): 573–74; *Acts of the Session of 1865–6 of the General Assembly of Alabama, Held in the City of Montgomery, Commencing on the 3rd Monday in November 1865* (Montgomery: Reid and Screws, State Printers, 1866); Alabama Governor (1865–1868: Patton), administrative files, 1867 Supplies for Destitute Administrative Files, SG023024, folder 21. For further discussion of Unionism in Alabama, see Margaret M. Storey, *Loyalty and Loss: Alabama's Unionists in the Civil War and Reconstruction* (Baton Rouge: Louisiana State University Press, 2004).

24. Flynt, *Poor but Proud*, 52–53.

25. Marcus Cruikshank Report to Governor Robert M. Patton, March 7, 1866, Alabama Governor (1865–1868: Patton), administrative files, SG23023–23026.

26. Marcus Cruikshank Report to Governor Robert M. Patton, March 7, 1866, Alabama Governor (1865–1868: Patton), administrative files, SG23023–23026.

27. Pike County Commissioners to Governor Robert M. Patton, May 5, 1867, Alabama Governor (1865–1868: Patton), administrative files, SG23023–23026; *Union Springs Times*, April 18, 1866; C. S. England to Governor Robert M. Patton, June 7, 1867, Alabama Governor (1865–1868: Patton), administrative files, SG23023–23026.

28. Louis Wyeth to Governor Robert M. Patton, April 2, 1866, Alabama Governor (1865–1868: Patton), administrative files, SG23023–23026; Gilmour, "Other Emancipation," 68; Fitzgerald, *Reconstruction in Alabama*, 80; Flynt, *Poor but Proud*, 52–53.

29. Letter to Governor Patton, May 16, 1867, J. M. Warren to Governor Patton, May 27, 1867, Alabama Governor (1865–1868: Patton), administrative files, SG23023–23026.

30. Letter to Governor Robert M. Patton, May 25, 1867, Alabama Governor (1865–1868: Patton), administrative files, SG23023–23026.

31. Flynt, *Poor but Proud*, 53–54; "Report of the Directors of the Sheltering Arms," Flyer, undated 1868, Alabama Governor (1865–1868: Patton), administrative files, SG23023–23026.

32. Marcus Cruikshank Report to Governor Robert M. Patton, February 1868, Alabama Governor (1865–1868: Patton), administrative files, SG23023–23026; Flynt, *Poor but Proud*, 53–54; *Gadsden Times*, August 13, 1869.

Conclusion

1. Glen Feldman, *The Disfranchisement Myth: Poor Whites and Suffrage Restriction in Alabama* (Athens: University of Georgia Press, 2004), 136; Alabama Constitution (1901), article VIII, sections 177–196; Jimmie Frank Gross, "Alabama Politics and the Negro, 1874–1901" (PhD diss., University of Georgia, 1969), 274–75.

2. Flynt, *Poor but Proud*, 64–65.

Bibliography

ALABAMA DEPARTMENT OF ARCHIVES AND HISTORY, MONTGOMERY, ALABAMA (ADAH)
Harris Hardin Averett Papers
Bostic Family Papers
Branscomb Family Papers
Henry Bray Civil War Letters
John F. Davenport Civil War Letters
Newton N. Davis Papers
Sarah Rousseau Espy Diary
Eliza Fielding Diary
W. V. Fleming Civil War Letters
Margaret Josephine Miles Gillis Diary
John Floyd Gwyn Civil War Letters
William Hobson Civil War Letter
Michael Holmes Civil War Letter
James W. Jackson Letters
William Riley Jones Papers
Leonard Land Letters
Kinnon Lee Civil War Letters
Jane Brooks Lindsey Civil War Letter
Mary Allin Loftis Letters
McCullough Family Letters
MG Milligan Letter, 1867
Simeon Orr Letters
Thomas R. Owen Civil War Letter
Pearson and Danielly Family Papers
Horace Mortimer Smith Civil War Letter
Thomas Smyrl Civil War Letters
Samuel King Vann, "Most Lovely Lizzie: Love Letters to a Young Confederate Soldier"
Joseph E. Wesson Civil War Letters
Robert Williams Civil War Letters
Cornelius Wright Civil War Letter

SOUTHERN HISTORICAL COLLECTION, UNIVERSITY OF NORTH CAROLINA-CHAPEL HILL, CHAPEL HILL, NORTH CAROLINA
James Caldwell Diary
John Gideon Diary
James Mallory Diary
Milner Family Papers

Stuart A. Rose Manuscript, Archive, Rare Book Library, Emory University, Atlanta, Georgia
James Preston Crowder Papers
James P. Garrison, Confederate Letters, 1862–1863
Nimrod William Ezekial Long Papers
James T. Norman Family Papers
William Anderson Stephens Letters, 1859–1891

Government Documents, Alabama Department of Archives and History, Montgomery, Alabama
Alabama Circuit Court (Calhoun County) case files, 1833–1926, Government Records Collections
Alabama Governor. Paroles, Pardons, etc., 1821–1825
Alabama Governor military volunteer family assistance reports, 1861–1866, Government Records Collections
Alabama Governor applications for military service exemptions, 1863–1864
Alabama Governor (1865: Parsons), Administrative files, 1864–1865
Alabama Governor (1865–1868: Patton), Administrative files
Alabama Governor (1861–1863: Shorter), Pardons, paroles, and clemency files
Alabama Governor (1863–1865: Watts), Administrative files, 1859–1865
Bibb County, Alabama. Chancery Court. Minutes, 1843–1853
Blount County, Alabama. Chancery Court Files
Public Information subject files—Civil War and Reconstruction Misc. SG 17 131 folder 18
Report on Indigent Families. From a brief summary compiled by Miss Carlotta P. Mitchell, for the WPA project #1584
Perry County, Alabama. Chancery Court Files
Russell County, Alabama. Chancery Court Final Record.
Talladega County, Alabama. Chancery Court. Final Record, 1847–1849.
Governor Thomas Watts records
Wilcox County, Alabama. Circuit Court. Final Record, 1831–1834.
Wilcox County, Alabama. Chancery Court. Minutes, 1848–1868.

Census Records
Abstract of the Fifth Census, 1830. America in Two Centuries: An Inventory (series), advisory editor Daniel J. Boorstin. New York: Arno Press, 1976.
1820 Manufacturer's Report—District of Alabama
1820 Manufacturer's Report—State of Georgia
1820 Manufacturer's Report—State of Tennessee
Historical Statistics of the Unites States, Millennial Edition, Volume 1, Population
Statistical View of the United States, Compendium of the Seventh Census, by J. D. B DeBow, Washington 1854.
U.S Bureau of the Census. Manuscript Census Schedules. Sixth (1840), Seventh (1850), and Eighth (1860), and Ninth (1870) Censuses.
_____. Slave Schedules. Seventh (1850) and Eighth (1860).

Newspapers
Alabama Beacon
Daily Richmond (Virginia) Enquirer

Gadsden (Alabama) Times
Livingston (Alabama) Journal
Mobile Tribune
Montgomery Daily Advertiser
Montgomery Post
Selma Morning Reporter
Sunday Mississippian
Union Springs (Alabama) Times

Published Primary Sources

Acts of the Second Called Session, 1861, and the First Regular Annual Session of the General Assembly of Alabama, held in the City of Montgomery, Commencing on the 28th Day of October and Second Monday in November 1861. Montgomery: Montgomery Advertiser Book and Job Office, 1861.

Acts of the Second Called Session, 1862, and of the First Regular Annual Session of the General Assembly of Alabama, held in the City of Montgomery, Commencing on the 27th Day of October and Second Monday in November 1862. Montgomery: Montgomery Advertiser Book and Job Office, 1862.

Acts of the Called Session, 1863, and the Third Regular Annual Session of the General Assembly of Alabama, Held in the City of Montgomery Commencing on the 17th Day of August and the 2nd Monday in November 1863. Montgomery: Saffold and Figures, State Printers, 1863.

Acts of the Called Sessions, 1864, of the General Assembly of Alabama Held in the City of Montgomery, Commencing on the Twenty-Seventh Day of September, 1864. Montgomery: Saffold and Figures, State Printers, 1864.

Acts of the Session of 1865–6 of the General Assembly of Alabama, Held in the City of Montgomery, Commencing on the 3rd Monday in November 1865. Montgomery: Reid and Screws, State Printers, 1866.

Acts of the Session of 1866–7 of the General Assembly of Alabama, Held in the City of Montgomery, Commencing on the Second Monday in November 1866. Montgomery: Reid and Screws, State Printers, 1867.

Blomquist, Ann K., and Robert A. Taylor, eds. *This Cruel War: The Civil War Letters of Grant and Malinda Taylor, 1862–1865*. Macon, GA: Mercer University Press, 2000.

Cutrer, Thomas, ed. *Oh, What a Loansome Time I Had: The Civil War Letters of Major William Morel Moxley, Eighteenth Alabama Infantry and Emily Beck Moxley*. Tuscaloosa: University of Alabama Press, 2002.

Griffith, Lucille, ed. *Yours till Death: Civil War Letters of John Cotton*. Tuscaloosa: University of Alabama Press, 1951.

Hallock, Judith Lee, ed. *The Civil War Letters of Joshua K. Callaway*. Athens: University of Georgia Press, 2014.

Hundley, Daniel R. *Social Relations in Our Southern States*. New York: HB Price, 1860.

Jackson, Harvey H., Jr., and Harvey H. Jackson III, eds. "Moving to Alabama: The Joel Spigener—William K. Oliver Letters, 1833–1834." *Alabama Review* 48 (January 1995).

Jackson, Alto Loftin, ed. *So Mourns the Dove: Letters of a Confederate Infantryman and His Family*. New York: Exposition Press, 1965.

Olmsted, Frederick Law. *The Cotton Kingdom: A Traveller's Observations on Cotton and Slavery in the American Slave States*. New York: Mason Brothers, 1861.

Posey, Walter Brownlow, ed. "Alabama in the 1830s: As Recorded by British Travellers." *Birmingham-Southern College Bulletin* 31, no. 4 (December 1938).

Robertson, W. G. *Recollections of the Early Settlers of Montgomery County and Their Families.* Montgomery: Excelsior Print, 1892.
Schwaab, Eugene, ed. *Travels in the Old South: Selected Periodicals of the Times.* Volume 1. Lexington: University Press of Kentucky, 1973.
Wood, Wayne, and Mary Virginia Jackson, eds. *Kiss Sweet Little Lillah for Me: Civil War Letters of William Thomas Jackson.* Birmingham: Ebsco Media, 2000.

Secondary Sources
Books
Abernathy, Thomas P. *The Formative Period in Alabama, 1815–1828.* Tuscaloosa: University of Alabama Press, 1965.
Bardaglio, Peter W. *Reconstructing the Household: Families, Sex, and the Law in the Nineteenth-Century South.* Chapel Hill: University of North Carolina Press, 1995.
Bellows, Barbara L. *Benevolence among Slaveholders: Assisting the Poor in Charleston, 1670–1860.* Baton Rouge: Louisiana State University Press, 1993.
Bergeron, Arthur W., Jr. *Confederate Mobile.* Baton Rouge: Louisiana State University Press, 1991.
Berry, Stephen W. II. *All That Makes a Man: Love and Ambition in the Civil War South.* New York: Oxford University Press, 2003.
_____, ed. *Weirding the War: Stories from the Civil War's Ragged Edges.* Athens: University of Georgia Press, 2011.
Bolton, Charles C. *Poor Whites of the Antebellum South: Tenants and Laborers in Central North Carolina and Northeast Mississippi.* Raleigh: Duke University Press, 1994.
Bolton, Charles C., and Scott P. Culclasure, eds. *The Confessions of Edward Isham: A Poor White Life of the Old South.* Athens: University of Georgia Press, 1998.
Brewer, George E. *History of Coosa County, Alabama.* Greenville, SC: Southern Historical Press, 1987.
Broomall, James J. *Private Confederacies: The Emotional Worlds of Southern Men as Citizens and Soldiers.* Chapel Hill: University of North Carolina Press, 2019.
Brown, Tommy Craig. *Deep in the Piney Woods: Southeastern Alabama from Statehood to the Civil War, 1800–1865.* Tuscaloosa: University of Alabama Press, 2018.
Bruce, Dickson D., Jr. *Violence and Culture in the Antebellum South.* Austin: University of Texas Press, 1979.
Bushman, Claudia L. *In Old Virginia: Slavery, Farming, and Society in the Journal of John Walker.* Baltimore: Johns Hopkins University Press, 2001.
Bynum, Victoria E. *Unruly Women: The Politics of Social and Sexual Control in the Old South.* Chapel Hill: University of North Carolina Press, 1992.
Campbell, Jacqueline Glass. *When Sherman Marched North from the Sea: Resistance on the Confederate Homefront.* Chapel Hill: University of North Carolina Press, 2003.
Carmichael, Peter S. *The War for the Common Soldier: How Men Thought, Fought, and Survived in Civil War Armies.* Chapel Hill: University of North Carolina Press, 2018.
Cashin, Joan E., ed. *Objects of War: Material Culture in the Civil War Era.* Chapel Hill: University of North Carolina Press, 2018.
Cecil-Fronsman, Bill. *Common Whites: Class and Culture in Antebellum North Carolina.* Lexington: University Press of Kentucky, 1992.
Clinton, Catherine. *The Other Civil War: American Women in the Nineteenth Century.* New York: Hill and Wang, 1984.
Collins, Bruce. *White Society in the Antebellum South.* New York: Longman, 1985.

Curran, Thomas F. *Women Making War: Female Confederate Prisoners and Union Military Justice*. Carbondale: Southern Illinois University Press, 2020.
Davis, Reuben. *Recollections of Mississippi and Mississippians*. Boston: Houghton Mifflin, 1890.
Dorman, Lewy. *Party Politics in Alabama from 1850 through 1860*. Wetumpka, AL: Wetumpka Printing, 1935.
Edwards, Laura F. *Gendered Strife and Confusion: The Political Culture of Reconstruction*. Urbana: University of Illinois Press, 1997.
_____. *The People and Their Peace: Legal Culture and the Transformation of Inequality in the Post-revolutionary South*. Chapel Hill: University of North Carolina Press, 2009.
Escott, Paul D. *Many Excellent People: Power and Privilege in North Carolina, 1850–1900*. Chapel Hill: University of North Carolina Press, 1985.
Faust, Drew Gilpin. *Mothers of Invention: Women of the Slaveholding South*. Chapel Hill: University of North Carolina Press, 1996.
Feldman, Glenn. *The Disfranchisement Myth: Poor Whites and Suffrage Restriction in Alabama*. Athens: University of Georgia Press, 2004.
Fitzgerald, Michael W. *Reconstruction in Alabama: From Civil War to Redemption in the Cotton South*. Baton Rouge: Louisiana State University Press, 2017.
Fleming, Walter L. *Civil War and Reconstruction in Alabama*. New York: Peter Smith Press, 1949.
Flynt, Wayne. *Dixie's Forgotten People: The South's Poor Whites*. Bloomington: Indiana University Press, 1979.
_____. *Poor but Proud: Alabama's Poor Whites*. Tuscaloosa: University of Alabama Press, 1989.
Forret, Jeff. *Race Relations at the Margins: Slaves and Poor Whites in the Antebellum Southern Countryside*. Baton Rouge: Louisiana State University Press, 2006.
Frank, Joseph Allen. *With Ballot and Bayonet: The Political Socialization of American Civil War Soldiers*. Athens: University of Georgia Press, 1998.
Frank, Lisa Tendrich, and LeeAnn Whites, eds. *Household War: How Americans Lived and Fought the Civil War*. Athens: University of Georgia Press, 2020.
Fredette, Allison Dorothy. *Marriage on the Border: Love, Mutuality, and Divorce in the Upper South during the Civil War*. Lexington: University Press of Kentucky, 2020.
Fry, Anna M. Gayle. *Memories of Old Cahaba*. Publishing House of the M. E. Church, South, 1908.
Gallagher, Gary. *The Confederate War: How Popular Will, Nationalism, and Military Strategy Could Not Stave Off Defeat*. Cambridge: Harvard University Press, 1997.
Genovese, Eugene. *Roll, Jordan, Roll: The World the Slaves Made*. New York: Vintage Books, 1976.
Griffith, Lucille. *Alabama: A Documentary History to 1900*. Tuscaloosa: University of Alabama Press, 1968.
Hadden, Sally E. *Slave Patrols: Law and Violence in Virginia and the Carolinas*. Cambridge: Harvard University Press, 2001.
Hahn, Steven. *The Roots of Southern Populism: Yeomen and the Transformation of the Georgia Upcountry, 1850–1890*. New York: Oxford University Press, 1983.
Harris, William J. *Plain Folk and Gentry in a Slave Society: White Liberty and Black Slavery in Augusta's Hinterlands*. Scranton: Harper and Row, 1985.
Harrison, Kimberly. *The Rhetoric of Rebel Women: Civil War Diaries and Confederate Persuasion*. Carbondale: Southern Illinois University Press, 2013.
Hyde, Samuel C., ed. *Plain Folk of the South Revisited*. Baton Rouge: Louisiana State University Press, 1997.
Inscoe, John C., and, Robert C. Kenzer, eds. *Enemies of the Country: New Perspectives on Unionists in the Civil War South*. Athens: University of Georgia Press, 2001.

Jones, Katherine M. *Heroines of Dixie: Confederate Women Tell Their Story of the War*. Westport, CT: Greenwood Press, 1973.
Jordan, Weymouth T. *Ante-Bellum Alabama: Town and Country*. Tuscaloosa: University of Alabama Press, 1987.
Kierner, Cynthia. *Beyond the Household: Women's Place in the Early South, 1700–1835*. Ithaca: Cornell University Press, 1998.
Lockley, Timothy James. *Lines in the Sand: Race and Class in Lowcountry Georgia, 1750–1860*. Athens: University of Georgia Press, 2001.
Martin, Bessie. *A Rich Man's War, a Poor Man's Fight: Desertion of Alabama Troops from the Confederate Army*. Tuscaloosa: University of Alabama Press, 2003.
McCurry, Stephanie. *Confederate Reckoning: Power and Politics in the Civil War South*. Cambridge: Harvard University Press, 2010.
——. *Masters of Small Worlds: Yeomen Households, Gender Relations, and the Political Culture of the Antebellum South Carolina Low Country*. New York: Oxford University Press, 1995.
McIlwain, Christopher Lyle. *Civil War Alabama*. Tuscaloosa: University of Alabama Press, 2016.
——. *1865 Alabama: From Civil War to Uncivil Peace*. Tuscaloosa: University of Alabama Press, 2017.
McMillan, Malcolm C. *The Disintegration of a Confederate State*. Macon, GA: Mercer University Press, 1986.
McPherson, James. *For Cause and Comrades: Why Men Fought in the Civil War*. New York: Oxford University Press, 1997.
McWhiney, Grady. *Cracker Culture: Celtic Ways in the Old South*. Tuscaloosa: University of Alabama Press, 1988.
Miller, Randall. *The Cotton Mill Movement in Antebellum Alabama*. New York: Arno Press, 1978.
Mitchell, Reid. *Civil War Soldiers*. New York: Viking Press, 1988.
Merritt, Keri Leigh. *Masterless Men: Poor Whites and Slavery in the Antebellum South*. Cambridge: Cambridge University Press, 2017.
Nelson, Megan Kate. *Ruin Nation: Destruction and the American Civil War*. Athens: University of Georgia Press, 2012.
Noe, Kenneth W., ed. *The Yellowhammer War: The Civil War and Reconstruction in Alabama*. Tuscaloosa: University of Alabama Press, 2013.
Owens, Harry P., and James J. Cooke, eds. *The Old South in the Crucible of War*. Jackson: University of Mississippi Press, 1983.
Owsley, Frank Lawrence. *Plain Folk of the Old South*. Baton Rouge: Louisiana State University Press, 1949.
Perman, Michael. *Reunion without Compromise: The South and Reconstruction, 1865–1868*. New York: Cambridge University Press, 1973.
Phillips, Jason. *Diehard Rebels: The Confederate Culture of Invincibility*. Athens: University of Georgia Press, 2007.
Phillips, Ulrich Bonnell. *Life and Labor in the Old South*. Boston: Little, Brown, 1929.
Rable, George. *Civil Wars: Women and the Crisis of Southern Nationalism*. Urbana: University of Illinois Press, 1989.
Rogers, William Warren, Robert David Ward, Leah Rawls Atkins, and Wayne Flynt. *Alabama: The History of a Deep South State*. Tuscaloosa: University of Alabama Press, 1994.
Ruminski, Jarret. *The Limits of Loyalty: Ordinary People in Civil War Mississippi*. Jackson: University Press of Mississippi, 2017.

Schweninger, Loren. *Families in Crisis in the Old South: Divorce, Slavery, and the Law.* Chapel Hill: University of North Carolina Press, 2012.

Sheehan-Dean, Aaron. *Why Confederates Fought: Family and Nation in Civil War Virginia.* Chapel Hill: University of North Carolina Press, 2007.

Southerland, Henry DeLeon, Jr., and Jerry Elijah Brown. *The Federal Road through Georgia, the Creek Nation, and Alabama.* Tuscaloosa: University of Alabama Press, 1989.

Storey, Margaret M. *Loyalty and Loss: Alabama's Unionists in the Civil War and Reconstruction.* Baton Rouge: Louisiana State University Press, 2004.

Sword, Wiley. *Southern Invincibility: A History of the Confederate Heart.* New York: St. Martin's Press, 1999.

Thomas, Daniel H. *Fort Toulouse: The French Outpost at the Alabamas on the Coosa.* Tuscaloosa: University of Alabama Press, 1989.

Trelease, Allen. *White Terror: The Ku Klux Klan Conspiracy and Southern Reconstruction.* New York: Harper and Row, 1972.

Varon, Elizabeth. *We Mean to Be Counted: White Women and Politics in Antebellum Virginia.* Chapel Hill: University of North Carolina Press, 1998.

Ward, Robert Davis, and William Warren Rogers. *Alabama's Response to the Penitentiary Movement, 1829–1865.* Gainesville: University Press of Florida, 2003.

Wetherington, Mark V. *Plain Folk's Fight: The Civil War and Reconstruction in Piney Woods Georgia.* Chapel Hill: North Carolina University Press, 2005.

Whites, LeeAnn. *Civil War as a Crisis in Gender: Augusta, Georgia, 1860–1890.* Athens: University of Georgia Press, 1995.

———. *Gendered Matters: Civil War, Reconstruction, and the Making of the New South.* New York: Palgrave Macmillan, 2005.

Whites, LeeAnn, and Alecia P. Long, eds. *Occupied Women: Gender, Military Occupation, and the American Civil War.* Baton Rouge: Louisiana State University Press, 2009.

Wiggins, Sarah Woolfolk. *The Scalawag in Alabama Politics, 1865–1881.* Tuscaloosa: University of Alabama Press, 1977.

Wiley, Bell Irvine. *The Life of Johnny Reb: The Common Soldier of the Confederacy.* Indianapolis: Bobbs-Merrill, 1943.

Williams, David, Teresa Crisp Williams, and David Carlson. *Plain Folk in a Rich Man's War: Class and Dissent in Confederate Georgia.* Gainesville: University Press of Florida, 2002.

Wray, Matt. *Not Quite White: White Trash and the Boundaries of Whiteness.* Durham: Duke University Press, 2006.

Wright, Gavin. *The Political Economy of the Cotton South: Households, Markets, and Wealth in the Nineteenth Century.* New York: Norton, 1978.

Wyatt-Brown, Bertram. *Honor and Violence in the Old South.* New York: Oxford University Press, 1986.

Articles

Ash, Stephen V. "Poor Whites in the Occupied South, 1861–65." *Journal of Southern History* 57 (February 1991): 39–62.

Bailey, Hugh. "Disaffection in the Alabama Hill Country." *Civil War History* 4 (June 1958): 183–94.

Baker, Paula. "Domestication of Politics: Women and American Political Society." *American Historical Review* 89 (June 1984): 620–47.

Bryant, Keith L., Jr. "The Role and Status of the Female Yeomenry in the Antebellum South: The Literary View." *Southern Quarterly* 18 (Winter 1980): 73–88.

Cashin, Joan. "Trophies of War: Material Culture in the Civil War." *Journal of the Civil War Era* 1, no. 3 (September 2011): 339–67.

Derbes, Brett J. "The Production of Military Supplies at the Alabama State Penitentiary during the Civil War." *Alabama Review* 67 (April 2014): 131–60.

Fitzgerald, Michael W. "Radical Republicanism and the White Yeomanry during Alabama Reconstruction, 1865–1868." *Journal of Southern History* 54 (November 1988): 565–96.

Forret, Jeff. "Slave-Poor White Violence in the Antebellum Carolinas." *North Carolina Historical Review* 81 (April 2004): 139–67.

———. "Slaves, Poor Whites, and the Underground Economy of the Rural Carolinas." *Journal of Southern History* 70 (November 2004): 783–824.

Hagler, D. Harland. "The Ideal Woman in the Antebellum South: Lady or Farmwife?" *Journal of Southern History* 46 (August 1980): 405–18.

Harris, W. Stuart. "Rowdyism, Public Drunkenness, and Bloody Encounters in Perry County." *Alabama Review* (January 1980): 15–24.

Holt, Sharon Ann. "Making Freedom Pay: Freedpeople Working for Themselves, North Carolina, 1865–1900." *Journal of Southern History* 60 (May 1994): 229–62.

Hyde, Samuel C., Jr. "Plain Folk Reconsidered: Historiographical Ambiguity in Search of Definition." *Journal of Southern History* 71 (November 2005): 803–30.

Jackson, Harvey. "Time, Frontier, and the Alabama Black Belt." *Alabama Review* 44 (October 1991): 243–68.

Jones, Catherine A. "Women, Gender and the Boundaries of Reconstruction." *Journal of the Civil War Era* 8, no. 1 (March 2018): 111–31.

Kyriakoudes, Louis M. "The Rise of Merchants and Market Towns in Reconstruction-Era Alabama." *Alabama Review* 49, no. 2 (April 1996): 83–107.

Neeley, Mary Ann. "Painful Circumstances: Glimpses of the Alabama Penitentiary." *Alabama Review* 44 (January 1991): 3–16.

Osthaus, Carl R. "The Work Ethic of the Plain Folk: Labor and Religion in the Old South." *Journal of Southern History* 70 (November 2004): 745–82.

Otto, John Solomon. "The Migration of the Southern Plain Folk: An Interdisciplinary Synthesis." *Journal of Southern History* 51 (May 1985): 183–200.

Sherrod, Ricky L. "Plain Folk, Planters, and the Complexities of Southern Society." *Southwestern Historical Quarterly* 113 (July 2009): 1–27.

Shirley, Michael. "The Market and Community Culture in Antebellum Salem, North Carolina." *Journal of the Early Republic* 11 (Summer 1991): 219–48.

Whites, LeeAnn. "Written on the Heart: Soldiers' Letters, the Household Supply Line and Relational War." In *Household War: How Americans Lived and Fought the Civil War*, ed. Lisa Tendrich and LeeAnn Whites. Athens: University of Georgia Press, 2020.

Wiener, Jonathan M. "Planter Persistence and Social Change: Alabama, 1850–1870." *Journal of Interdisciplinary History* 7 (Autumn 1976): 235–60.

Winters, Donald L. "'Plain Folk' of the Old South Reexamined: Economic Democracy in Tennessee." *Journal of Southern History* 53 (November 1987): 565–86.

Dissertations

Gilmour, Robert. "The Other Emancipation: Studies in the Society and Economy of Alabama Whites during Reconstruction." PhD diss., Johns Hopkins University, 1972.

Gross, Jimmie Frank. "Alabama Politics and the Negro, 1874–1901." PhD diss., University of Georgia, 1969.

Index

Abernathy, Thomas Perkins, 8
Adams, Thomas, 30
African Americans, 12, 27, 153, 157, 159, 162–63, 165, 168–69, 174–75. *See also* enslaved people; race; slavery
Alabama Beacon, 91, 117
Alabama government: and favoring elite interests, 136–39, 145; and paternalism toward common whites, 6, 8, 17, 58, 91, 117, 119, 131, 136, 153, 161; and postwar policies effecting common whites, 164–65; on reaction to criminal activity, 135–36, 161; and releasing prisoners for military service, 142–45; on salt distribution, 134–35; on wartime aid for common whites, 131–36; postwar economic agenda of, 158–60. *See also* antebellum political culture; crop failures; exemptions; Parsons, Lewis E. (Gov.); Patton, Robert M. (Gov.); poverty relief, postwar; Shorter, Gov. John Gill; Watts, Thomas H. (Gov.)
Allen, C. S., 101
antebellum political culture, 21–23, 35–36
Atkins, Leah Rawls, 21

Barbour County, 144
Bass, John, 52–53
Bates, John, 151
Berry, Stephen, 14
Bibb County, 48–51, 113
Black Belt region, 11–12, 21, 24–25, 28, 170
Black Warrior River, 35
Bolton, Charles, 4
Bonner, C. H., 87
Bonner, D. D., 63, 72, 107
Bostic, Henry, 78, 85, 134
Bowden, William, 143

Brandon, Francis Lawson, 59
Brandon, Hines, 66, 88
Brandon, James, 64, 66, 88
Brandon, Zillah Haynie, 59–61, 64, 66, 88–89
Branscomb, James Zachariah, 63, 98
Branscomb, John Wesley, 83
Branscomb, Louis, 123, 153
Bray, Henry: on camp conditions, 70, 73; and concern for family reputation, 81–82; on home front conditions, 103; on lack of furloughs, 73; sentimentalism of, 84; on soldiers' pay, 79; and use of masculine bravado, 65–66
Brown, Anna M., 46–47
Brown, Ellen J. Vandasdel, 151
Brown, Eps, 165–64
Brown, John W., 151
Brown, Leonidas, 144
Brown, Morgan G., 46–47
Brown, Tommy Craig, 7, 28, 136
Buckner, Samuel B. (Maj. Gen.), 147
Bynum, Victoria E., 40

Calhoun, John C., 27
Calhoun, W. B., 138
Callaway, Dulcinea, 102
Callaway, Joshua K., 102
camp life, Confederate military, 82, 88, 106–7, 123, 161; conditions of, 70–72, 92–98; illnesses in, 99–100. *See also* soldiers, common white
Carroll, Pat, 144
Cecil-Fronsman, Bill, 5
Chambers County, 68, 87, 140
Chaudron, Adelaide V., 147
Cherokee County, 32–33, 59–60, 144
Civil War Alabama (McIlwain), 7
Clark, James, 42–43

Clark, Nancy, 42–43
Clark, William, 139
Clarke County, 30
class, 2, 21, 34, 59, 144, 161; conflict with elites, 3, 14–15, 100–101, 120–25, 137–39, 149; differences, 4–8, 11–13, 24–25, 28–31, 55, 176–77; identity, 4, 12, 27, 178. *See also* common white(s); legal system, Alabama; planter elites; poverty relief, postwar; race
Cobb, Williamson Robert Winfield, 22–23
Colbert County, 171
Coleman, George W., 143–44
Collier, Augustus, 47–48
Collier, Mary Ann, 47–48
Collins, Bruce, 4
Collins, P. E., 138
Committee on Destitution, 164. *See also* Cruikshank, Marcus; poverty relief, postwar
common white(s): antebellum culture of, 5, 32–35; definition of, 3–5; gender identity of, 3, 14–15, 36–37, 80; in the New South, 153, 175–76; political agency of, 5–7, 14, 68, 121, 145, 152–53, 163–65, 173, 177–78; postwar conditions of, 152–58, 160–61, 163–66; and their response to calls for wartime sacrifice, 14, 58–59, 68, 83, 91–92, 117, 149. *See also* Alabama government; class; crop failures; family/families; gender; men, common white; poverty relief, postwar; race; soldiers, common white; women, common white
Conecuh County, 167
Confederate economy, 99, 126–27, 149
Confederate government, 67, 114, 116, 120, 122, 125–27, 135, 146
Confederate military, 94, 105, 127, 155; conscription policies of, 61, 101–11, 128, 133, 136–38, 149, 152; and impressment of civilian supplies, 6, 104–5, 119, 126–29, 149, 152. *See also* camp life; soldiers, common white
constitutions, Alabama: 1819, 21; 1901, 173
Coosa County, 25–26, 34, 61, 70, 75, 77, 165

Coosa River, 23
Cotton, John, 61; on camp conditions, 70, 73; and instructing wife, 75–76; on the material condition of family, 125; and resentment toward elites, 116; sentimentalism of, 64, 84–85; and wavering commitment to war 103, 106, 109, 113–14
Cotton, Mariah, 75–76, 109, 113–14
Covington County, 60, 73, 96, 126, 136
crop failures, 153, 163–64, 166, 173. *See also* Alabama government; common white(s); poverty relief, postwar
Crossman, Egbert, 39–40
Crossman, Nancy, 39–40
Crowder, James, 87
Cruikshank, Marcus, 164–66, 168–69, 171–73. *See also* Alabama government; Committee on Destitution; Freedmen's Bureau; poverty relief, postwar

Dale County, 141
Dallas County, 102, 131
Danielly, Elizabeth, 64, 77
Danielly, Frances, 64–65, 69, 71–72, 81, 84
Davenport, John, 63–64, 74, 81, 86
Davenport, Mary Jane, 63–64
Davis, Bettie, 87
Davis, G., 87
Davis, Newton, 87, 98–99
Democratic Party, 9, 16, 158. *See also* Alabama government; antebellum political culture
divorce, 15, 38–39, 53, 151; abandonment as cause for, 41–42, 45, 50, 53–54; adultery as cause for, 40–41; and domestic violence, 45–53; gendered arguments for, 36–37, 39–40, 42–45, 54, 151; studies of, 37–38. *See also* legal system, Alabama; men, common white; women, common white
Dortch, Amanda, 50–51
Dortch, James, 50–51
Dye, James, 51, 53
Dye, Margaret Jane, 51–53
Dye, Weldon, 51–53

early settlement, Alabama, 8, 11, 20–21

Edwards, Laura, 37, 53, 161
egalitarianism,12, 20, 36, 176
Elliott, Thomas, 52
Enemies of the Country (Inscoe and Kenzer), 9
England, C. S., 170
enslaved people, 23, 35, 37, 44, 49, 59; in freedom, 157; management of in wartime, 138–39; and poor whites, 4, 13, 28; in relation to common whites' status, 11–12, 14, 26; whites' postwar views of, 156, 158, 168. *See also* African Americans; race; slavery
Escott, Paul D., 8
Espy, Columbus, 69
Espy, Marcelleous, 154
Espy, Sarah Rodgers Rousseau, 32–33; antebellum domestic life of, 59–60; on behavior of male kin, 82; and home front conditions, 100–101; and postwar conditions, 153–54; on regional conflict, 60–61, 66; on religious faith, 88; and resentment toward elites, 122
Espy, Thomas, 32, 59
exemptions, 119, 137–42. *See also* Alabama government; class; soldiers, common white

family/families: as cause for Confederate support, 2–3, 13–16, 58, 62–66, 68; declining wartime conditions of, 102–5; gender roles within, 31–32; as a means of sustaining morale, 16, 58–59, 73–74; postwar conditions of, 152–56, 163–64, 171; reason for wartime discontent, 3, 16, 92, 115, 122–23, 126–27, 177; source of emotional support, 66–68, 83–89, 108–10; as a source of power, 2–3, 6, 13–16, 31–32, 131, 145, 152, 163–65, 175–77; wartime dependency on, 66–68, 90. *See also* Alabama government; common white(s); gender; household supply line; men, common white; religious life; sentimentalism; soldiers, common white; women common white
Fayette, city of, 1, 77
Fielding, Eliza, 155–56
Figures, Henry Stokes (fig. 3), 93
Fleming, W. V., 71, 84, 95–96, 110

Flynt, Wayne, 7, 168, 173
Forret, Jeff, 4
Forsyth, Byrd, 43
Forsyth, Mary, 43
Franklin, James, 41
Franklin, Nancy, 41
Fredette, Allison Dorothy, 38
Freedman's Bureau, 153, 164–66
freed people. *See* African Americans; poverty relief, postwar
frontier conditions, antebellum Alabama, 7–8, 19–21, 24–25, 38, 176
Fry, Anna Gayle, 12

Gadsden, city of, 157, 160, 173
Gadsden Times, 160
Garrison, Harriet, 95
Garrison, James, 1–2, 17, 87, 95, 102
gender, 2–3, 7, 11, 13–16; in arguments to support the Confederacy, 62–64, 132; and changing roles in wartime, 67–68, 70, 73–77, 85–86, 92, 101–2; postwar concepts of, 161–63, 166–67, 177; and postwar roles, 154–56; and prewar identities, 35–37, 39, 43, 55. *See also* family/families; men, common white; soldiers, common white; women, common white
General Assembly, Alabama, 132, 164–65, 168, 170. *See also* Alabama government
Genovese, Eugene, 27
Gibson, Bennett, 41
Gibson, Elizabeth, 43–44
Gibson, Lucinda, 43
Gibson, Robert, 43–44
Gibson, William, 143
Gillis, Margaret Miles, 32, 69, 156
Gillis, Mollie, 69
Goodman, R. C., 139–40
Green, Antonello, 53
Green, James, 53
Greene County, 155
Griffin, A. J., 140
Gwyn, John, 77, 94, 105

Hale, George, 140
Hamilton, Thomas, 19, 54
Harrell, Henry, 165

Harris, William, 4
Henry County, 61
Herring, Allen, 142
Hickory Flat, city of, 140–41
Hill Country, 9, 11
Hobson, William, 81
Hodges, Rodden, 141–42
Holcombe, D. G., 71–72
Holloway, Elizabeth, 53–54
Holloway, Washington, 53–54
Holmes, Mike, 61
household supply line, 67–68, 95–96, 129
Hubbard, Hiland, 26, 35
Hunt, Henry, 43–44
Hunter, Lucinda Branscomb, 62, 69, 83, 86, 122–23

Inscoe, John, 9
Isham, Edward, 4

Jackson, Benjamin, 61; on camp conditions, 71–72, 99, 105–6; and familial concerns, 77, 98, 126; sentimentalism of, 87–89; on supplies from home, 69, 95, 99; and wavering commitment to war, 110–11, 114–15
Jackson, James, 61, 69
Jackson, Martha, 61, 66, 72, 77
Jackson, Mary, 60
Jackson, Mary Ellen, 74–75, 87–88, 104–5
Jackson, William Thomas: on camp conditions, 70; and concern with wife's behavior, 80; on condition of family 104–5, 126; on desertion, 114; and farming instructions, 74–75; sentimentalism of, 87–88; and wavering support for war, 107–8
Jackson County, 29
Jefferson, Campbell, 41
Jefferson, Lydia Margaret, 41
Jenkins, Edwin, 54
Jenkins, J. D., 124
Johnson, Andrew, 157, 161, 168. *See also* Reconstruction
Johnson, Elizabeth, 47–48
Johnson, Huldah, 50
Johnson, James, 41–42
Johnson, Mary, 41–42

Johnson, Spencer, 50
Jones, Fannie, 73, 77, 83, 102–3
Jones, John S., 155
Jones, William Riley, 73, 77, 83, 102–3
Justice, Appleton, 78–79

Kenzer, Robert, 9
King, Anna, 142
Knight, Joseph, 139, 158
Ku Klux Klan, 158

Land, Leonard, 73
Lauderdale County, 30
Lawrence County, 31
Lee, Kinnon, 73–74, 77–78, 126
Lee, Mary, 126
legal system, Alabama, 29, 46; courts, 30–31, 36–39, 41, 45–47, 49, 53–54. *See also* divorce
Lewis, Daniel, 144
Limestone County, 155
Lindsey, Jane Brooks, 77
Lipscomb, Smith, 23–24
Littlefield, William, 140–41
Loftis, Mary, 63, 69, 72, 86–87, 107, 124

Macmillan, Duncan, 24
Madison County, 28–29
Malloy, Charles, 78–79
Mansell, John, 48–49
Mansell, Mahala, 48–49
Marengo County, 139, 168
Marshall County, 170–71
Martin, Bessie, 7
Martineau, Harriet, 24
McConnell, Felix Grundy, 22–23
McCormick, Mary, 145
McCormick, William, 145
McCullough, Martha, 115
McCullough, William, 61, 74, 99, 107, 110, 115
McCurry, Stephanie, 14–15, 125, 145
McGuire, John, 143
McIlwain, Christopher, 7
McKinnon, Malcome A., 40
McKinnon, Sarah, 40
McMillan, Malcolm, 7
McPherson, James, 62

men, common white: antebellum gender concepts of, 13, 31–32, 36, 39, 43; antebellum political rights of, 9, 21–23; importance of work, 33; protection of honor and public reputation, 35–37; social activities of, 33–34. *See also* Alabama government; antebellum political culture; common white(s); divorce; family/families; frontier conditions, antebellum Alabama; legal system, Alabama; poverty relief, postwar; religious life; soldiers, common white; violence; women, common white

Merritt, Keri Leigh, 4, 28, 30
Miller, Julia, 166–67
Milligan, Martin Gateway, 157
Mitchell, J. C., 29
Mobile, city of, 19, 29, 71, 109, 140
Mobile, food shortages and riot: 6, 145–48. *See also* Alabama government; common white(s); women, common white
Mobile County, 166, 172
Mobile Tribune, 147
Montgomery, city of, 19, 24, 63, 65, 98, 103, 131, 159, 170
Montgomery County, 63
Montgomery Courthouse, 37 (fig. 1)
Montgomery Daily Advertiser, 119–20, 131
Moxley, Daniel ("Newton"), 78–79
Moxley, Emily, 57–58; and emotional strain of separation, 85, 90; and the death of, 153; on conflict over family finances, 78–79; on family's material conditions, 100–101; on religious faith, 88
Moxley, William, 57–58; and concern with wife's behavior, 80; and emotional strain of separation, 85, 90; on conflict over family finances, 78–79; on death of wife, 153–54; on family's material conditions, 100–101

Native American peoples, 20

Olive, Guilford, 54
Olive, Elizabeth, 54
Oliver, William, 23
Olmsted, Frederick, 24–26
Osborne, Eliza, 54

Osborne, Francis, 54
Osthaus, Carl E., 4
Owsley, Frank, 27

Palmer, J. C., 165–66
patriotism, Confederate, 62, 64, 68, 96, 123
Patton, Robert M. (Gov.), 158, 166–72. *See also* Alabama government.
Parsons, Lewis E. (Gov.), 160–61. *See also* Alabama government.
Pase, A. E., 165
Perry County, 25, 42, 48, 53, 131, 151
Pemberton, Gen. John, 147
Pickett, J. F., 139
Piney Woods region, 11, 13, 28, 60, 136, 169
Pike County, 139, 151, 170
planter elite(s): as a class, 5, 8–9, 15–17; common whites' resentment toward, 28, 95, 120–23, 136–37; government favoritism toward, 26, 116, 119–20, 123–25, 137–39, 149, 152; shared culture with common whites, 6, 8, 12, 20, 22, 24, 55. *See also* Alabama government; antebellum political culture; class; common white(s); gender; race
Poor but Proud (Flynt), 7
poor whites, 3–5, 7, 12–13, 21–22, 28, 37
Populist Party, 176
poverty relief, postwar: community and county efforts to provide, 172–73; corruption and partisan favor in, 167–69; gendered appeals for, 153, 166–67; geographic and funding obstacles in, 170–72; and racial bias, 168–69; structure of, 164–66. *See also* Alabama government; Committee on Destitution; Cruikshank, Marcus; Freedmen's Bureau; Sutherlin, J. M.
prisoners. *See* Alabama government; legal system, Alabama
Pritchett, James, 107
Progressive era, 176
Pulliam, Thomas, 141

race, 6–7, 11–12, 15, 26–27, 162, 168–69. *See also* African Americans; enslaved people; slavery

Radical Republican(s), 157–58
Raly, Jackson, 139
Randolph County, 64–65
Rea, Benjamin Frank, 167
Reach, Jeremiah, 49–51
Reach, Zelpha, 49–51
Reconstruction, 149, 152, 157, 174–75. *See also* Alabama government; Committee on Destitution; Cruikshank, Marcus; Freedmen's Bureau
religious life: churches, 25–26; concerned with morality, 34–35, 82–83; source of comfort, 59–60, 83, 88–90, 156
Riley, James, 112
Robertson, W. G., 12
Russell County, 41–43, 54, 97

Schweninger, Loren, 38
Secession, 5–6, 9–10, 13, 58–61, 176
Selma Morning Reporter, 112, 130, 137
sentimentalism: role of food in, 87–88; romantic expressions of, 92, 108–10; as a source of emotional comfort, 59, 64, 83–85, 90
Shelby County, 140
Shepard, Sam, 140
Shorter, Gov. John Gill, 62, 131–32, 134–36, 138, 140–42, 144–45, 147
slavery: antebellum South social hierarchy, 3, 38, 176; cause of Civil War, 1, 9, 58, 89–90, 128, 177; common whites' relationship to, 4–5, 8, 11–12, 27–28. *See also* African Americans; enslaved people; race
Slough, R. H., 147
Smith, Horace, 95
Smith, Patrick, 165
Smith, William Russell, 23
Smyrl, Thomas, 72, 74, 85, 97–99, 123–24, 127–28
soldiers, common white: and attempts to maintain familial roles, 2, 58, 73–82, 105; desertion of, 6–7, 112–16, 120–21; and fears of family safety, 101–2, 104–5; furloughs for, 73, 83, 89, 110–14, 116, 124; and hiring substitutes, 111–12, 119, 133, 137, 142; masculine bravado of, 65–66; religious faith of, 82–83, 89–90; and their conflict with military leaders, 99, 129–30; and their masculine duty to serve, 62–65; and their wavering support for war, 92–96, 105–8. *See also* Alabama government; camp life, Confederate military; exemptions; family/families; household supply line; sentimentalism; women, common white
Spigener, Christianah, 32, 35
Spigener, Joel, 23–24, 32
St. Clair County, 41, 141
Sterling, W. J., 138–39
Storey, Margaret, 7, 9–10
Strom, H. S., 71–72, 87
Stubbs, Benjamin, 79
Stubbs, J. M., 72
Stuart, James, 26
Sutherlin, J. M., 130

Talladega County, 40–41, 51–52, 69, 103, 141
Taylor, Grant, 65; on camp life, 70, 72, 94–95; on desertion, 116; on furloughs and substitutes, 111–12; and his concern with wife's behavior, 80–81; and his wavering commitment to war, 105–6; and the material condition of family, 103, 134; postwar life of, 155; religious faith and sentimentalism of, 83–85, 89, 108–9; and resentment toward elites, 128–30
Taylor, Malinda, 65; on desertion, 116; on furloughs and substitutes, 111–12; and her husband's concern over behavior, 80–81; and the material condition of family, 134; postwar life of, 155; religious faith and sentimentalism of, 84–85, 89, 105, 108–9; and resentment toward elites, 128–30; on seeking husband's advice, 76–77
Tennessee Valley, 11
Turnbull, Joseph, 29
Tuscaloosa County, 30, 65, 102, 128
Tuscumbia, city of, 171

unionism, Alabama, 5, 7, 9–10, 163, 168–69

Union Springs, 62, 159
Union Springs Times, 159–60

Vann, Samuel King, 85–86, 94, 106–7
violence, 24–25, 28, 34, 145; in defense of honor, 29–30. *See also* legal system, Alabama; Alabama government

Warren, J. M., 171
Washington County, 73
Watts, Thomas H. (Gov.), 130, 136, 139–40, 142
Wesson, Joseph, 69, 84, 98, 103, 110, 116
West, Daniel, 30–31
Wheeler, Madison, 144
Wheeler, Thomas, 144
Whig Party, 9. *See also* Alabama government; antebellum political culture
White, David, 45
White, Jemimah, 45
Whites, LeeAnn, 67, 69
Wilcox County, 39, 45–46, 53–54
Williams, Eliza, 42
Williams, Mittie, 65
Williams, Robert, 65

Williams, Thomas, 43
Wiregrass region, 9, 11, 163
Winston County, 171
Womble, C., 167
women, common white: antebellum gender concepts of, 33–34, 45–46, 54; home front roles of, 68–69, 74–77; political agency of, 14–15, 68, 146–48; postwar life of, 153–56; social activities of, 34; wartime conditions of, 100–101, 131; and wartime discontent, 16, 122–23. *See also* Alabama government; common white(s); divorce; legal system, Alabama; men, common white; Mobile, food shortages and riot; poverty relief, postwar; religious life; sentimentalism; soldiers, common white
Woodhall, Mrs. Tarlton, 172
Woods, James, 94
Wyeth, Louis, 170

Yancy, James, 143–44
Yancey, William Lowndes, 9
yeomen/yeomanry, 4–5, 8, 12–13, 21–22, 24